Three Sheep
and a Dog

Three Sheep
and a Dog

An Insider's View of
New Zealand Sheep Dog Trialling

John Gordon

REED

To the memory of Cyril Perry MBE

1917–1988

Published by Reed Books, a division of Reed Publishing (NZ) Ltd,
39 Rawene Rd, Birkenhead, Auckland. Associated companies, branches and
representatives throughout the world.

ISBN 0 7900 0624 3

Illustrations © 1998 Jamie Boynton

Editors: Anna Rogers, Peter Dowling
Designer: Sunny H. Yang
Cover photograph: Graham Meadows

First published 1998

Printed in Singapore

Contents

Acknowledgements

I'd like to thank all the shepherds, whoever they were, who thought that their dog was better than the other fellow's and therefore founded sheep dog trialling. My thanks also to their modern colleagues who have given me a lot of help and support over the past twenty years. Although only some of them get a mention in the following pages, that doesn't mean that I haven't appreciated any contribution they may have made towards my various activities in and around trialling.

I am especially grateful to fellow writer and triallist Ian Sinclair, who assisted with a lot of background material and, from his own pen, has contributed many facts and a fair amount of colour. Ian also read the manuscript, as did John and Deirdre Bartlett, and all three contributed to the book's accuracy.

The other fount of knowledge I frequently tapped was Alf Boynton who, as manager of Pikarere (the property on which I live and where I am tolerated as a volunteer shepherd), faced at least twelve months of questioning and came up with the answers. Alf's son, Jamie, provided the book's excellent illustrations — the result of natural talent and of having spent his formative years within earshot of plenty of dog trial conversations.

Some of my material is drawn from articles originally written for the *New Zealand Journal of Agriculture* and the *New Zealand Farmer*. I wish to acknowledge that, and the contribution made by the *Farmer* through its century-long coverage of sheep dog trialling by publishing endless results and informed comment from writers of the calibre of Peter Newton, Ian Sinclair and Alan Box.

To Anna Rogers, my long-suffering editor and defender of the grammatical faith — with sufficient flexibility to adjust to the variations that occur in pastoral New Zealand — thank you. Thanks also for christening this book. Finally to Kereyn, my partner (who has observed, 'Writers get quite odd when they're writing, don't you think?'), thank you for your patience and support.

Introduction

Horse sports aside, New Zealand's two best-known rural contests are sheep shearing and dog trialling, both of which have emerged from the development and importance of the most intensive sheep farming industry in the world. Of the two, dog trialling is my favourite, not only because I'm a triallist, but because there's far more to this particular following than getting a trained sheep dog to control a few sheep, which, very often, isn't all that easy to do! This book represents a personal view of sheep dog trialling, which is a competitive extension of practical stock work on New Zealand farms. By developing this kind of contest between shepherds and their dogs, this country's pioneer stockmen were no different from many other rural groups throughout the world. In Britain, harvest workers made a sport out of sheaf tossing, rough-riding American cowboys developed the rodeo, and rival Canadian bushmen started racing each other with sharp axes and crosscut saws. In this country we have turned oyster opening, possum skinning, shovelling coal or gravel, and erecting farm fences into competitive affairs.

My aim is to explain the intracacies, trials and tribulations of dog trialling, and to celebrate its development, traditions and continued existence in New Zealand's rural community. As with any pursuit, there are a few variations from the norm, but 'the norm' is the backbone of trialling here, which is based on a competitor (human) with one dog (canine), working three sheep (ovine). The dog can be one of two main types or breed: the silent heading dog (a Border collie derivative) and the noisy huntaway (the result of plenty of planned breeding and quite a few unsupervised incidents).

All the standard events at authorised trials are run under the auspices and rules of the New Zealand Sheep Dog Trial Association, with two separate classes for each breed. For heading dogs, these are the long head, and short head and yard. Both of these begin with the dog being cast out to head three sheep from the uphill side. The trio were placed up there, in a pre-ordained spot, by a person called a liberator, who was helped in the task by a hooked fence of wire netting on the uphill side. The dog behind them, the sheep are then pulled straight(ish) down to the boss who, in the case of the long head, waits in a ring, 20 metres across, where the run will end. In the so-called shorter event, there is a set of hurdles for the sheep to be steered through before, it's hoped, they're put into a 2-metre-square pen to finish the run.

There's a time limit which, for heading events, is usually twelve to fifteen minutes, though judges usually warn of the inevitable march of time by calling out 'two minutes' when that's all that's left. There's only one judge, who marks out of 100. This is the total every competitor starts with, but very rarely receives. Scoring is a matter of elimination and the greater the number of errors, the further from 100 the final tally will be. After the dog, the only other assistance or weapon a trialist can have is what a British shepherd would call a crook, but to us is simply a dog trial stick. This is much shorter than an overseas trialist's crook — it can't be longer than a metre — and it can be used only to wave at sheep, not to touch them. It is, however, quite remarkable how, in times of great pressure and urgency, sheep can run into a trial stick that just couldn't be got out of the road in time!

The huntaway is New Zealand's own breed and works in noisy reverse to the heading dog, by barking at the trio and urging them uphill — hunting them away from the triallist. This is done on two different courses. One of these has three sets of markers 20 metres apart on it, forcing the sheep and dog to change direction on two separate occasions, which is why it's called the zigzag. On the other huntaway course, the sheep aren't supposed to deviate from a true line, so it's known as the straight hunt. In both cases, liberators release each competitor's sheep at the foot of the hill, a short distance from competitor and dog. The time limit for both hunts is between eight and twelve minutes, but because of the course and the type of dog that works on it, most runs are well and truly over — one way or the other — long before the judge calls 'time', signalling that time has run out.

There are many more things I could say and explain about sheep dog trialling, especially since I'm both a triallist and trialling commentator, as well as a countryman-columnist who believes in the importance of upholding a wide range of rural traditions that are now disappearing. The last bastion of many of these can still be found in and around our dog trial grounds. From these venues, with all the goings-on at their annual events, there's enough information, anecdote, history and folklore to fill a book — which I have.

1

FROM A TYKE TO A MIKE

Some sheep dog triallists are quite literally born to it. Not only do they have a natural aptitude for handling stock and an inborn eye for country, but there's also an established tradition of stockmanship in their family, and the likelihood of a long-standing association with dog trialling. Others, who possess the same ability and enthusiasm, come to trialling by a longer route. My journey was certainly rather tortuous, compared with, say, Ginger Anderson of Omarama or Dan Murphy from Whangamomona, both third-generation competitors. I hasten to add that I would never claim to have the same ability with stock as Dan or Ginger, but my affinity for the whole practice of handling livestock, via the medium of a working dog, is much the same as theirs. If I didn't share their keenness, I couldn't have survived the many public 'trials' and embarrassments that I have suffered — or maybe I'm just pig-headed.

To be a successful triallist, at any level, you must not only possess an affinity for stock but, deep down, you also need to be a masochist. This means being able to take the punishment being meted out, in public, by a disobedient dog ('and he's been so good at home!') or sheep that won't even stay put long enough to make a decent hoofprint in soft mud. In addition, you need to be able to withstand successive failures yet run the risk of it all happening again when you have another go next week --- and pay an entry fee for the privilege!

My development into a fully fledged masochist began by mustering without a dog. There was a canine present, but he was following me and more than happy to have the shoulder-high bracken fern bashed down for him, to allow easier passage for his shorter legs … no, he wasn't a dachshund. This was on Pigeon Island, the largest of three islands towards the top end of Otago's Lake Wakatipu. At that time Central Southland farmer, Clive Gray, leased The Islands and, since I worked for him, that's how I found myself on the middle beat of my first muster. The dog, Jack, was Clive's and, being given to occasional bouts of tenor-pitched barking, he could be described as a huntaway. To ensure that he couldn't run back to his owner at a crucial moment, we were connected by a couple of lengths of baling twine. The testing moment would either be when I most needed him or, if we were in earshot, when Clive whistled his team into action for the first time. Although the lead ensured that my team of one would always be at hand, it did hamper a usually free-running, noisy dog, reducing his effectiveness by about 70 percent. Mind you, sheep will show at least some respect to a person with a dog in tow, more than to someone with no dog at all.

That first morning I leaped, dashed and yelled at the sheep — Merino Leicester half-breds — and they ran well. I followed them with total enthusiasm and the dog followed me, the baling twine allowing no choice in the matter. By the time we had negotiated several clearings, blocked alternative routes round rocks and collected various woolly waifs and strays on the way, two things became very obvious: I was getting a bit puffed, tired and hoarse, but Jack was getting a lot more interested in proceedings. This was fortunate because, with all my haste, to say nothing of a reluctance to allow the sheep to pause and consider other options, Jack and I arrived at the island's rather make-shift yards well ahead of the rest of the gang, and had to get the animals in on our own. This required extra effort. Not just fancy steps, jumping and 'ho-ho-ho-ing' either, but waving both hands and side slapping as well. The result was that I relinquished my grip on the lead and Jack was free. Fortunately he decided against bolting into the distance, from which the boss could now be heard in full cry with his team, and started to help me.

By throwing in a very effective salvo of barks to the right of the yard gate, he turned the sheep straight over to me on the left. They were in fact bolting, as they'd been startled by the sudden arrival of a new and alarming noise. All I could do was flap my arms helplessly and watch them go straight past. Jack, however, now fully committed to the task, arrived to cover the left and, with a very effective stiff-jaw tackle on the leading runaway, brought everything to a halt. By this time I found myself in the middle of a not very wide gateway, which also happened to be the main entrance. It didn't matter; the impact of Jack's new persona had been so effective that the sheep ignored me and dived into the yards and safety. At least I was in the right position to close the gate on my mob which, over 35 years later, I'd like to think was of close to 100 head, rather than the 30 or so it surely was. It turned out that shutting the gate quickly was a good idea as Jack was one of those dogs who, whenever he saw an open gateway, got a rush of blood to the head, whipped round the nearest mob and shoved them through it.

The set up on The Islands was rather rough and ready, as there was neither full-time management nor a permanent residence there, just a collection of ancient huts and sheds in the middle of some of the most beautiful country in the world. The part-time approach meant that certain parts of the sheep-yards had quite literally drifted on to the adjacent beach and, when a gap appeared in the rails, you duly combed the shore for a replacement. Accordingly, each part of this twisted and gnarled, stone grey complex relied on the next segment for support; any illusion of combined strength was completely optical. It was, therefore, a good idea to get the sheep into a separate pen so that Jack could take the pressure off our mob and I would not tempt fate when the main gate had to be opened for the rest of the flock. I well remember taking the mob through a couple of pens. I'd open the gate, my colleague would shove them through. Simple, really, and no need to use commands — he ignored them anyway — but I issued plenty. It felt important and, if there was anyone watching, it might seem that I knew what I was doing!

A couple of days later Jack and I went over to Pig Island, just a ten-minute row away, to be part of that muster. Apart from the start of the beat when we were near the others, the twine connection between the pair of us wasn't necessary and allowed a freedom that meant we did equal amounts of work. I think at one stage we had a mob each and were almost racing, but not too quickly, as the yard set-up on Pig was in the singular and lacked the luxury of separate pens. Because of this, forward planning was necessary to ensure that we joined the main mob at the right time, so there'd be just the one gate-opening ceremony. This, fortunately, was the way it all turned out, no doubt to Jack's great disappointment.

Despite the fact that, one way or another, I had shifted plenty of stock before, especially down country, on flatter and more productively pastured land, this was the first time I'd felt more like a shepherd — amusterer even. Being on an island towards the top end of Lake Wakatipu was certainly the place to get that feeling. Up there, the lake is bounded on either side by steep, tussock-clad mountains, slopes that have been grazed and mustered since Rees and Von Tunzelman brought in the first mobs of sheep in the early 1860s. Looking from the islands, on our eastern shore was Mount Creighton Station, and to the west you looked across to two other well-established High Country runs, Elfin Bay and Greenstone. To the north on either side of the head of the lake lay Glenorchy and Kinloch and, towering above them, one of New Zealand's more dramatic-looking combinations of rock, ice and snow, Mount Earnslaw. In those days, this part of the back country was very isolated, as there was no road access up the top half of the lake — Queenstown to Glenorchy — and the stations on either shore. These were serviced by the SS *Earnslaw*, an ancient soot and smoke spreader that is still a tourist trip fixture on shorter trips out of Queenstown. We, too, used the old steamer for our mustering, shearing and dipping trips to the islands, all of which added to what I thought was the glamour of the whole enterprise.

This was the legendary High Country, a region where the traditions of shepherding and dog handling really began in this country, and developed in a way without parallel elsewhere. The early Scots shepherds who, with their collie dogs first worked this country, also organised the first sheep dog trials. Many of the unwritten rules of stockmanship to which we still try and adhere were created on this class of country. It was a logical place to be smitten by the shepherding bug, especially as I'd read everything our great back country author, Peter Newton, ever wrote. His first book, *Wayleggo*, must be regarded as a New Zealand classic.

The next stage in my journey was my first dog. An unusual-looking, long-coated, tri-coloured (chocolate, tan and white) fellow, he was called Tyke and was well named, as he began with a bit of unplanned mischief. The first property I worked on after leaving school had a very good heading dog called Bob and a very busy, fluffy-coated huntaway bitch with the rather fitting moniker of Fuss. Among the sort of company I keep these days, that sort of cross is frowned on as it's neither one thing nor the other. That's fine for the purist, but to a teenage farmhand having a dog who could both run round to the front of a mob (head) and throw a bit of noise about, was very useful or, to use the colloquial description of a canine jack of all trades, handy.

Versatility certainly became a key element in Tyke's life. He heeled and hounded beef cattle, brought in dairy cows, mustered sheep, learned to have nothing to do with pigs and loved annoying the hell out of bulls — from a safe distance. At one stage we were living on a pot plant nursery in Christchurch and he, looking for more satisfying activity than sitting around watching begonias grow, wandered off to the Addington Saleyards for a look. There he was picked up by a lorry driver from whose clutches he escaped some six weeks later and returned home, with a little bit of help from the Addington Borough Council. Tyke taught students at the Telford Farm Training Institute how to work him and sired a litter of Springer spaniel-huntaway cross pups, at least three of which became useful farm dogs, especially during the duck shooting season. Tyke learned to put up with the many other dogs who came and went and, by the time he was a teenager (the human equivalent of 80-plus), he had worked in various parts of both islands; from southern Southland to South Auckland.

The last place we worked on together was in the central King Country. We'd been sharemilking and came to a shepherding job, dog light. There were just the two: a very likely-looking young heading dog, who wouldn't work for me (nor, as it was later proved, anyone else) and Tyke. He, alas, was showing his years, plus the vocal effects of an operation to control cancer in a very male part of the anatomy. To reduce the deficiency, I went to a dog sale at Te Kuiti and bought a huntaway named Jock who, along with the rest of his team, was put up for auction by a shepherd who was heading overseas. Jock looked and sounded the part and after the sale I stood with fingers firmly hooked into his collar, contemplating my purchase. At that point a man came up who'd had a major part in organising the proceedings and demonstrating, on sheep, six different dogs, none of them his own. They had belonged to the recently deceased dog triallist, George Herbert of Pongaroa, and being able to work someone else's dogs at a public sale like that was quite a feat. The man who achieved this, however, wasn't your run-of-the-mill cockie, but Cyril Perry, then vice-president of the New Zealand Sheep Dog Trial Association. He commented favourably on Jock and wished me well with him, uttering a phrase I was to hear a lot more in years to come, 'You're going to have a lot of fun with that dog.'

Unfortunately Cyril was wrong, but not through bad judgement. The first week or two were a battle of wits and wasted commands, Jock preferring his whim to the orders of a new boss. This meant that whenever he spotted a goat, and there were plenty around the King Country's hills in those days, he'd whip away and give some nanny or billy a quick workout and a nervous breakdown. Within a day or so of us attaining some sort of working relationship,

Jock was wiped out by a slow-braking truckie, while moving cattle between properties on State Highway 4. It's no fun being on the other side of the road from a dog you've begun to appreciate and watch him come towards you while you're yelling at him to stay there — and he doesn't hear a thing because of the noise of a heavy truck and trailer braking and changing down far too late. It's the most helpless situation you can ever be in, seeing, screaming and knowing, all in the same millisecond, that the inevitable is going to happen. So it was down to the old firm, Tyke and me. The property was typical of the central King Country, very steep and no longer suitable for an old dog. This was noted by the boss, John Gemmell who, during one muster where I took one side of the hill and Tyke the other, wryly advised me to 'slow down, your dog can't keep up with you!'

It wasn't long after that that I left the land and went to town to become an assistant rural broadcaster with the NZBC, based in Hamilton. Tyke came too and, apart from finding good patches of sunlight to bask in, his main role was the care of two toddlers, who became the bane of his life as he neared the end of his. Not that he was unused to town. On many occasions he'd camped in various urban outhouses and garages while I visited relations, both permanent and temporarily prospective. As a shepherd, the deepest into the hinterland I got to was Makarora Station, on the Otago side of Haast Pass, which, in the 1960s, was about five hours drive from either Dunedin or Invercargill. The prospect of journeys of that length always led me to pop a dog or two into the Morrie 1000 for company, which always seemed a good idea at the time. Until, that is, you reached town where, usually sooner than later, there would an incident. Generally these centred around family cats, flower beds or beautifully polished hub caps. The most unusual involved the leg of the lady of the house, who was hanging out the washing when Tyke mistook her leg for a post. This, in every meaning of the term, was extremely close to the Last Post for the dog. Over a decade later the young Gordons were exacting a kind of urban revenge, and he didn't mind a bit.

It was as a rural broadcaster that I had my first close contact with a championship dog trial. I'd been to trials before and had competed in casual events, with all the success you'd expect of a bottle-happy picnicker. By covering the 1974 North Island Championships at Ngongotaha, near Rotorua, I met the leading triallists of the day and was drawn to them both as a group of genuine people and as real shepherds. I also met up with Cyril Perry again who, by this time, had become national president. Typically, he not only remembered our brief meeting of two years earlier but asked how I'd got on with the dog. At that time, the standard form of radio coverage meant that each evening of the week-long event, the rural broadcaster of the parish where the champs were being held, would be presented with the call to that stage of the trial. The call is a list of the top seven competitors and their dogs in each of the four events. As those leading competitors' points or placings couldn't be disclosed, this didn't make for great radio, especially to those who weren't close followers of the sport. I decided to liven things up by inserting small excerpts of commentary. At the beginning of the week the commentator was Ken Hindman, an established triallist. Not many days had gone by, though, before I had a go myself. It was great fun and, apart from my getting the straight hunt and the long head confused, and coming out with something quite impossible called the straight head, all went well. One of the memorable runs of the week was in the final of the long head which, but for the fact that she ran out of time, would have been won by Pauline King. I had a marvellous time, gauging whether the job would be finished in time by saying, 'Will she … ooh … will she…?' This was to become a bit of a trademark in later years but, for once, the audience was spared these rhetorical questions. On his way to complete the run by getting a balanced hold in the ring, Pauline's Boy ran rather wide and included my tape recorder in his route — it was on the ground in front of me — turning it off with a hastily passing paw. One way or another, this was not to be the last time that a dog would leave me speechless.

Early the following year I covered the Expo International trials in January and again had a wonderful time. The highlight was watching, at first hand, trialling's best ever heading event exponents, R.M. (Bob) Wilson and Gary Brennan, in what became a needle match. In the final, and after stalling at a very contrived water obstacle for what seemed like an age, Bob achieved the miracle of the last four obstacles in 90 seconds and won. Exciting stuff, and as I was able to do live commentaries for the local radio station, it certainly provided plenty of verbal fuel for a tyro commentator. Perched on top of an aging NZBC Land-Rover, I was well on the way to being hooked on both ad lib expression and dog trials. At the other end of the same year I was one of the team who were to do three days of live and pre-recorded television coverage of the Royal Show in Invercargill. As a Southlander I was more than happy to be involved in a major production on home ground, though a touch nervous at the prospect of appearing on camera. This was eventually overcome while explaining and demonstrating the intricacies of a portable cattle crush, which I managed without the major freeze-up in explanatory patter that I had feared. Nor was it too obvious that, for the last part of the item, my hand was jammed in the head gate's trip mechanism, meaning that the planned walk down the side of the crush, to finish the item, could not eventuate.

From my point of view, the big moment was to be the final of the Royal Show's Sheep Dog Trial Championship. A commentary position had been incorporated in a scaffold camera tower by the main stand. To a commentary newcomer, this was the pinnacle since, along with the necessary microphone and headset, there was a monitor so I could match my words to the vision; it all seemed very professional. The plan was that I would pre-record an introductory piece to camera, then climb up the tower to prattle on throughout the final. This, too, I was assured, would be recorded, not live. As the time approached I was summoned to the main ring, just out from the grandstand to do the set-up piece. I did think it strange that the floor manager gave me such a precise countdown for a recorded piece, but gave that only brief consideration as something much serious was on the horizon. Four local youths had spotted the TV paraphernalia, as well as someone presenting to it, and decided to volunteer their services as some sort of drunken chorus.

Whenever a presenter is working to camera he or she is always accompanied by a floor manager, who is the director's link with the studio floor or paddock, and all those in that area who are involved. In this case it was the very experienced Peter Short who, though his height ran fairly true to his name, was solidly built, with a direct and practical approach to proceedings. Noticing the alarm my eyes registered at the approach of the mini-mob, Peter spun, summed up the situation as being too late for diplomatic negotiation, took one step forward and put the group leader's lights out. The lad fell to his knees, his colleagues stopped, aghast at what had befallen their leader, and nearby onlookers in the grandstand went 'oooh'. With my eyes out on stalks and my jaw dropped in amazement, I stopped talking. Hearing this, Peter spun back in my direction and made a circular hand signal that meant 'For God's sake keep going', and somehow I did. The

would-be interjectors disappeared into thin air and I went on to what I thought was the end of the piece. It wasn't. Peter had returned to his usual post beside the camera lens to indicate, with a repeated, two-handed stretching motion, that I was to keep going, which I managed to do. Not long after he appeared beside me — by now they were covering the course with another camera — and held up a little blackboard saying, 'Describe the course', so I did. Then, another blackboard message appeared: 'Keep going'. That, too, was achieved, though I've no idea what I said, which, I'm sure, is a very good thing.

While delivering that desperate ad lib, I was led to the edge of the show ring and parked against the recently painted, red railing that topped the fence round the oval. Even from that ground level vantage point I could see that there was quite a bit of action on the course, as the first competitor was under way. Accordingly, the dreaded blackboard reappeared: 'Commentary for 15 minutes'. So, without a bird's-eye view of the action from the tower, a seat or a monitor, I did as I was told and described the action. On at least two more occasions the blackboard bearing the same message was held up. There we were, floor manager and caller parked at ringside and, to all appearances, just another pair of onlookers — except that one of them didn't seem to be able to shut up! It all looked so normal, especially me blathering on, that a couple of old school friends stopped by for a chat. This being far less challenging than our earlier visitation, Peter was able gently to move them and arrange a more convivial meeting at day's end.

The afternoon was oppressively hot and humid, with bright sun beating down, but great banks of dark purple clouds building up away to the sou'-west, as they always do an hour or so before the southern cloudburst and thunderstorm. It became so hot that the new paint on the railing I'd been backed on to melted into my trousers. Not that I cared; in fact the gluey substance probably stopped me from subsiding onto the ground and into oblivion. It was a very good final and although the competitors came from throughout the South Island, it was won by one of Southland's better known triallists, Bill Hazlett.

The total package ran for nearly an hour and, as these were the days of not very commercial television, wasn't interrupted by advertisements.

And, contrary to what I'd been told, it was all live, from my eventful introduction to Peter's final blackboard message: 'Wrap up and throw to Finlay McCullough at the Meat and Wool Cup'. I would be lying if I said that, as the final went on, I wasn't aware there was more to the situation than a recording session. After all, professional floor managers don't normally take their job title quite as literally as Peter, quite correctly, felt he needed to. As an introduction to television commentary it was a very useful experience; by comparison nothing else would ever seem that nerve-wracking or under-resourced. And, not that I had any inkling of it at the time, for the next twenty years I was to get at least one annual outing on TV as a dog trial commentator.

In the two years that followed an annual outing was quite literally the case, at the Christchurch A&P Show doing their dog trial final live on local television. On the second occasion Frank Torley, who had flown down from TV One's rural office at Avalon to share fronting duties, brought a message from rural producer Tony Trotter, who was planning a competitive sheep dog trial series — 'Was I interested in being the commentator?' I hesitated for at least a zillionth of a second, and said yes! Over the next five months I learned that the series would be called … *a Dog's Show*, have an eight-week run on air and involve eight leading triallists from each island. All were heading dog competitors and half would compete on a singles course (one dog working three sheep) and the rest in the doubles (two dogs and six sheep). After a few technical hiccups, incredibly bad weather and three recording sessions on two different locations, the series went to air. Despite the fact that it was given what had been regarded as a very bad time slot, late afternoon on Sundays, the series was extremely well received and rated highly. The biggest surprise was the urban reaction; city audiences accepted it right from episode one, and most of them were still with us sixteen years later, when the last series screened. With the normal uncertainty broadcasters show while waiting for a new programme to go to air, we had consoled ourselves by saying, 'At least the farmers will like it.'

Most of the criticism the programme did receive — and no programme is critic free — came from very rural addresses, their main concern being 'that stupid man with his inane and irritating comments.' Other letters were more explicit and, being written by the truly heroic, they were unsigned. No doubt I had some rather annoying habits, such as continually using the expression, 'My word, he's going extremely well', but no one ever complained about those. What they were reacting to was the fact that, all of a sudden, dog trialling had jumped from the steep faces of the backblocks to the front rooms of the suburbs. This new profile involved all the trappings of entertainment, including an effusive and repetitive commentator, and some had trouble coping with that. After all, the essentials of shepherding and sheep dog trials had changed little since the 1870s and, a century on, many weren't ready for trialling by television and the excitable elements that accompanied it.

2

A SEPARATE WORLD

One of the things that first fascinated me about sheep dog trialling was that, to an outsider, it appeared to be a separate society with its own values, language and traditions. It could never, of course, be described as a secret society, with strange rites of induction conducted behind closed doors — a triallist's introduction, alas, is very public! At the same time, uninformed onlookers can wonder what's going on, and what on earth the shepherd is actually saying. Deciphering the whistles and commands can be difficult, as there are some unusual words and phrases such as, 'come by', 'way-err', 'keep oot', 'that'll do' and 'get in'. They're used as commands for the direction or side the dog is required to take and, since different people use them for either side, precise knowledge can be difficult to come by. Then there's the great New Zealand shepherd's cry, 'wayleggo'. This can also be pronounced or spelt — not that the dog's fussy — 'awaileggo' or 'wareleggo', and can mean 'let go' or 'come away out of that' or 'come in behind me' or all of the above. 'Wayleggo' can also mean something completely different, which an individual shepherd and his dog will have arranged between themselves. And, to throw a little more fog over the subject, any given spoken command can mean different things at different times, when it's delivered at different sound levels or intensity. It's not what you say, it's the way that you say it.

Eavesdropping on a conversation between a couple of triallists can be just as puzzling as the communication between man and dog. To me, this reinforces the mystery and separatism any special interest group can develop, especially one that has emerged from practical stock work on New Zealand farms and stations, otherwise known as shepherding. Having worked for the last 25 years in a basically urban environment, for me the escape to a trial ground — to another world — has been very important. Sure, I had been to a few district and Young Farmers Club trials when I was shepherding and working on down-country places. I'd even organised and judged a dairy farmers' cow dog event in the Waikato, but my main interests on those occasions were social. Working on the first couple of series of ... *a Dog's Show* served notice that both dog trialling, and its followers, were very special. This was confirmed, in 1979, when I was asked by the daytime television programme, *Today at One*, to be part of an invitation series where several individuals were given a 30-minute episode of their own. This entailed selecting and presenting all the content, with only one major drawback: it was to be in quite a small studio and to go out there and then, live. In this context the term 'live' can often mean the opposite.

When asked what I would include in my show, I ended my wish list with, 'And we'll finish up with a dog trial.' 'What!' said a very wide-eyed Frank Torley. Frank is a long-standing rural colleague in broadcasting who, at that time, was working towards his director's ticket on *Today at One*. It was he who suggested I be included in this guest series and, therefore, I insisted that he should share the risks of live TV and direct the show. The first piece of good news I was able to give Frank was that I wouldn't be using sheep in my 'trial' but ducks. That was the only good news he got throughout the whole episode, and it wasn't much. Fortunately for both the director and Avalon's cleaners, a reasonably calm trio, with conveniently clipped wings, had been located and brought to the studio on the appointed day. At around the same time, the dog triallist for the show arrived — Bob Wilson of Kirwee, near Christchurch.

Bob, as I've mentioned, was one of the country's two most successful triallists (the other was Gary Brennan) and had had his first contact with trialling some 54 years earlier, in 1925. Back then Bob was a

Mid-Canterbury drover with a little blue heading dog, Mac, who impressed those who saw him on the road with his ability and intelligence. They reckoned Mac should be entered at the upcoming Ashburton trials. Mac was, and he won, the beginning of a habit Bob Wilson and his dogs never lost. When he finally retired from trialling, a couple of years before his death in 1986, he had won 1274 events with 66 different dogs. Included in this were seven New Zealand titles and another sixteen at South and North Island Championships. Goodness only knows how many placings Bob would have had in major events. If a list were compiled, it would begin at the first New Zealand event in 1936 when, in the short head and yard, he won the first round. This gave Mac, the original Mac's son, the North Island title and, in the seven-dog national final, he was joined by two kennel mates, Fly and Miss Mac. This led to Bob and his trio taking second, third and fourth places, respectively, which has never been done since. To me, a trial hanger-on, he was a god. Yet, true to the unwritten traditions of trialling, here he was, aged 76, prepared to chance his arm on live television, against the unknown ways and wiles of three pekin-muscovy cross ducks.

Accompanying Bob were two long-time travelling companions, both female, and each with a special place in dog trialling's annals. Zoe — Mrs Wilson to the likes of me — was always at Bob's side at trials and kept an immaculate record of both the breeding and competitive performance of the Wilson kennels. There was no more successful member of that establishment than the representative nominated for duck duty that day — Rose. Winner of three New Zealand titles, the first some seven years earlier, Rose had also won the Expo International trial and the Ashburton A&P Centennial Show Trial; on the latter two occasions I'd been armed with a microphone, so I was used to saying good things about her. I'd also been in the gallery when Rose won her second national title, and on other occasions when she and Bob made difficult sheep look like goody-goodies from Sunday school, while for everyone else they were behaving like runaways from reform school. By the time Rose found herself at Avalon, she was at least twelve and had been retired from trialling for a couple of years with a tricky hip.

This made running the hill in standard events rather difficult but the studio floor wouldn't be a problem, and nor would the ducks.

The set construction people had made a pair of hurdles, a bridge and a yard, all of duck-like proportions. Before the studio we set it all up in a garage so man and dog could introduce themselves to the poultry and iron out any major behavioural problems in private. There weren't any, apart from the usual amount of indignant quacking and feather bristling, but that's the way it is with ducks, and it's only for show. All it needed was one of Rose's 'You're going to be good, aren't you' looks straight at each would-be troublemaker, and the web-footed ones were waddling in the right direction. This, of course, was a rather odd, though arresting sight. Despite that, I remember looking up at Bob at this stage and seeing a slow smile of satisfaction spread over his face. With the feathered trio's obvious acceptance of the dog's control, he well knew that they wouldn't create any major problems or public embarrassment. At this point I realised just how lucky I was having this great pairing, with over 60 years of trialling experience between them, on what the programme's producers insisted was to be called *The John Gordon Show*. Not for fee, fame or fortune either, just Bob's belief that appearances of this kind were good for dog trialling's profile.

The duck dog trial was to finish the programme, which it did, and in some style! After I introduced Bob and Rose, the full studio lights went up to reveal our miniature trial course and feathered sheep. Even the studio audience, all of whom knew what was going to happen, gasped at the sight of it all. Rose then began to deftly work her magic and steer things in the right direction. Over on the other side of the poultry Bob calmly shuffled behind — ducks aren't quick on their feet — and, like everyone else, I was transfixed, and completely silent. Speechless for long enough to move Martin Didsbury, my producer in *Country Calendar*, to bend down from the uppermost tier of our hay-bale grandstand and utter in gravelled tones, 'Go on, commentate!' I did, and added very little. It was such a fascinating sight and there was no need for comparisons with previous scores or competitors. There was a result, though: Rose, three (ducks in a little yard); ducks, one (dog glowering between the yard rails).

About this stage I became aware that some of the fears people had expressed about the difficulties of covering a duck dog trial in a small studio had been realised. Not the least of these was the fact that each of the studio's four walls had a camera backed on to it, pointing to the action in the centre. This is known in the trade as a 'fool's firing squad', meaning that each camera operator can shoot his or her counterpart on the other side. Anyway, that was Torley's problem, not mine. I was intent on having a chat with Bob and, walking towards him, managed, in turn, to obscure the view the two safe cameras were getting of Rose and the ducks staring at each other. It was while talking to Bob that I realised there was an air of uncertainty about the place — panic, even!

That can be contagious, especially if it brings on the realisation that you have no idea which of those isolated islands of electronic wizardry you're going to be smiling at, come time to close the programme. Fortunately I had the wit to ask Bob one more question, not that I should have since, apparently, we were already four minutes over time.

The question I asked was about Rose or, to be precise, the relationship between Bob and Rose. If you ever ask a real dog man about his dog, and the animal's at hand, he'll never look at you, just at his workmate while talking of their time together. That's precisely what Bob Wilson did, enabling me to leave him to it and dash across the studio to ask the floor manager what camera I was to close to. He didn't know and, at that stage, who really cared? When I got back to Bob he was still looking at and talking about Rose. When he finished he looked up at me and smiled. I smiled back, thanked him, and that was it. What happened after that I have long since put into the conveniently blank file. What I will never forget is that while all about her were in varying stages of distress or panic, Rose stood like a statue, eyeing her charges. Looking down at her with nothing short of absolute affection in his eyes was Bob, talking about her. What passed between them was timeless. It proved to me that the relationship between a good shepherd and a good dog is not only of great practical use, it is extremely precious. If sheep dog trialling does nothing but demonstrate and strengthen those bonds, then it is a following well worth participating in and talking and writing about. That's what I've done ever since, and I'm still at it.

The century or so of history and consolidation that came between the first dog trials and my introduction to top-level competition and competitors was, for the most part, very discreet. The concept of a shepherd proving his skills in competition grew quietly in tandem with the development of New Zealand's pastoral industry, and the communities that developed around it. Just as hunt, racing and football clubs were founded, so too were annual gatherings, such as dog trials, sports meetings and A&P shows, each bearing its district's name. Many of the original trial grounds were inaccessible to the general public, lying at the end of dusty tracks or very muddy roads, where the early enthusiasts found the flat-bottomed gullies, steep slopes and tussocked faces necessary to test man, dog and, quite often, the sheep. Even today, it seems that the more isolated and difficult to reach a course is, the better it'll be. As a result, the tensions, trials and tribulations that attracted television viewers from the mid-1970s to the early 1990s were well hidden from the public. Aside from appearances at A&P shows, the faithful were able to practise their rituals between themselves, consenting dogs and, occasionally, consenting sheep. As the numbers of sheep, shepherds and sheep farmers grew, so too did the sport, both here and overseas.

The exact date and place of the world's first public sheep dog trial is not really known, although plenty has been said and written on the matter. According to experts from Britain, the first man, sheep and dog contest was held at Bala in the North Wales hills in 1873. We now know that the Bala trial wasn't the first, because a trial held near the town of Forbes, New South Wales, in either 1871 or 1872, preceded that of old North Wales by at least a year. The final word on the matter is from a New Zealand perspective and is the result of the work of Robert Pinney, the author of *Early South Canterbury Runs* and *Early Northern Otago Runs*. While researching these books, Pinney found newspaper reports of our earliest trials. The *Oamaru Times* (now the *Oamaru Mail*) of 9 July 1869 carried a report of the third annual Wanaka dog trial on 22–23 June of that year. This proves two things: that the Wanaka club held their first event in 1867 (six years before the Welsh), and that the time it takes clubs to get their results in the paper hasn't speeded up in 130 years!

There is no doubt that Bala is the world's longest established, competitive sheep dog trial club, although it did go into recess during both world wars. This gives the distinction of holding the longest running annual trial to New Zealand's oldest club, Waitaki, which celebrated its centennial in 1985. In fact, the first trial in the Waitaki Valley region was a one-off event held on Waitangi Station in 1868. A year later and upriver, in the Mackenzie Country, there was a trial on Black Forest Station, which was reported in the *Timaru Herald*. 'The conditions of the trial were to put three sheep into three separate pens in half an hour, the sheep having half a mile start.' I assume that the reference to a half-mile start means that the dog had to run out and head the sheep, bring them home, then make them heartily sick of going in and out of a yard. The neighbouring property, Haldon Station, ran a trial in 1870 that included the first ever competition for New Zealand's own breed, the huntaway. The following year the Black Forest trial boasted prize money of £11 12s 6d for the McKenzie Sweepstake, for heading dogs, and huntaways competed in the Mount Cook Stakes for a stake of £5 2s 6d. 'J. McDonald of Black Forest with his Bob was equal first. With Bob hunting six sheep half a mile between sets of flags 20 yards apart at an angle of 45 degrees.'

Much more will be said about the huntaway later in this book. For now, the definition of former *Auckland Weekly* rural columnist Rupert Sharpe will suffice. All his early working life was spent as a shepherd — 'the 25 years in which a team of dogs helped me earn a living' — followed by 'five happy years on the government gravy train as a valuer'. Sharpe then became a journalist, wielding a somewhat irreverent pen. 'A Huntaway is a cheerful, childish sort of creature that barks when it runs, or when you suggest it.' Sharpe's portrait of a heading dog is a little more tongue in cheek: 'A heading dog's natural inclination is to run quietly around to the far side of any group, muster them into a mob, and then kill one and eat it! After a little training it will run round the sheep and then pull them back towards the man who started the dog.' The second approach is the only one that would give any chance of gaining a place at a dog trial.

The dogs run at these early events were immediate descendants of those the original Scots and Border shepherds brought out with them. The dogs, it was soon realised, were at least as useful as their owners, and nowhere more so than on the extensive tussock and mountain grassland runs the early graziers took up in the South Island. These men, whether they were shepherds, overseers or runholders, played a major role in establishing sheep dog trialling here and, at the same time, embedded the principles of stockmanship in the sport. Their intentions are still an important part of the Aims and Objects of the New Zealand Sheep Dog Trial Association, despite being written in the usual legalese of this kind of document, which I helped to update. Article 4-01 (a) states: 'Foster in stockmen and the wider community, a full understanding of the skills of handling stock and working sheep dogs.' Browsing through the records of club after club, it's impossible to ignore the role Scots settlers played in starting most of the early clubs and establishing traditions that are still upheld today — their national beverage is still consumed at every trial. The lists of early office bearers are loaded with MacKenzies and McKenzies, Mathesons and Mathiesons, McDonalds and Macdonalds, to say nothing of all the Andersons, Hamiltons, Scotts and McKays. It would have been people of that ilk, true shepherds who believed in the natural strength and ability of their own dogs, who held the first real dog trial.

This unofficial meeting would have happened long before the events I've already mentioned, and been much easier to organise. It would have been the result of a wager between two shepherds from the same property or nominated shepherds from neighbouring stations. This rivalry was based on the personal bias all dog owners have, which is why trialling still exists, and is nicely summed up by the writer Donald McDonald. 'Your dog and my dog are all right. My dog is necessarily a better dog than yours. It is not a matter of opinion, or of partiality, or of prejudice; it is a matter of fact, proved by experience all the world over. … I am willing to admit certain virtues in your dog. But their comparative merits form a topic upon which anything like agreement is quite impossible.' As is still the case today, any form of agreement is left in the hands of an independent authority, a judge, who'll deliver a result that won't always meet with universal approval. In the case of my imagined first trial, the owner or overseer would have acted as judge. As often happens today, though, there may not have been the need for an unbiased opinion. If one man's dog headed the hill well and brought the sheep safely down a big spur and into the sheep-yards, both he and the judge would be satisfied. If the other's effort ended with one sheep in the middle of a creek, another cowering behind a matagouri bush and the third a mere wisp of dust on the lip of a distant ridge, deciding who won the half-crown, or the bottle of mountain dew, wouldn't be difficult.

One-on-one contests of that nature were very close to the heart of Peter Newton, Canterbury's High Country author, who was also a competitor, judge and lifelong supporter of sheep dog trials. 'Where each man is only as good as his dog.' That still holds true, but the problem can be that, as the moment of truth approaches, would-be competitors may, understandably, have mounting doubts about whether they and their dogs are good enough. It was also the case in the earliest days of trialling itself, especially at a district's inaugural trial, where everyone was having their first run in public. This was certainly what happened at Porangahau in 1889, where the East Coast Club's trial was the North Island's first. This event was hampered by a widespread attack of nerves, which, according to club records, led to a serious outbreak of withdrawal symptoms. 'Of the 25 entries in Class I only nine started and of the seven entries in Class II, only a modest two faced the judges — and the criticism of the spectators, which was probably more pungent, if less expert. In the Huntaway, Hugh McDonald's Glen was unable to put his sheep between the flags, but had enough force to put them through a wire fence! Never the less, in the judge's estimate he showed enough knowledge of hunting away to gain him first place.'

After their nerve-wracked, but otherwise successful first trial, the East Coast club went into recess, though no one seems to know why. They reconvened in 1896, when two other North Island clubs, Martinborough and Mohaka, got under way. I've been a member of the Martinborough Collie Club — the MCC — since the early 1980s and their first trial had much in common with conditions that can still occur: strong winds and sheep of uncertain temperament. The creatures they tried to work in 1896 weren't just temperamental, they were well nigh impossible, as past president and patron Murdoch McLeod recalled 50 years later. 'The sheep were Merinos from Whatarangi Station and few of them waited at the flag long enough for the dog to head them. I owned a splendid dog who ran out well, but the sheep had disappeared. He eventually tracked them down to the boundary fence and brought them down another ridge under good control, but three-quarters of an hour late!'

Looking back on those first trials, it's fair to say that, in most cases, neither sheep nor dogs were really up to it. The result was shoddy work or none at all, when the dog failed to find the sheep. This must have been what happened during at least one of Waitaki's earliest trials, prompting a long head judge to say to the locals: 'You fellows must be good shots.'

'Why?' he was asked.

'Well,' he said. 'How the hell do you get your mutton?'

Despite disasters and embarrassments, and with the exception of the seven-year pause at Porangahau, all the country's clubs ran annual trials, with their competitors coming back for more the following year. Reading newspaper reports, such as this from Waikari's 1893 trial, you'd wonder why. 'Short Pull and Yard (12 entries). Results: First, Jasper Stewart's Dash. This was the only man to yard. He succeeded in getting the sheep into the yard but was not quick enough in closing the gate and two escaped. He rushed into the pen and pushed the Merino's horns through the bars of the hurdle [at the back], and tied them with a piece of flax. He then tried to pen the other two, but time was called.'

In similar vein are notes from the Methven Collie Club's first gathering in 1897. 'Course I Heading and bringing back three merino wethers about 500 yards (19 entries). Mr R. Pollock's "Wily" made some zig zag work and was lost sight of and eight minutes elapsed before he was seen again. Mr A. McFarlane's Doll — After some fiddling, the sheep were sighted and headed, a little noisily. "Yarrow" trialled by F.W. Clarkson, headed his sheep well. He brought them back steadily and quietly but was slack getting them into the ring. Then to the amusement of the onlookers he started to talk to his dog. "If you don't hurry up, then time will be up … and then you will get fits!" ' The extra talking-to worked — Yarrow came second.

By the turn of the century at least ten New Zealand clubs held an annual trial. Along with Waitaki, Methven, Waikari, Martinborough, East Coast and Mohaka, clubs were established in the Mackenzie Country, at Moawhango near Taihape, at Kaiti in Poverty Bay and at Hawke's Bay's Taradale. The original Taradale grounds have long since become part of that town's suburbs, and they're now in the safety of the hills, some 15 kilometres inland. It was there that they celebrated their centenary in 1993. As jubilee programme after club history after anniversary booklet invariably states, the first meeting called to discuss the idea of forming a collie club, collie dog club or sheep dog trial club (there are six or seven variations) was called by runholders and other sheep men, 'with an interest in improving the quality of stock work and dog handling in this district'. Other clubs have begun for reasons much more personal. It is said that the Weber club in southern Hawke's Bay was begun by a Mr Crosse of Kelvin Grove Station, after he had seen Colin Thom and his huntaway Glen in action. Thom was an experienced triallist from the South Island High Country who mustered on Kelvin Grove at the same time as A.R. (Bob) Mills. Years later, Mills wrote, among others, the book *Huntaway*. 'He [Mr Crosse] was so impressed that he, there and then, decided to form a Dog-Trial Club at Weber. The first trial [during the First World War] was a great success.'

The stimulus that led to the formation of a club in the Mangamahu Valley, near Wanganui, emerged in a railway carriage, when the valley's two practising triallists were returning from competing at Waitotara. They were uncle and nephew, Alan Campbell and Don McKinnon, respectively, who felt that 'what other districts could do, Mangamahu could do'. It certainly did, and very quickly. Just two months elapsed between their conversation in the carriage and the first trial in July 1923. Because of the rush there was no time to build obstacles for the trial course or holding yards for the sheep. As a result, all the valley's gateways looked like an eight-year-old's mouth, as every available gate was simply lifted off its gudgeons (known to southerners as dogs) and pressed into service at the trial. Despite holding the event in midwinter with 'mud up to the neck', there were more than 100 entries on the two courses, a head and a hunt.

The Tokarahi club in North Otago came into being in 1935 because a long-established club, Ngapara, had gone into recess. They, too, suffered from a lack of equipment. 'The secretary [Arthur Hore] sat on a soapbox in a tent and took entries. Truly a case of "simple sat on a soapbox" — it being only the second trial he had attended.' Some years later when Tokarahi had erected a cookshop and headquarters building they decided they needed to have the phone on. They simply went out to the roadside, hooked into the local line and intercepted calls from the party line they'd tapped into. That worked very well until one year a Post Office engineer — they ran the phones in those days — stopped at the side of the road to watch the trials while he had smoko. Obviously the runs weren't all that good and, as his gaze went skyward, it hardened into a civil service scowl, and that was the end of Tokorahi's contact with the outside world.

Naturally enough, sheep dog trialling's expansion followed the opening and development of new farming districts, a trend that has continued to the present day. It was no coincidence that the Mohaka club's inception in 1896 coincided with the opening of the Napier-Mohaka road. The Taupo club was formed in 1967 as a result of the extensive development and settlement on the Central Plateau. As many of the settlers and Lands and Survey staff had been involved in trialling elsewhere, it was inevitable that they'd form a club of their own. Over towards the eastern lip of the same plateau, the country's youngest club, Rangitaiki, has held an annual open trial since 1995. This is on Lochinver Station, a very large property developed by Sir William Stevenson and his family from the 1960s on. Much of this harsh upland environment had been quickly and effectively transformed into farmland. With similar efficiency, Lochinver's staff, and those from nearby Landcorp properties, established, virtually overnight it seemed, a trial that immediately ranked with the best in the country. In all these matters, though, if you look behind the scenes you'll find someone with dog trialling in their blood. In the Rangitaiki club's case, Lochinver's stock manager, Colin Gray, has a trialling pedigree which, through his father and uncles, reaches back to the stations and trial grounds of the Canterbury High Country.

It would be impossible to estimate but at least half of our 170 clubs would probably have been formed as a direct result of an experienced triallist moving into the area. That was certainly the case with Peter MacKenzie, who moved from Hawke's Bay to Northland around 1917. His dogs were the envy of his neighbours and spectators at northern A&P shows, where he gave demonstrations. In time, his influence led to the formation of the Northland Club, of which Peter was the first president and his brother, Jim, the secretary. This club was established with the ambitious aim of holding an annual trial, in three different districts, Kaitaia, Herekino and the district whose name and trial survives today, Broadwood. By 1942 the concept of using three different grounds on a roster had been dropped and the club moved to a new site at Rockfield. There they got on with building new facilities in a way that seems a lot less complicated than today. Or it could be in the telling, by long-time club member and patron, Eric Carman. 'A pavilion was required, so we went into the bush and felled a tree, took it to Herb Hodges' mill where Eric McGraith is now, milled it and taking it back erected a pavilion.' It sounds so easy, though there was a ten-year gap between Broadwood's arrival at Rockfield in '42 and the pavilion's official opening in '52. 'We had forty two enjoyable years at Rockfield, it was a beautiful spot with pigeons flitting around in the patches of bush.'

One of my favourite accounts of a club's inaugural trial is a letter written by Mr J.H. Thompson of Northland. He addressed it to the Maungakaramea secretary, after making a mistake with the dates of that club's fiftieth jubilee trial, and missing the entire celebration. Mr Thompson was competitor at Maungakaramea's first trial in 1913. 'Seventeen dogs ran and Mr Sloane won with Fly, who had the last run. I only remember one event that year which was a long head. We all took our own sheep away. Donnie McClennan boiled the billy and we had six loaves of bread and butter and a leg of mutton afterwards. It was more of a field day. There was plenty of beer and whisky.'

With one or two exceptions in the staunchly Presbyterian south, the aforementioned lubricants and whistle-wetters have played quite a part in dog trialling. There have been many occasions when a competitor has gained more pleasure, albeit temporary, from an hour or so in the bar, than a few minutes of hell on the trial paddock. This was surely the case at the Omarama Collie Club's first trial, held in 1915. 'The trials lasted two days, after which the visitors departed, but the local aftermath occupied the rest of the week.' On other occasions, certain incidents would provide fuel for gossip or leg pulling at many trials to come. 'We were up on the old Ruahine course, and the old man, well, he'd lubricated himself pretty well — the old bugger — and the bar was a fair way from the cars. To go the shortcut meant you had to jump the creek. So I said to him before I left, "Don't forget, get over there by that drive and go down the walkway, you'll never make it over the creek." No way was he going the long way.

' "Hell, I can get through there," he reckoned.

'The next thing we saw, he was flat on his back in the middle of the bloody creek with his watch, whistle, glasses and teeth all under water. A week later Kingi Lambert saw the old man at another trial and came up to him and said: "I was up the Ruahines the other day, crossing the creek," he says, "and you know what, I saw this bloody great eel and it had false teeth and was wearing glasses"!'

Moawhango, on the lower reaches of the Napier-Taihape road, held its first trial in 1899. In those days, and in many cases right up to the 1950s or 1960s, each of the three or four events — long head, short head and yard, zigzag hunt and maybe a straight hunt — were run in sequence, usually on the same hill. Not like today where, with a few exceptions, there are three or four separate courses, with everything running concurrently. Running each event in turn in districts like Moawhango, then a very isolated community, meant that when every-one came out of the nearby hills, they were there to stay, and play. 'Usually everybody took three days holiday, with Sunday to recover and return home. A smoke concert was always held on the first night, with a big ball to finish proceedings on the Saturday night.' In com-munities such as this, their dog trial was the event of the year, and catered for a wide range of tastes and interests. Dog men could run their dogs, drink beer and tell lies. Local school children would get at least a half holiday, and the ball meant that the women of the district could appear in their newest and finest. In some districts the ball was of such importance that it warranted separate coverage in the local paper. In 1938 the *Oamaru Mail* gave a very full account of the Tokarahi Collie Dog Club's annual knees-up. After praising the decor — red white and blue paper chains and 'luscious ferns' — it carried on with a fashionable form of roll call. 'Among those present were —

Mesdames A. Gardiner, midnight blue Chenille velvet; A. Henderson, red lace and Georgette; A. Sutton, blue satin Romaine; R. Simpson, black frock Oriental coat; Rona Blanchard, pink net; E. Conlan Angel skin lace …'

When the early Scots shepherds and runholders decided to organise competitions which, they hoped, would establish who had the best dogs, they provided a basis for much more. Very few rural communities in this country have been without a dog trial at some stage or another. Today, with better roads and vehicles, along with rural depopulation and forestry expansion, many district clubs, sports meetings and annual occasions have fallen by the wayside. In many instances, the last club or yearly gathering that bears an individual district's name is the sheep dog trial.

3

HAVING A GO

There are times when you'd think that it might be easier to start a dog trial club than to encourage, cajole or even threaten some extremely reluctant individuals into beginning a competitive career. Some people develop a great fear of competing yet are quite prepared to have a go at such life-threatening activities as unofficial rally driving, rock climbing or bungy jumping. Maybe they think a broken neck is better than a red face. There's no doubt that walking out to the mark at a trial can be a rather a lonely and nerve-wracking experience, aptly summed up by Marlborough triallist, Lionel Winstanley: 'You have no friends. The judge, the sheep and sometimes the dog, are all against you.' There's no doubt that a fatalistic feeling can wash over you, when you realise you're at the mercy of your dog — with whom you wish you'd spent more time — and three sheep, creatures from the same mob as those you've watch bury the hopes of the last five competitors in a row. You also get the feeling that all eyes are upon you, and waiting for something to happen that will provide a good laugh. But unless you've been going round the grounds shooting your mouth off about how good you and your dog are, the only looks you'll attract will be those of support.

The fact is, most regulars couldn't give a toss about a competitor's track record, or complete lack of it, and take little notice of who's walking to the foot of the hill for the next run. They will, however, sit up and pay close attention when they see good work, especially if they realise it's a newcomer. I do have to admit, though, because it can provide very good entertainment, that they also enjoy watching a dog who, full of fire, frenzy and very little apparent common sense, makes some spectacular, but rash, moves towards the sheep. The woollies, in turn, put in some flash moves of their own — in the opposite direction — and, after the initial flurry, an abrupt end to the action is the result. In a huntaway event, the sheep are supposed to climb uphill, away from the competitor. One silly move, however, can offend the sheep so much that, all of a sudden, the dog's above them and they're hurtling back down the hill, straight at you.

On heading courses, where the dog can be sent out to fetch three sheep, waiting on the mark up to 800 metres away, the first hope is that it gets there. Hope number two is that, when the dog does make contact, this is by sight only. If things do go wrong up there, before you know it, three innocent-looking sheep have turned into woolly missiles — aimed straight at you. Top triallist, and trainer of men and dogs, Les Knight, has a good description of a similar incident in his book, *A Guide to Training Sheep Dogs*. It concerns a young, but very quick and fiery heading dog called Belle who '… soon woke up to the fact that on trial days she could pull my leg a little, without coming to any harm, so proceeded to make the most of it, to the extent that she ran the big Te Anga hill [in the northern King Country] in record time, and came home just as quickly. Sheep and dog passed me at a flat gallop, not slowing until there was a crash at the road gate. Only then did Belle look around for me.' Les has won four New Zealand titles and another twelve at North and South Island Championships and one of those was won by Belle, just a year later, after graduating from Les's finishing school. Seeing something like the Belle incident occur to one of the guns is inclined to put off those of us who were thinking of having a go. Mind you, some might react with the thought, 'Well I can't do any worse!' Yes you can. For all her dash and bash behind her sheep, Belle did head them, on a very big and difficult hill, and probably without any points off, either.

There's one important point about running, or not running, at trials that's well worth considering. If your dog has little aptitude, interest or you've simply forgotten to break the poor blighter in, then whipping your name off the list of runners is probably a good idea. I suspect that was the reason why so many would-be competitors at Porangahau, back in 1889, pulled out. For the first time, many would have seen the level of command necessary to control three sheep, within a predetermined course. They would also have noted how the sheep were behaving, and that may well have settled the matter. At the Paparangi club's first trial (north-west of Wanganui) in 1913, the mixed aged wethers for the long head were so wild that they were carted to the mark by a horse and dray, with pig netting over the top, to stop them leaping out.

Watching that kind of carry-on, no one would blame you if you put the start of your dog trial career on hold.

The most succinct reason I've come across for not taking proven station dogs to a dog trial was given by Joe Condon from the Waitaki Valley. For 44 years Joe was a shepherd, then head shepherd on Waitangi Station, and retired to nearby Kurow in 1931. Because of his ability on Waitangi's hills he was asked, 'Why don't you go to the dog trials, Joe?' His reply: 'I've got a good reputation and I'm going to keep it!' Those who have a dog with promise should have a go. Then, and only then, will they find how much more there is for them and their dog to learn. Les Knight, for example, went to his first trial because someone had commented to him that his young dog, Tyke, had the potential to be a trial dog. 'At that stage I didn't know what a trial or a trial dog was, but decided to have a go anyway. It was at a little club called Kaeaea (now Aria) that Tyke first ran, and I was lucky enough to have some of the experienced men tell me what was required. It was that air of helpfulness and good sportsmanship that has always attracted me to trials.... we performed well enough to win the maiden and place fourth in the open. That was enough to seal my fate, making me an addict for life.' Later that season, Les and Tyke won their first open event. Since then Les has won countless opens, with the more than 50 dogs he has broken in.

Having success of some sort at a first trial is not all that uncommon, but winning an open event, as Bob Wilson did at Ashburton, is extremely rare since the open is the top class. The grade immediately below is the intermediate, and then comes the maiden, for dogs who, when it comes to winning, have been perfectly chaste. When a dog wins a maiden it then competes as an intermediate and when it wins an open event, it becomes an open dog and can compete only at that level. Whatever the classification, though, everyone competes on the same course, the only difference being the prizes for which individual dogs are eligible. A maiden dog, therefore, is also in the running for intermediate and open prizes and can gain places in all three classes, at the same time — even win them. When that happens, the owner can be seen patting the dog some days after. Some clubs also have a prize for the best run by a novice, who is having their first public outing.

Some 45 years after making his trial debut at Oxford with Rock, a huntaway, Peter Newton certainly remembered his first run. 'Needless to say I was as nervous as a cat, but my ordeal didn't last long — ten seconds at the most, I'd say. Rock was worse than useless on a few sheep in hand [close by], and his first three bounds wrecked everything completely. Those three sheep got the quickest change of grazing they'd ever had. But the beer was good and I'd had a good day.' For many years Peter Newton was the South Island dog trial correspondent for the *New Zealand Farmer* magazine. The man who covered North Island trialling at the same time was Ian Sinclair, who spent many years mustering on the big stations along the Taihape to Napier road, otherwise known as the Inland Patea. Ian has as quick and clever a turn of phrase as any New Zealand writer, and his book, *Boot in the Stirrup*, contains many colourful descriptions of mustering, musterers and sheep dogs. Its foreword, like Ian, is a touch unconventional. 'I've written this book solely for my own amusement. If it amuses you, then you must have a peculiar sense of humour.' One of the many incidents he described occurred in 1945. 'It was during this year I made a singularly unsuccessful debut in the dog trialling world. None of my dogs went further up the hill than halfway. This also included my heading run, as well as my three huntaways.' The trial ground was at Mataroa, just out of Taihape, and 30 years later, in the *Farmer*, Ian summed up his debut day as a series of opposites: 'I ran four dogs there. My heading dog didn't head, but my huntaways did!'

For newcomers it's easy to think that an unfortunate first run has been an absolute disaster, to brand trialling immediately as an impractical and impossible form of recreation and to decide to have nothing more to do with it. I suppose there are times when I wish I'd taken that attitude but such thoughts last no longer than a grumbling, mumbling, minute or two. Then you start thinking about running on the course next door and march towards it, reinflating your typical dog triallist's chest, in which hope always springs eternal. Dog trialling is all about optimism, with a touch of masochism, enabling you to take a beating and bounce back for more. Of course, if the right amount of preparation hasn't been put in beforehand, then no amount of luck or hope will ward off the inevitable. Those who walk away from an initial disaster with a determination to learn and return, do exactly that — gain just reward, and become real dog triallists. The blighters then become addicted, as Les Knight did, and hang around the trials for years keeping the rest of us out of the prize money. Debutantes who walk away soured by an unfortunate experience, and do little to avoid the same thing happening again, will never be dog triallists —and that's all right too.

The journey towards my first real run at an open dog trial began in the spring of 1980, in Pinehaven, a suburb of Upper Hutt, near Wellington. The great attractions at that year's school gala were Bob Bryson with Bruce and Trump, a son of Bob Wilson's Rose. This was the team who were runners-up in the doubles event (six sheep, two dogs and two yards) in that year's series of … *a Dog's Show*. They put up just as good a performance at Pinehaven, too, with sheep borrowed from Wallaceville Animal Research Station, who were steered round an unfenced course in the middle of the school playground. For the necessary obstacles we had brightly painted red and white hurdles and yards which, as someone said at the time, looked just like 'the ones they have on the television'. They were. Bob's eleven-year-old son, Guy, brought his dog with him and had two runs, ending both by coolly and calmly penning his three sheep. The bitch he ran, Jet, wasn't young, but as she'd been one of the best in the country, popping three sheep in a yard for a young fellow she obviously liked and listened to wasn't a problem.

Jet had in fact been in the first series of … *a Dog's Show* in 1977 with her previous boss, Ted Morrow, who was the pick of the North Islanders that year. Ultimately, though, Ted and his team came second to the South's Ginger Anderson, with Boss and King. Ted was getting on in years, approaching 80 I think, and was asked, during an on-screen interview, 'When will you retire from dog trialling?' As quick as a flash he barked: 'When I bloody well die!' A couple of years later Ted decided that Jet should retire and he gave her to Guy Bryson. This was despite the fact that he had once turned down a lot of money because he didn't want to part with her. Guy got Jet because 'A boy needs an old dog to start with … show him what to do'. You'll often see a young girl or boy have their first trial run with a dog who knows much more than they do. Often this will be on an enclosed, special, show ring course for heading dogs. Working their way through this, the youngster may look a little tentative and unsure, but the dog just does the business. On more than one occasion, especially as a judge, I've said to my timekeeper, 'They're doing well, is this really their first run?' You're quickly informed that it's 'so-and-so's daughter' and, although this is her first outing, the dog is a veteran. 'That's Glen, who he [so-and-so] got in a couple of island [championship] run offs with.' The best example I've seen occurred in the mid-1980s, when I judged the show ring special at Taupo. The young gentleman making his debut was twelve, a few months older than the dog, who, I think, was called Bob. They usually are.

In the North Island, show ring events are run within a confined space, usually an oblong shape, and contain several obstacles — parallel hurdles, a narrow race, a gateway, a bridge — then finish with a yard. The normal procedure with obstacles is that, when the sheep have completed each of them, the competitor follows them through; the dog doesn't have to. In this particular run Bob and the boy were on either side of the entrance to the hurdles and the sheep were nicely positioned, about a metre back from the entrance. After the normal amount of hesitation and prick-eared heads in the air looking round for an alternative route, the trio went through. The lad, anxious to hold the balance and keep them going straight, started to move forward on a line 2 metres parallel to the hurdles, not between them. Over on the other side, the dog seemed to sense that the boss was going to do something quite wrong and stopped. As if it was he who was being worked, the lad stopped. Old Bob (his full name) looked up at him, then at the hurdles, and back at the boss, repeated the routine and, finally, the lad took the hint — or the hesitation gave him time to remember — and passed through the hurdles. I found out later that not only was the dog an experienced triallist, but this was the third member of the family he'd escorted round a trial ground. I would like to finish this tale by describing how the duo finished their run with a full yard. Alas, by the time they all got to the mouth of the second to last obstacle, the bridge, the sheep had worked out that Bob was a rather nice old gentleman — maybe a bit soft even. So they just edged themselves across the mouth, to park on a wing at the edge of the ramp, and there the blighters stayed, staring at him, until I had to call time.

There have been times when I've thought, 'Why didn't I try and get myself a veteran of the hill to start with?' It's certainly what I did when I started working on farms, and to bulk up the team when I was shepherding. Scots born Bert Grierson, who became a successful Taranaki triallist, was just fourteen when, in 1913, his first boss introduced him to his first dog. 'Noo laddie, yon will be your dog. His name is Help. You'll often think the dog is wrong, but he won't be. It'll be you who are wrong.' How much easier it might have been in this, my second time round with sheep dogs, if I had had a Help, not a dog that's also learning. But no, if there's a difficult path, I'll give it a crack.

As the Pinehaven event wound down, the Brysons crossed the road to our place for afters. Later, as they were leaving, I said to Bob, somewhat hesitantly, 'Look, if you ever have a spare pup, I'd be happy to try and break it in … see what I can do.' For someone living in a city, without access to sheep, or any sort of training support, that wasn't the best idea since sliced bread. 'Anyway,' I later thought, 'Bob'll probably forget about it. Everyone wants one of his line.' I was, though, always aware of a hankering for some kind of practical involvement in trialling, to say nothing of having a dog again. The following autumn the phone rang and Bob, in his direct and economical way, informed me that 'There's a pup here for you. From not a bad-looking litter. Gary Brennan's getting one of them so they must be okay.' (Gary's five-time national winner, Dick, was the father of the other very good Bryson dog, Bruce.) Bob went on: 'I've picked which one it'll be. In your position you need a decent-looking dog, not some ugly beggar, and it's a bitch. Living in town, you don't need a dog that's going to go round peeing on car wheels or looking for hot bitches all the time. And she's half Wilson blood, half Brennan blood … should be all right.'

All that remained after that was to organise an expedition to Makuri, east of Pahiatua, where Bob was managing, and collect the creature. It should be said that, at Bob's insistence, no money changed hands; it was a gesture to get me started. The eight-week-old bundle of black fur with a white-tipped tail, blaze, ruff and four white paws was put on the floor of the Volkswagen where, at different stages of the journey we learned, as they say, that all systems were go. She became known as Peg, after Peg Taylor, the venerable publican and main character in the documentary series, *The Southlanders*, I was working on at the time. Peg became part of the family but, apart from the first few weeks, was an outside dog with her own motel, a little to the right of the clothesline. As she grew, her natural instinct to eye and herd became apparent in playing with a then three-year-old person called Rebecca, whose every move was closely followed. The moment Beccy climbed aboard her tractor-trike contraption, Peg would put in a quick block. Beccy would then turn to move in the other direction, but the pup would be there already. She'd naturally assume the classic stalking pose: eyes full of intent, three paws on the ground and paw number four poised between lawn and jaw, ready for the next move. In time a wail from a completely corralled child would bring parental assistance and one youngster or the other would find itself inside its house.

Some aspects of Peg's training were unusual. The run whistle — by the way, she was a heading dog — was first put on as a 'get up' command, on to the front patio. This was gradually lengthened by moving further down the lawn. We then crossed the road to the park and gained greater distance by running her out to two of her best friends, John and Rachel, the elder of the Gordon children. I was lucky, she loved to run and, as she got older, I kept her fit for very different terrain by running her from one end of the Pinehaven park to the other end of the school playground on whistles alone. By then commands were sufficient, which was just as well, as the children had long since got sick of being treated as sheep. Her sides — the left and right commands — were put on by walking her towards me and using various forms of body language. Once they seemed to have sunk in I simply turned her around, to apply them as she went away from me. This was preparation for fetching woolly trios off the top of all these big hills we were going to conquer. Talk about playground dreams! At no time did I use training equipment that I now know to be of use, such as a training rope, pole or harness, and certainly not an electric collar. That would have created all kinds of suburban misunderstanding. As it was, enough happened to cause complaint. Apparently my whistles were too loud, especially for the genteel folk who played tennis or wanted to sleep in of a Sunday morning. Not that I ever had much interference. To the average urbanite I was obviously right off my trolley and it's a well-known fact that people in such a state should be humoured, not accosted.

After almost two years of city living Peg had still not seen what she was born to work — sheep. A camping holiday in the King Country fixed that. Under the benevolent guidance of Cyril Perry, a campsite had been selected for us in a beautiful valley, west of Pio Pio. This was on dog triallist Barry Murphy's property and, with the surrounding ridges topped by spectacular limestone crags, a trout stream below and paddocks full of sheep all about us, it seemed like heaven. Well, to me anyway, and when the sun shone and the creek wasn't in flood, Adrienne and the children thought it was all right too. Peg saw sheep, chased sheep, began to work sheep and, at all times, ran like the wind — which, at the time, I did wonder about. While we were shifting his sheep, Barry talked a lot about the coming dog trial season, especially the first major outing in that part of the world, the Whanga' trip. This involved three or four trials over the same number of days, though attending them all depended on your stamina and where you lived. The first three ran in a westerly line between Taumarunui and Stratford: Tokirima, Whangamomona and Tututawa. Then it was on to Paparangi which, being quite near Wanganui, is a fair way from the others, so northern triallists usually gave it a miss. Not so southerners, on their way back to base.

The more I heard of that trip, the more determined I was that I would give it a go and make it a full-blooded initiation to real trialling. Looking back, it wasn't one of my better ideas. With consecutive events, I wouldn't be able to return home, lick my wounds and undertake any special counselling that either party required, until it was all over. I did leave a day early, arriving at Tokirima around noon, on day one of their two-day trial. The plan was to watch what everyone else did, soak up the atmosphere and run the next day, when Cyril Perry and the King Country branch of the Murphy clan would arrive. The first thing I noticed was that people were noticing me. By that time I'd been commentator for six series of … *a Dog's Show* and, for the last three years, the on-screen presenter as well. This, combined with the somewhat incredulous reaction to my turning up to run a city-trained dog, meant that it wouldn't be an anonymous debut.

Later in the day I wandered down the road to the short head and yard course, sat beneath a willow's shade and studied the challenge. The sheep were parked in the liberation area, some distance up a fairly steep hill. Below that was an L-shaped flat for the drives (dog taking one side, man the other) with the hurdles at the base of the 'L', and the yard at the end of it. I also took note that, through those areas, a major mowing job had been done on what must have been a forest of tall, dense rushes — the rest of the flat was covered in them. Sitting there in casual country comfort, watching others run their dogs, the more I saw, the more nervous, and foolhardy, I became. I decided that I'd run that day and not wait until tomorrow, having worked out that there'd be a far bigger crowd to watch the action. As it was, Les Knight was there and because he had suffered the pressures of trialling on television he took some pleasure from seeing me visibly deteriorate with nerves. I remember saying to him, 'This is ridiculous, there are only half a dozen people here and I'm more nervous than waiting for a cue to go live into the network.' To which Les (rubbing his hands with glee) merely replied: 'Ooh, I'm enjoying this, I'm enjoying this!' He then went on to give a little pertinent advice, well knowing that screeds of helpful hints are useless.

With Les's 'Good luck, hee hee hee' ringing in my ears, I went to the quad at the hill end of the flat and in due course the judge gave us the go. Like a bullet, Peg shot across the flat, quite literally flew over the fence and nearly knocked herself out on the hill; the steep face at that point went straight up from the foot of the fence. The orthodox run out or cast on a dog trial hill is on the triallist's right of the sheep, the idea being to come round them from that side, at a good distance, and stop directly above them. The dog also needs to be far enough from the trio in the liberation area so as not to frighten them. Because she had ignored what right-hand whistles I had managed to issue on the way up the hill, Peg arrived on the left side and, just as unfortunate, was beneath the sheep. So the strategy quickly moved on to Plan B: a swift lift (moving the sheep downhill) before they walked all over the dog — she was only 30 centimetres away from them! It was swift all right; the trio bolted straight down the hill on a line as straight and pure as a liberation area fence. When that ended, they immediately did a 90° dart to their left, and sped towards more open ground. I quickly realised we needed to move on to Plan C: the hard left on Peg to catch and block the trio, and pull them down from there. That was only 33.3

percent successful. One ewe started to march downhill towards me, while the other two kept tearing across the hill at 50 kilometres an hour. We then went through Plans D to W. Peg sent to catch the runaways; Peg lost in the long grass; John's mouth now dry and whistleless; the duo in overdrive, and close to the horizon. At the same time, and without any help — or hindrance — from the dog or me, the solo runner came to a halt about 10 metres in front of me, and got there on a straight line, too. At that point I knew that, as far as a competitive run was concerned, it was all over. The job itself wasn't, though, as I still had to get my three sheep in safe custody so that the next man could have his run. So into the tall rushes I went and in due course, rather like a church caretaker after a windy wedding, I swept up all the confetti and sanity returned to the trial ground.

As I slunk back in front of the few who were present, wishing they hadn't mown the rushes on that side of the paddock, I waited for comments such as, 'It's much harder than talking about it, isn't it?' It was, of course, the opposite. 'By Jove, you're going to have a lot of fun with that dog,' said Les. 'She got her sheep and now she knows they're up there she'll get better all the time.' With support and encouragement such as that, how could you withdraw from running in the long head the next morning? It was an option I'd considered, as I trudged towards the car park after our first attempt. For a team such as Peg and I, Tokirima's long head is more suitable for pulling out of than for pulling sheep down — the second of this event's two main aims. The first is to head sheep that wait towards the top of a steeply sloping valley. To get up there the dog has to cope with very rough country, with more wrinkles in it than a bunkhouse blanket, as the slope tumbles down from a razor-back ridge. Again, Peg was off like a bullet. Because she was more accustomed to the firm, flat footholds of a football field, the rushes, rocks and hollows had her on her nose, back and in the air as much as she was on the ground. But, as Les said after her previous run, 'she got her sheep'. After that there was little more to report; we cleared up the mess as best we could and the trial got going again.

The next day we were still surrounded by steep hills, though we'd moved to the Taranaki back country and the Whangamomona trial. I had heard talk of the challenge of the long head here and, expecting to see something impressive and difficult, I wasn't disappointed. From the flat centre of a small but attractive, willow-fringed basin there's a demanding leading ridge for the dog to follow and, after a lung-loosening journey, finally gain access to the first of the twin peaks. Having scaled those heights, the dog takes a left turn to traverse a blind basin (meaning it can't see the sheep) to reach the second peak. Below this, hidden beneath a steep lip, the sheep await … often for very long periods at a time. With heart and whistle intermingling in my mouth, I heard the judge, Ivan Grice, say 'Just when you're ready, John.' About 1998 Ivan! (It was 1983.) Kind of him, though, as they usually snap the blankness with a resounding 'ti-i-i-me'. On the other hand, he had witnessed my first run at Tokirima. For a while at least, this was to be different.

I gave Peg her run whistle and away she ran, and how she ran — and on the correct line. Up the ridge she soared, literally flying over rugged country, and reached the rushes under the first peak. She wheeled left to traverse the hanging basin and came below the second peak to the brow the sheep were just beneath. It was magnificent stuff, and you must forgive me for my owner's eloquence, but to this day there is nothing that gives me a greater thrill than to see a dog, especially my own, run a big hill with pace and purpose. Down on the flat you can have all the flash drives, perfect hurdles and penalty-free yards you like; seeing a heading dog doing what it was born to do, head sheep on big hills, is the ultimate. W.V. McIntyre, one of trialling's earliest guns and characters, certainly thought so. 'It was in 1945, good gracious me, there's this tremendous bloody hill, man … a veritable mountain. There's all this burnt scrub and rubbish right across the bottom of it, then clear ground, then more bloody undergrowth. My God, man, a terrifically long run. I started the wee Scott … like an arrow from a bow, you should see him go. He got tangled up in some bloody lawyers and stuff, before the black stuff, and while he's doing that, the sheep left the mark. By God, man, I put the hard whistle on … you know, my hard whistle. God, he came in a bit and he came out and, God, he kept going and went all through this big ground. Over the next brow, through that stuff. My God, man, he finally headed them clear and clean, and straight behind them. My God, man he travelled over a thousand yards! A beautiful run. The wee Scott ... by God, man ... I was crying.'

Whangamomona's long head could even have been the very hill 'the wee Scott' ran. Peg's run out finished with her at the back of the brow and the trio in front of it. From here on the story becomes harder to tell. Peg did not cross the brow that separated her from the sheep she deserved to have. All the whistles, warblings and suggestions I could fling from the foot of the hill, imploring her to walk forward to where she'd see what I was getting so excited about, were to no avail. She didn't believe the sheep were there and, in a private search for her quarry, got lost. I then lost sight of her. Ivan, the judge, helped out here too, spotting Peg when she finally returned to our side of the hill. She had been away so long, she could have been halfway to Stratford. While she was up there I did get her to try again, but she couldn't — or wouldn't — believe there were any sheep to be found. On the neighbouring short head course I had to carry the blame for that run grinding to an early halt. As Peg was heading towards the top of a reasonable head, I managed to blow the call off whistle rather than the keep out. She stopped dead in her tracks and looked downhill, as if to say, 'What on earth are you up to?' Good question! After another three closely connected manmade mistakes, a run that only used two of its allotted fifteen minutes hurtled to a conclusion down on the flat. The rest of my activities that day were purely social.

The next day was the third leg of the quadfecta, Tututawa, where the trial is now held, although the club is called Mangaehu-Stratford. Nothing in dog trialling is as straightforward as it first seems. Over the years Tututawa's short head has become one of my favourite courses and not just because there are no hidden vices or traps on the course itself. They have the same sheep every year, Jack Hann's Romney two-tooths, which also lack apparent vices — if you don't annoy them into developing some. We didn't that day, and haven't since, but this was the occasion that guaranteed there would be more trials in the future. The hill for the run out leans away to the right of the sheep and deceives a narrow running dog to the extent that it runs wider than normal. This meant that the sheep's nerves and stability weren't put to an early test. In fact Peg and I went all the way and made it to the yard, opened the gate and, three minutes later, when the judge called 'time', we shut it — on a still empty pen. This was the first time either of us had seen such a contraption and, frankly, we didn't know what to do. Despite that failure, when you're a beginner, everything is relative, and I regarded reaching the gate as both an achievement and a great thrill. This was one of Bert Grierson's last trials — he was then 84 — and watching me give Peg a pat and walk off, he turned to fellow onlooker, Michael Wedd, and said, 'That'll be enough to addict him for life.'

Having the habit meant that two weeks later, when I went to the South Island in the course of other duties (or used them as an excuse),

I took Peg to try our hand at trialling on the Mainland. The first stop was St Bathans in the Maniototo, where time and the pressure of entries meant we were limited to the long pull, as the long head is known in the South. Given a choice, I would have chosen the short head, because when you look at that particular course, you can very clearly see the sheep as they wait on the mark. To the naked eye, all that the daunting rock, scree and tussock of the long pull has to crown its upper reaches is an old 44-gallon drum lid painted white, and not a woolly in sight. The sheep are actually immediately below the white disc, though you'd never really know whether they were there or not, unless the dog came back empty handed. The Merinos they run on this big hill are too far away and too similar in colour to the tussock to be seen. After a courageous run out, where I was silly enough to ask her to ascend a rock face and she did, Peg got behind the white bull's-eye. In unsighted situations like this you have to use your imagination, and that's one thing I'm quite good at. For instance, I reckoned that when I did see Peg flick between the alpine plant life, there was a very good chance that the sheep would be in front of her. In time I realised that the small group of tussocks moving downhill was in fact the sheep. When the trio finally arrived in the ring with me, they stopped in a huddle on the far side, leaning on each other for support. It had been a hard season and if I'd gone over and taken out the middle one, the other two would have fallen over. But they didn't collapse, nor had my run, though it had some major holes in it. Nonetheless, when we went over to the bar at the end of the day, there on the notice board at the very bottom of the long pull results was our first mention in dispatches: 'Long Pull: Maiden, 3rd J. Gordon Peg, 82.' I was so pleased you would have thought I had won a national title. Not long after, the results from all the courses came out, and one of dog trialling's finest gentlemen, Charlie Crutchley, had won both heads with his bitch, Sue.

On courses of St Bathan's difficulty, this was a real achievement. Yet, to my eyes at least, Charlie seemed far more pleased about my very minor first ticket. 'You'll have a drink with me, John,' he said in his soft, burred Central Otago voice. I did, and we had another one too; in fact, there could even have been more. But we had a lot of fun celebrating our relative levels of success. That's why going through the uncertainty and embarrassment of your first start at a dog trial is worth the hassle. When everything's taken into account, there's far more to dog trialling than just running a dog.

4

AS LONG AS
IT WORKS

'Yeah, I'll take it — as long as it works.' That's not only the standard reaction to the offer of a new dog from a fellow shepherd, farmer or triallist, it's also why we have sheep dogs. In the whole business of genetics and selection, the only breeding programme that will benefit New Zealand pastoral farming, is one which produces dogs that work, and not just at dog trials either. For every dog that does compete, there's another thousand who, day by day, do the basic slog among the most intensively farmed sheep population in the world. When animals are bred for a sole purpose, such as stock work, a whole heap of mystique and breeder-babble is taken out of the equation. If the creature in question doesn't work or comes from a long line of downright lazy beggars, then it doesn't matter a tinker's cuss how lovely its coat looks, or what colour its bloody eyes are, it's history! This attitude is best defined as the most practical form of genetics there is — natural selection. If the progeny of a particular cross works, naturally it stays. A young dog which has no interest in stock or which unsettles everything for miles around, will, naturally, be a goner. If that youngster's litter mates showed similar traits, you can guarantee that cross won't happen again — another natural decision.

It would be wrong to assume, though, that our breeding approach for the last 150 years has been simply to sort out two good workers of opposing gender, and let them get on with it. Sheep dog breeders, farmers and triallists are no different from any other special purpose group. No matter how good the current model is, they'll want something better, or at least as good. That means looking for certain characteristics in the bitch or dog to which an owner is putting their dog, with the aim of improving working ability yet avoiding severe constitutional faults. Among these are shark jaws (badly overshot), cow hocks (lower hind legs turned out), dicky hips (hip dysplasia) and heritable blindness. It is very difficult, though, to resist the temptation to breed from a dog which has tremendous working ability, but is liable to leave a glaring constitutional fault, such as a ringtail. Unlike Australia's ringtail possum, this has nothing to do with the way a dog's rudder is marked, but how it's constructed. It's an over-long tail piece, held high in the air, so that the top half can flow forward to form a perfect arch or ring over the dog's back. If the dog were a basket, it would be easy

to carry. From what I've seen, dogs with this affliction always make their tail much more apparent, when there's a good-sized crowd to wave it at, while poncing about on tippy toes, ruining a promising run. Conversely, if a dog is doing an excellent job and attracting attention with its working ability, it's possible to ignore an exterior flaw or two.

Some individuals have practical preferences that relate either to their country's contour or to the type or breed of stock they run. Others will choose a specific dog to add a trait they reckon their line needs, such as stronger running, bigger noise or a more tractable nature. But don't be fooled, some sheep dog people have very personal preferences, verging on the idiosyncratic, and do little harm by sticking to their notions. This is the great advantage of breeding for the one main trait of working ability; after that, the world's your oyster. There are no breed inspectors running round with a measuring tape and a breed standard listing the shades and body part shapes that must be adhered to. That's why, when you see mustering teams on big stations or look around dogs at a trial, you'll see such a variation in body size and coat colour and length. The differences will usually be more pronounced between teams than within them. Individual preferences could mean, for example, that a heading pup will be kept only if it's a well-coated black and white with four white feet. The rest of the litter would not be terminally disposed of but either sold or given away. As foretelling the future of a young pup is impossible, one of those you put in someone else's hands could easily go on to win a major title — and wouldn't that gap your axe!

There are as many theories about how to select the right pup as there are litters. The bottom line is that there's no sense in taking a dog to work every day, and feeding it nightly, if you can't stand the sight of the damn thing. William Whyte, in his 1919 publication, *The Sheep-dog*, gave some very colourful advice. 'The skull should be broad and of sufficient dimensions to contain the all-important brain matter. Avoid the pinched-in, pimple-skulled, sharp-nosed excitable specimen, with the piercing, treacherous looking eye, to whom the mere sight of sheep is signal for the explosion of dangerous emotional passions.' Some heading dog people will retain only smooth-haired, tri-coloured dogs (black, tan and white); others will want a full-coated (longer-haired) dog. Many prefer bitches, others, dogs (males). Whatever their preferences, if you scratch hard enough you'll find they once belonged to a distant predecessor, invariably referred to as 'best dog I ever had.'

With huntaways there's an even wider visual and physical variation and some families (human) have striven through the generations — human and canine — to retain a particular strain. This is certainly the case with two separate beardie type, huntaway dogs bred by the Calders of North Canterbury and the Busckes of Poverty Bay. They've preferred smaller, whiskery fireballs, have bred for that and have done the industry a favour by maintaining distinctive bloodlines. As a result, they've done themselves a favour or two, winning many major titles. Generally these strains are lighter framed than others, though I've noticed that those off the Calder assembly line have got bigger of late. The bigger type is what many other huntaway exponents prefer, though they wouldn't want you to think they were inflexible. As Ian Sinclair says, 'I don't care what colour, shape or size it is, as long as it is big, black and tan, and smooth-haired!' There is an exception to every rule, though, because Tadpole, a dog Ian acquired in 1950, 'became the best huntaway I have ever owned'. Tadpole — 'by Mick Murphy's Frog out of Pat Murphy's Tess' — was in fact a big, smooth-haired, black and white dog who 'had tremendous power but was easy to handle. He was a steel fist in a silk glove and I only saw him beaten once, in a bout with a house cow with pitchfork antlers, which nearly disembowelled him, so I called him off.'

It would be wrong to assume that all the notable matings that yielded progeny who made their name on big hills, stock-yards or the trial ground, were intentional. Some errors of circumstance, best described as 'by midnight out of the drover's ute', went unobserved. Similar accidents, which were seen or at least deduced, often went unannounced, a reticence that could owe its origins to the old army saying, 'don't complain, don't explain'. Some of these breeding whodunits are still puzzled over today, stimulating plenty of creative speculation, and folk-lore or, to put it another way, lots of little black and white or black and tan lies. As long as these creative theories aren't used to wring money out of the unsuspecting, then that's okay. After all, just as the rites of complete truthfulness are waived for gatherings of anglers, so too for dog triallists, and not only on trial grounds. It's a lifelong abstention, assumed when you're able to hold a dog whistle between your teeth, and not swallow it, while yelling 'wayleggo' and running up a steep ridge at the same time.

When a dog has erred in fairly disastrous fashion, its breeding is always the first aspect to be questioned, though this will only cover the poor devil's immediate parentage. In more rational moments, a dog owner will consider family trees that reach back to the earliest days of both our types of sheep dog, and our form of farming. I should point out that, for all my folklore-ish approach to some aspects of lineage, family histories are maintained and studied before many mating decisions are made. The New Zealand Sheep Dog Trial Association and the Working Sheep Dog Stud Book Association, which preceded it, have produced stud books since 1940. All dogs which win an open event or qualify for a New Zealand or island championship must be registered, which ensures a standard of practical excellence. Delving into over 50 years of volumes and the breeding histories of at least three-quarters of a century can be very rewarding, as long as you're tenacious and know what you're looking for and how to interpret it. Ian Sinclair certainly does, as he demonstrated in the *Farmer* in 1971. With the assistance of George Herbert of Pongoroa, Ian started his journey into history with three litter brothers, huntaways Ben, Wait and Claude. These belonged, respectively, to three other brothers, Norman, Alf and Sam Boynton. Each of the Boyntons has won at least one New Zealand title, Norman being the most successful with six. That entire bag was gathered by Ben alone, making him the most successful dog in trialling history. Ben, Wait and Claude were out of Sam's bitch, Queen, by Norman's Paul. It was Paul's side of the tree that Ian followed into the depths of time.

'Paul was out of Warwick Atkin's Peg (B. Fisher's Bo — T. Mitchell's bitch), by Reg Mullooly's Paul I. Reg's Paul was by Ken Bruce's Paul (Alec Thompson's Lad — K. Bruce's Mick), from H. Sheriff's Peg. Peg was out of J. Gardner's Nell (R. Moore's Dan — H. Sherriff's Nell). This last Nell was by a son of H. Boyce's Nap, but this is digressing.

Sherriff's Peg was by George Herbert's Joe. One year, out of 23 starts, Joe had 10 wins. How does that grab you? George said he never had to tell Joe how to hunt sheep, he only had to be able to stop him. This is a problem I understand very well! Joe was out of D. Trevithick's Lou who was by S. Jackson's Ned from S. Jackson's Fly. I wonder if this was Sam Jackson who was on "Pokaka" at Moawhanga about the end of World War 2? Joe's father was George Herbert's Sandy. George says that Sandy was the best dog he ever owned for working ability … a very noisy huntaway and a strong-eyed leading dog with plenty of brains and full of guts.

'Taking you on a trip back through Sandy's breeding, he was by Tom Herbert's Don out of Jim Mcleanon's Bell (Jim Mcleanon's Joe — Jim Mcleanon's Beauty). Don was by Stan Meech's Sweep from Harold Herbert's Nell who was born about 1918. Sweep was by W. Rain's Sweep. Nell was by Alan Meech's Roy from Eddie Meech's Speed. Roy was by old boundary rider, Billy Wright's Laddie out of old Bill Meech's Fan. Laddie was bred by Dick Harmon's Baldy, who was born around 1900, out of Dick Harmon's Nell. Baldy was by Jim Murray's Sweep, and that is as far as I can go.' Ian got right back to the early 1890s, over a century ago. What's even more remarkable about that lineage is that it goes back 50 years before the first volume of the stud book was published. And for a huntaway, too; the breed that emerged from the tussock and scrub of early pastoral New Zealand, with mists of uncertainty hanging over some of its origins.

Much of our early canine genealogy was passed on by word of mouth, particularly by those who got so good at it that they could trot out a family tree at a moment's notice. All it required was a tremendous memory, coupled with a speech pattern and attitude that brooked no argument. Such a man was Bob Guthrie who, as a teenager, first ran at a New Zealand championship in 1938. He and his brother were both placed in the same huntaway final that their father won. Three decades later, Bob, too, won a national hunt title. On matters of pedigree, he was exceptional. The first time I took Peg to his then club, Pahiatua, he took one look at her and in his typical staccato, rasping delivery said, 'Bob Wilson's Glen, 1939.' A few weeks later I was thumbing through a dog triallist's scrapbook and there was a photo of Wilson's Glen. Bob was absolutely right. They both had the same bits of white, a three-quarter coat and distinctive curling waves running down the backline. In Peg's case, some triallists reckoned I'd created the curls by getting her coat permed, but those waves were much more permanent; they were part of her genetic make-up and, 40 years on, Bob remembered the gene bank they'd come from.

He was always at his finest when others, at a club trial or championship, were trying to come to grips with a particular dog's background and not succeeding, as Arthur Harrison well remembers. 'Here at Te Ore [near Masterton] there was a group of us arguing over the breeding of a dog that was running. One bloke said, "She's by so and so, out of ..." Another said, "No! She's out of something else." All this went on for a while, with no one agreeing. Old Bob was down the road walking towards us. He had a dog with him and got to within a chain of us and said — no one had asked him anything — "She's by so and so, who was by such and such and he was by Ned Dahm's Jink, who was out of ..." He kept going, without stopping, till he was a chain away. Seven generations in 44 yards ... thank you Bob.'

Of our two main breeds, the heading dog is the easier to trace because the majority of its bloodlines stem from the collies of the Borders of Scotland and Northern England. The Scots agricultural scientist, J. Herries McCulloch, in *Sheep Dogs and Their Masters* (1946), has the most logical explanation of both the Border's evolution, and the emergence of its ancestors. 'Probably about 150 years ago, from a mixed ancestry of more rugged looking and less sensitive dogs, including the Bob-tailed Sheep-dog, the Bearded Collie and the Harlequin Collie [the multi-coloured English or Lassie collie].'

From that rugged, intelligent stock, McCulloch says, evolved the much smaller Border. 'Here and there noticeably clever little dogs and bitches would appear, as the result of the inexplicable variations of breeding.' They were noticed by others, bred from and 'spread through the Border country, and in course of time, the large, rough and noisy dogs would pass out of favour'. Much of that is also relevant to the evolution of our huntaway, with obvious noise in the original stock. Among all the variations which must have occurred, they identified the type that best suited their purpose. In the Border's case this was brainy wee dogs who silently shifted and minded stock. This improved blood is concentrated by line breeding.

In Herries McCulloch's description the next stages in the Border's evolution ran parallel to other developments: 'improved roads, railways and big annual sheep sales, so that these dogs would spread much more rapidly over the Border country, and beyond. Then came the first dog trials, which brought about a further concentration of the blood of intelligence.' The original dogs which accompanied our early immigrant shepherds aside, most of the significant dogs to come here were from breeders who were able to provide plenty of pedigree paperwork. In quite a few instances they also were able to list some impressive dog trial results in Britain. This was certainly the case with those imported by the Northumbrian born, Country Antrim reared, and Southland domiciled breeder and importer, James Lilico. 'My name is known throughout the Empire as a breeder of sheep dogs.' He arrived in 1893 to work as a shepherd on 30,000-acre (12,000-hectare) Morton Mains Station in Southland and 'had the misfortune to strike about half a dozen brainless mongrels, and anyone who knows anything about sheep, will understand the trial it was for me to be afflicted with them.' The result was that Lilico imported Captain, a dog he'd left at home but had broken in for sheep work at 22 months of age. Before that Captain had been a town dog and knew nothing of sheep. (At this stage I'd be grateful if no parallels were drawn between Captain and Lilico, Peg and Gordon!) 'Forty-eight hours after I got him I could hold a few wild black-faced ewes with him in perfect style.'

After an eight-month journey to the other side of the world, including quarantine, Captain was not only a success at station work, but quickly became Lilico's first stud dog, and sired R. Fraser's regular trial winner, Lilico. James Lilico watched his namesake's performance with all the interest you'd expect from a dedicated breeder and shrewd marketer. 'His winning was so consistent that at certain trials he was handicapped in points, about five, I think, in a possible of thirty, and yet he continued to win.' Over the next 40 years James Lilico imported hundreds of dogs and bred even more pups, all of the strong-eyed variety. 'I have imported the class of dog I considered was most needed in New Zealand and that I was justified in my predictions has been abundantly borne out by the demand to secure them.' This was the first major infusion of blood to be used over the lines bred down from those who followed our earliest shepherds. Many of these so-called colonial dogs were what's known as plain-eyed and could best be described as gathering or stopping dogs, who headed off would-be escapees and collected them together. They avoided the direct, eyeball-to-eyeball confrontation we'd expect to see from today's heading dogs, especially when challenged by bold sheep. Hence, plain-eyed, the opposite to Lilico's Border imports, which would arrive behind the sheep to grip them with the steady strength of a well-positioned stare.

For some 40 years, starting from the mid-1890s, James Lilico spent a total of £7,000 importing sheep dogs but, being a canny Border shepherd, there was a bob in it for him. The last trial he competed in was at Mosgiel, where he ran Border Boss who, in 1907, as Moss I, won the major British event, the International Championships. 'I failed to yard [at Mosgiel] but got full points for everything else. They [the judges] had never seen a dog pulling or under such command as Boss. I came out easily on top from a financial standpoint, as I booked over £60 worth of pups.' His average annual income from pup sales would have been over £500 and his record year grossed him £735. The effect of all this, according to one old Canterbury shepherd, was that it 'shook the living tripe out of the High Country sheep dog world in New Zealand'. Another sheep man, George Hurley, of The Shades, near Kaikoura, said; 'They are not dogs, they are magic.' I doubt that Mrs Lilico thought as highly of the whole business, as her kitchen was taken over by huge pots of puppy porridge, simmering daily on her coal range. Lilico's were not the only imported or locally bred dogs who played an important role in the heading dog's development. One of the most influential on the North Island's east coast was a Tasmanian dog, Cranswick's Dictator. The bloodlines that hark back to him show Dictator was of the benign variety, not a despot. Fraser Smith's

Highland King played a major role on the North Island's west coast, and Lopdell's Ring and Speed, who carried a fair bit of Whyte's Boy blood, also had a major influence.

Despite the infusions of imported blood, there's a big difference between our heading dog and the current model of working Border collie in Britain. Invariably, they are long-coated, black and white, with a shorter leg and a more cobby, compact body. Many of their New Zealand counterparts are smooth-haired and tri-coloured, with the tan usually appearing around the points, legs and jowl. They're also a longer, leaner, faster and more upright type of dog, who'll stay on their feet and not clap, as most British dogs do. Clapping is a Border trait: when they stop behind sheep they immediately drop to the ground — clap. New Zealand shepherds like to see their dogs up on their toes and the only time they'd want to have anything to do with clapping would be after a very good run at a dog trial. The lengthy black and white coat of the modern British dog hasn't been considered essential either, especially as the original dogs here, just as they were in Scotland and England, were of a wide range of colour combinations, coat style and length. They had tri-colours, black and tans, red and white, even fawn and white. Others were smooth-haired and jet black, all white or a deep red. An example of the range that existed in Scotland would be one of the foundation members of Australia's Kelpie breed. This was an imported, smooth-haired, prick-eared collie bitch who was called Kelp, and her coat was the same deep liver red that's a hallmark of today's Kelpie. Another of that breed's foundations came from a cross between two imported Scottish black and tans who produced a red pup, Caesar. He eventually sired a bitch pup called Kelpie, winner of Australia's first dog trial at Forbes, New South Wales.

There have been rumours of a dash of 'pepper and salt' being added to the New Zealand heading dog in the form of whippet and fox terrier. It's a good story and true, but extremely unlikely that it had any influence on later bloodlines. When W.E. (Billy) Whyte, one of tri-alling's earliest champions, retired to town, a dog with an odd back-ground went with him. Whyte was famous for his Boy heading dogs and won several North Island titles with them. He mated Boy III to 'what may be termed a whippet bitch, the mother of which was a pure bred greyhound and the father a pure bred fox terrier'. I would have liked to have seen that particular mating take place! By the side of the woolshed, from the top of the landing stage? The result of the next cross down the line, which the old gent kept, was obviously given a fair bit of schooling, then taken out to a friend's run in the Hawke's Bay hills. It showed enough heading instinct to go to the far side of the mob and, being a streamlined, whippety thing, it got there very quickly! 'My dog was going great guns, appearing to be only skimming over the bumps, on the outline of his cast. Causing me to remark that such a dog was too fast and fearless for that class of country, and likely to break his neck over a cliff.'

About the only bone that Billy Whyte's rocket didn't break, was his neck. 'Failing to notice a turn in the cliff until he was too close to avoid it, and travelling at a terrific pace, he was precipitated over the side, falling about 60 feet [20 metres] in one sheer drop to the floor of the canyon.' That was not only nearly the end of the dog but, Whyte thought, it would also stop him from running his canine express at a few trials, to show what could be done with an outcross. A year later, a miraculously recovered dog, though one-eyed and a touch lame, went trialling with Whyte. 'I ran him at five trials, in high class company, out of which he was placed 4th, 2nd, 3rd, and 1st, besides winning a cup for the best exhibition in Class II [short head and yard].' It seems an unusual mixture to make a point, but Whyte wanted to show that crosses had occurred in the past and that 'no doubt many strains of modern sheep-dogs have a degree of setter blood in them, if only it could be traced'.

The supposition in Whyte's time was that the instinct to eye stock was a result of early collie types being crossed with setters and other sporting breeds. I, and many others, don't believe this is the case, as the eye our dogs show goes all the way back to the earliest canines stalking their prey. After centuries of breeding, selection and discipline, this stealthy approach has been harnessed and become what we now regard as a very special skill which plays an important part in filling many millions of stomachs, not just that of a hungry dog in a European forest.

Herries McCulloch objects to describing the effect of 'The Eye', as he calls it, as mesmerising. 'The sheep is not dazed and the dog does not display diabolical or hypnotic powers. It merely "holds" the sheep with its eager and watchful eyes … its expression seems to say: "there's no use trying to make a bolt for liberty, for I'm watching you carefully, and I can move a great deal faster than you can, if it comes to that".' What has misled some as to whether eyeing is a form of setting, was a reference in the *Cyclopaedia of Modern Agriculture*, of almost a century ago, stating that, in the early 1800s, 'the then Duke of Richmond was not above crossing one of his famous Gordon Setters with a black and white Collie bitch, the property of a well known poacher, with the object of improving the intelligence of his dogs.' An interesting twist that, as in gun dog circles the Gordon is known to be the most intelligent of all the setters, which doesn't surprise me at all!

I think that what William Whyte's greyhound-fox terrier heading dog cross proved was that, physically, the dog may have thrown to the outcross, but its brain-box was full of Boy III. The Boy line was the most successful of its day and, between 1911 and 1935, won six North Island titles — the first national championship was in 1936 — five other places and runner–up to a national title in 1937. Whyte's outcross creation had another important influence in its favour too, his tremendous ability as a trainer. I always remember Cyril Perry saying of the country's leading operators that 'some of these blokes could train a fox terrier to win a hunt'. Billy Whyte did something similar, again to prove a point: properly trained, an intelligent dog can do anything. As a result, one of his Boy dogs was trained to hunt sheep and won an open event. Legend has it that, to wring the necessary noise out of him, Whyte would give Boy a stop whistle then, holding a white hanky aloft, he'd drop his arm, a signal that extracted a bark or two. My feeling is that the intervening years have allowed the legend to outstrip the dog's ability to hunt.

It's worth remembering that, up to the 1960s and 1970s, nearly every district in the country had a rabbit board. The rabbiters they employed had teams of the ugliest mixture of confused bloodlines imaginable. Some of them were the result of unplanned and unusual liaisons with sheep dogs. Others, given the opportunity, were only too keen have a go. Family pets and gun dogs were also a source of outside blood and some, as with the rabbbit pack cross, worked sheep very well. There was, however, always the risk of them reverting to their other type. In his book, *Droving Dogs and Sheep*, Sonny Osborne of Apiti, near Feilding, wrote of a retriever-heading dog cross, Bob, who came to him as an orphaned Napier survivor of the 1931 Hawke's Bay earthquake. On returning to country life, Bob drew on half of his natural leanings and became an accomplished stockman, 'but,' wrote Sonny, 'when I was doing a lambing beat at home, a mystery arose. Nobody seemed to know why there were so many pet lambs in the back yard. It was not until Bob was seen gently carrying a lamb back down the track that the mystery was solved! It seemed that every lamb I mothered up, Bob went back later and brought it home.'

One of the most distinctive strain of heading dogs to arrive here was the blue and white collie type known here and in Australia as the German collie, on the Scottish Borders as the Bilton Blue and in the United States as the Australian collie. The German has a very distinctive blue-black to blue-grey and white coat, and can fall prey to a hereditary form of mange over the back. This causes a form of baldness which, though not infectious, is rather unsightly. The breed's most distinctive characteristic, though, is a strong susceptibility to wall eyes, known in the States as glass eye. In such an eye the iris is blue, not brown, as in most other canine eyeballs. Hence a friend of mine who recently bred a litter with two wall-eyed dogs, kept one and calls it 'my blue-eyed boy'. I dare say the name will stick until young 'blue eyes' starts work and, at some stage, refuses to do what he's told. The gene that determines wall eye (often there'll be one blue, one brown) is recessive and, therefore, appears only when both parents carry the gene. As a separate breed or strain, the German has long since been crossbred into anonymity, except that when the blue coat or eye appears, you know where they've been. I know of several very good heading dog families where the grey-blue coat appears regularly, as do dog trial prizes and placings. Ian Sinclair describes the original versions as 'mostly rough haired and the colour was merled blue and black patches; often with a tan muzzle and legs.' Ian also describes the old German collies as handy dogs, meaning they could head, show eye and, when required, could speak up with purpose. As a result, they also made a contribution to the evolution of the huntaway.

The other handy breed which had an input to both our breeds was the Bobtail or Smithfield. This is not to be confused with Australia's Smithfields, who are long-coated, beardie type dogs, whose predominant colours are smoky shades, and dark grey and white, blended with stray strands of black and light tan. The New Zealand version came in a wide range of coat colours and lengths and often had a natural bobtail — a stump — which was long enough to wag, but too short to be any use as a duster. The last of its type I saw was a black and white bitch, Lee, in the early 1980s, worked by Graeme Pollock, who had got her from Pongoroa in Southern Hawke's Bay. She was a smooth-haired dog, mainly black with a white blaze and was smarter than a tin of Dulux. She was regularly placed in heading events, though in some judge's eyes Graeme would have blotted her copybook by occasionally giving his sheep spoken directions. I remember another Bobtail on a muster at Mount Linton Station in Southland. This, too, was black and white, though rough coated and out on the hill, he kept himself as busy as a lint picker in a blue serge suit factory. One minute he'd be using good eye and balance to pull a small mob down a face, and next thing he'd appear behind the main mob with which he'd just married up his stragglers. Then he'd become a huntaway and give full vent to some very useful noise, while his little bobtail kept time to his chorus.

The Bobtail is a recessive gene and as the law of averages now seems to rule against two gene bearers of opposing gender being in the right place at the right time, it would appear this trait has receded into history. That's a great pity. Geneticists often talk of pathways, where a gene carrying, say, very coarse hairy wool in Drysdale sheep will bear other traits with it. With Drysdales these would include short stubby horns and a stubborn nature that makes it impossible for a soft dog to shift them. For the Bobtail-Smithfield, the pathway would include industry, intelligence, natural stock handling ability, noise and eye. Ian Sinclair has a very clear memory of three Smithfields being worked by a shearing contractor and farmer, Arthur Walsh, while drafting sheep in the Te Horoa Station yards. 'He was using three dogs all out of the same bitch. Two were bobtailed, and the third, a rough haired black and white was not. The third dog was keeping the diamond full. The second, a multi-coloured dog, was backing (as I think all three would) in the crush [backing means working on top of yarded sheep], and the third dog, a black and tan, was keeping them going up the drafting race. It was a fantastic performance and I have never seen anything to equal it since.'

The essence of that exhibition was the use of well-trained dogs, with stock sense, who added impetus to the whole operation by using natural noise. That's why in New Zealand conditions we need two main types of sheep dog: the noisy huntaway, and its keen-eyed collie cousin, the heading dog — the perfect combination. Of these, the heading dog owes much to its ancestors in the Border country, but it cannot be classed, in Kennel Club terms, as a Border collie, since it's a separate breed. Clever, popular and attractive as the Border may be, it now has little in common with our calm, strong running and commanding heading dog, which plays such a vital role in New Zealand's livestock industry.

5
HAS IT GOT GOOD NOISE?

Of all the questions that can be asked about a working sheep dog, the standard enquiry about the quality and quantity of its noise will be asked only in this country. There are dogs elsewhere that will bark a bit when under extreme pressure in the paddock or, when excited, yip and yap in the yards. But only one breed uses noise as its prime means of shifting sheep — the huntaway, one of the most distinctive dogs in the world. It is also the only breed of dog to be developed in New Zealand and, in the land of the long white fleece and lots of lean and lengthy lambs, it was for a very logical reason: to shift sheep. The decision to use well-spoken dogs to move livestock can not be put down to one person or a particular property. In every respect, the evolution of the huntaway is aptly summed up by the old cliché: necessity is the mother of invention. The sheer size of many of our early flocks and the high ratio of sheep to shepherd created part of that need. The long distances sheep had to be moved on large properties was another factor; something special was needed to give a flagging flock a hurry up. When a large mob was on the move, and being worked only by silent heading dogs, the great majority didn't have the faintest idea that there was a dog in the vicinity. Noise was also required to handle and gather awkward sheep in the open, clear a hill face with a few well-placed barks and then move the mob to the yards. Once the sheep were there, similar amounts of noisy persuasion were, and still are, needed to keep the drafting race full and to ease bottlenecks at gateways.

Dogs which bark and work with sheep in farm, sale and trucking yards are found in other countries. Australia is a good example, with a beardie type they call the Smithfield, the German Koolie, the Kelpie and crosses between all three of them, with some Border collie thrown in for good measure. Known simply as yard dogs, they do a lot of work, and a fair portion of this will be without noise though, when required, they'll do plenty of yapping, particularly the Smithfields and Koolies. As a rule, these dogs aren't used in the paddock, as Australian stockmen fear how far their mobile Merinos might run if something frightens them by yelling in their ear.

In New Zealand, the huntaway is at its best out in the open, vigorously moving — hunting — stock away from the shepherd. A well-trained huntaway can, however, do virtually anything. It can move sheep in any direction and, if required, silently and capably head a mob. It would find it very difficult to come on to the sheep, to lift or move them if it wasn't allowed to give full voice. At its best, on the farm or competing at a dog trial, the huntaway will be in front of its boss and behind the sheep, delivering its noise either rock steady or on the move. In a perfect world, this canine music (to my ears and many others) is delivered with intent, not thrown aimlessly into the air. There's little to be gained from barking at nearby mountains or passing seagulls; noise needs to be aimed directly at sheep which, the dog firmly believes, require its counselling and control. For this reason we often talk about hunting the lead, though the dog is at the back of the mob. Even from there the message is directed to the leaders both to steer them and to keep the whole mob as a compact unit. By moving out to, say, the right, but still behind the mob, the dog remains on balance with the lead and warns against any further leaning to that side. If the sheep were to be turned or slewed to the left, a well-noised huntaway, able to get good effect from a distance, would angle further to the right and literally blow the mob left.

A lesser dog, more suited to yard work, would either hurl itself alongside or, worse still, into the mob and scatter them forward at speed. Even more disastrous would be arriving right in front of them, to take the lead off so effectively that, in a matter of seconds, the sheep would be tearing straight back at the shepherd. He or she would, by this stage, be a very troubled person, making at least as much noise as the dog. The latter, in turn, would probably have just enough grey matter to go into safety mode, and keep its distance from both shepherd and sheep. A good huntaway's main means of control is the steady, almost calming, presence of its noise. A dog with a bark which doesn't frighten, yet rings with authority, will settle sheep to the extent that they come to depend on both the barking, and its source. When the barking is properly applied, sheep move into a kind of comfort zone and, time after time, you'll see them quite literally glued to the noise and conditioned into almost total obedience. It's as if they're contained within an invisible net, but should it break — the barking stop — the spell will be broken and, all of a sudden, controlling them can become quite difficult. This is especially the case at a dog trial, when three sheep are being marched up hill with all the co-ordination of a military drill team. Yet, any change in the way they're being handled, such as a lull in the dog's noise or an off-balance move, will switch the whole affair from one of pending triumph to one of instant despair. This can be brought on by the triallist, through a lapse in concentration or obvious increase in tension and anxiety. An intelligent huntaway will not only sense this but, very often, react rather unexpectedly.

A good example of how a dog can sense a change in circumstances concerns a competitor who, away from home on a trialling trip, was having a very convivial time. He and his impressive huntaway were also having a top run on a zigzag hunt course. As the sheep neared the markers at the top of the hill, with the dog walking and talking just beneath them, it looked to be the run to beat — unbeatable, even. At the foot of the hill, the man obviously thought it was the latter. With a can of beer in one hand he turned right round to his mates, who were watching from behind the judge's box, and said, 'Theer-ya'rr-yoo-jokerss, that'ss thu way ya hunt sheep.' He then fixed the gallery with a lingering stare and defiantly jutted jaw that said, 'Beat that if you can!' With full ceremony he turned slowly back to the hill to savour the end of his run. There was nothing there! When the man had first turned to crow, the dog noticed the relaxed and uncommanding note

in the bosses' voice, to say nothing of a complete absence of instructions, and obviously decided that, since the pressure was off, the job must be over. He simply flicked out to the right of the sheep and hurled abuse in their ears. They responded by taking a sharp left turn, to depart the scene just before the all important finish line. Then, with the dog close behind, urging them to keep up the pace, they all disappeared round the corner. In seconds, the winning run had become an also ran.

Working a top huntaway with plenty of lung and larynx power can be very demanding, especially early in the day, when its oxygen tank is still full. To see an animal of that ilk in full cry is also an extremely exciting spectacle, with plenty of noise to accompany the action. None of this, though, should be confused with the excitement of the chase, as in fox hunting. Hunting sheep is all about shepherding, not chasing, and can't be carried out at pace. If it is, sooner or later the sheep will run out of puff and either fall over and roll downhill or dive under a bush to have a nervous breakdown. If that happens on the trial ground, the run's history. If it happens at work, the shepherd should be history. And work is what the huntaway was bred for, which means 70 to 80 percent of the day-to-day work with New Zealand's flock of around 55 million adult sheep. On the hill, the flat, sheep-yards, cattle-yards, stock trucks and abattoirs — whatever the situation, a properly trained huntaway can cope with it, and look and sound as if it means business. It's the finer points of those skills that go under the microscope at a dog trial, and even though there are just three sheep to work with, we still expect to see the power that would be applied to a big mob. That's very important to a devout huntaway man such as Ian Sinclair: 'My hackles rise when I watch an airy-fairy huntaway, silk-handkerchiefing three sheep up a trial course'.

The huntaway is 100-percent New Zealand bred yet, paradoxically, all from completely imported stock, raw material which, in its country of origin, would not have resembled much of what we'd now describe as a natural huntaway. There is no doubt that noisy dogs had their place in early Scottish and English shepherding, especially since the main sources of the modern, working Border collie all had noise. The earliest reference I've found to a dog being used in a manner we'd describe as hunting is in 'An Evening Walk', by William Wordsworth, written in 1793, a good 50 years before extensive sheep farming got under way in New Zealand.

> Waving his hat, the shepherd in the vale
> Directs his winding dog the cliffs to scale
> That barking, busy 'mid the glittering rocks
> Hunts, where he points, the intercepted flocks.

The huntaway was developed because our early musterers and run-holders saw the benefits of properly applied noise. They then set about breeding and selecting for that trait from dogs who also showed good stock sense. In doing so they founded a unique breed that is admired here and around the world. In the *Pastoral Review* of 1919 James Lilico wrote that 'when it comes to clearing huge tracts of rough country in in a minimum of time, or forcing big mobs up a race, then I say that the high grade New Zealand huntaway is the finest dog in the world.'

In his book, *Sheep Dogs*, the Australian geneticist, Dr R.B. Kelly, described the huntaway as 'probably the most specialised of sheep dogs used to assist in the movement of sheep.' To another geneticist, Dr Clive Dalton, who's from the English side of the Borders and has worked here for 30 years, the huntaway is 'probably the best example in the world of an animal bred for performance alone, and not ruined by breed societies' rules and regulations! A wonderful example of how to use a pool of genetic variation, out of which you select what is needed to do a specific task. It's modern genetic theory, used before such theory was worked out!'

In the earliest days of the huntaway's development, the genetic pool Clive refers to wasn't large. Even so, we can't define all the material swimming in it, because no one specifically set out to establish a new breed; it emerged as the result of individuals defining a need. No committee of earnest people sat down to design a new dog — and just as well or we'd have ended up with a camel! Accordingly, there are no minutes or records to be discovered nor, save for a few oral exceptions, are there any details of the earliest parent stock. Even in 1919 James Lilico had no idea: 'The origin of the natural huntaway is somewhat hard to trace.' Without being able to point to any form of pedigree, Lilico did answer the question in general terms, with considerable assistance from Charles Darwin. 'It is simply a case of a distinct race being evolved by selection and environment. Darwin in his original *Origin of the Species* argues that acquired characters may become hereditary ... and our huntaway is an instance of this.'

To take this a stage further, a plain-eyed heading dog with some inclination to bark could, therefore, be turned around and taught to hunt sheep away. By breeding from that dog and, in each subsequent generation, selecting those with both noise and stock handling ability, real progress could be made. It was too, especially by some of our earliest shepherds and musterers. From the 1880s up to the First World War, the Boddington brothers, Bob, George and Ernie, worked on the Marlborough and North Canterbury runs of Molesworth and St Helens. Early in their working careers they developed a huntaway line and stuck to it. It was from different streams of the same bloodline that the Calder and Buske strains descended from, and others too. This includes a North Canterbury strain that began by mating Rose, a black and white Boddington bitch, with Alan Ede's Joe. The outcome was Ede's Maid, who became the founder of the strain that bore her name for 60 years. Some 30 years after the original Maid's birth, Alan Ede competed at the Malvern dog trials with two direct descendants, Maid and Cash, who were typical of his breed. Peter Newton saw them run: 'In the hunt, Cash put up an impressive run; full of vigour and noise. He was a bit too aggressive and overdid his hunting, but Alan then stepped out and ran him in the drive and yard. That dog, naturally a bold huntaway, won that event, the highlight of the run being a full point pen.'

Ede's Cash was a great example of a dog who, in the right hands, could switch off one set of characteristics — brash noise — and switch on another — quiet balance. This strain were all small, black, long-coated dogs, similar to many of their ancestors. In parts of Scotland where the bracken is at its tallest, and the black-faced sheep at their most elusive, there has always been a strain of rough-coated, noisy dogs known there as 'hunters', and in England as 'chasers'. It is logical to assume that these hunters played an important role in the huntaway's development, providing noise, hardiness and a name. An extract from *The Book of the Dog* describes how they worked: 'These are noisy dogs which work across the hill in front of the shepherd, barking almost incessantly. Once out in the open the shepherd will probably call the hunter back to heel and finish the journey with a wearer [heading dog].' To follow sheep trails among the bracken, hunters used their nose, as much as any other sense. One of these senses was never to go past the last sheep in a mob, an attribute some modern huntaways I know of seem to have lost!

Among the noisy and handy (head and hunt) dogs that came here, one of the most important was a half beardie which, with its shepherd owner, came out from Scotland to work on Molesworth in the early 1880s. Rose, the Boddington bitch who was put to Alan Ede's dog, was a direct descendant of this dog, making this one strain we can trace directly back to the Northern Hemisphere. Another important source, especially in other parts of the country, was the much stronger eyed Border collie. As a result of line breeding and careful selection they are now, give or take the odd yip or yelp, completely silent; their ancestors were not. This was especially the case when they were working in the yards, which James Lilico called forcing. 'I can remember three which my father took, over to Country Antrim, from the Borders in 1870 — Tip, Yap and Laddie — the two former big, rough-coated black and tan, and the latter smooth, black and white. All these dogs had any amount of eye and style and yet they were powerful forcers with plenty of noise, though perfectly silent when out in the open. When I left the Borders in 1894, dogs of this kind were quite common.' Many of the dogs Lilico imported could give voice when required. 'A bitch pup I sold … went direct to [the] freezing works to pen up and developed into a first class forcer and backer.' In the North Island William Whyte's Boy I not only appears in the heading dog breeding records of early this century, but can also be found in the genealogy of the northern huntaway. Charlie Hay's Tweed, who won the hunt event at the 1913 North Island Championships, was a son of Boy I. Tweed's half-brother, Boy II won the short head at the same championship.

The beardie played an important role in the early days, especially in the Molesworth dogs and many other early strains. Although beardies didn't come in all shapes and sizes, because all the early photos indicate they were small, they were certainly of a variety of shades, and still are: deep blues, bluey-greys, light greys, yellow, white and black. There have been others, of an even more distinctive hue, such as orange, light rust and liver. There's even been, as Ian Sinclair once reported, a pink one, and Pink was her name too, 'because in some lights she was really pink in colour.' This was a conversational pearl Ian once shared with fellow triallists. 'For this remark I received some very peculiar glances and pitying looks. However she was pinkish and because she was a beautiful mustering bitch, she was line-bred. Had she been no good, she would have been in-bred.' Pink was a Waiouru dog, from one of the two High Country areas that played a major role in fixing the breed in its earliest stages. Obviously strains emerged from various districts around the country but it's impossible to trace them all. The huntaway bloodlines whose development I have followed have been chosen because there's good anecdotal material — with a touch of folklore — and some written evidence. The Taihape-Waiouru area, through to inland Hawke's Bay, which was always known as the Inland Patea, was an important huntaway nursery. The big upland stations of this region, the North Island's equivalent of the South's High Country, were then running Merinos on open hill and tussock, a challenging combination that has always attracted top shepherds with good dogs. It wasn't any different before the turn of the century, as this was where William Whyte was shepherding when he first developed his Boy dogs. As confirmation of their influence, their distinctive yellow coats kept cropping up over many generations.

The other major huntaway nursery (and the one with the best records) was North Canterbury and Marlborough, especially the huge Molesworth and St Helens Stations. Shepherds there needed dogs which could cope with hard, open country and Merino sheep; this meant mobility and sheer guts, the kind of motor that keeps a dog going on a summer's day when its throat and lungs are telling it that it's been too long since it last visited a creek. This same inner strength was also needed so that, though their pads might be sore, even raw, from running on scree, they'd still take the run whistle and go again. It was a tough school, and as most of the mustering was on shanks's pony, the men got pretty footsore and thirsty too. Four main hunt strains came from this region, one of them with the unlikely name of Clown. They, too, were descendants of Molesworth's Scottish import and were white with blotches of either liver or black. As with all these strains, Clown dogs were, as they said back then, 'very clever', which meant that they could head and hunt, and were also quite happy to stand around and quietly mind sheep for some hours.

Another strain with an unusual name was Bill Carney's Weed breed, from the Mid-Canterbury back country. The best known of this strain was Harold White's Bounce. This was an all white, full-coated dog who, when White was working on stations east of Arthur's Pass, such as Grassmere, Flock Hill and Mount White, was virtually unbeatable on a trial ground. Bounce had also been trained to perform tricks way beyond the normal brief of a station huntaway. One of these required Harold to grip the top of his dog trial stick (or crook) with one hand and the bottom with the other, then hold it out to one side. This would form a rather squarish hoop through which Bounce, with his long white coat glowing and flowing, would gaily jump. The story is told of the pair of them performing this trick, some time in the late 1920s, at a gathering in Christchurch's Cathedral Square. The audience included two older women, one of whom turned to the other and said, 'Isn't he brave, holding his stick up like that for that polar bear to jump through!' Another exceptionally clever huntaway of that time was Bob Innes's Lloyd, who also has a line bearing his name. Lloyd, a yellow and white dog, was a regular trial winner and was second in the hunt at the first ever South Island Championships in 1932. A newspaper report of that same year described Lloyd's antics when he and Innes were running at Methven's club trial. 'While competing Lloyd left his owner and trotted over to the judges' tent, went inside and raised a paw for the judge to shake, and then returned to work for Mr Innes.' The report did not say whether Lloyd gained a bonus for good manners or a penalty for taking a break from the job.

All these early strains had rather unusual names, and the Lunn breed was no exception. They were black with a grey muzzle, could be either smooth- or rough-coated and, like all the rest, could both hunt sheep away and pull them back again. As mentioned earlier, Ede's Maid breed was important, though it's now known as the Parson's Corby breed. Dudley Parsons of Parnassus and his dog of the the Maid line, Corby, won the New Zealand Straight Hunt title at Tai Tapu in 1966, which gave the strain a new lease of life and name. This is a typical occurrence in the development of any breed. When a top sire is identified, it's lined with bitches from miles around and if the progeny turn up trumps, then all credit goes to the sire. All going well, the old fellow's name can live on for ever, even when the progeny are many generations removed, yet still spoken of as 'one of the old breed'.

One such line was the Rag breed, which was started by Lew Mead, who saw a litter of outstanding pups on a Marlborough station and bought the sire and dam, Rag and Rose. According to his nephew,

Rex Mead, the line was kept going while Lew was away at the Boer War, and he returned to several young dogs of the line, but didn't have anything to mate them with. 'He raked up a bitch pup that no one would own, out from under the Waihopai pub, and this was his brood bitch of the future. She would go miles but never pass the shoulder of a sheep; she was a direct huntaway, yet her descendants would head or hunt.' The dogs of those days were clever, rather than powerful, as brains were essential to cope with many of the situations they faced. A good example would be a story that early musterer and breeder, Bob Pollock, passed on to Rex Mead. 'Once he saw Rag [the first of the line] following a mob of Merinos up a steep face; one knocked up and lay down and Rag immediately hid in the tussock. Every now and then he would raise his head to see if the sheep had stood up. When it finally caught up with the mob, he carried on.' When it comes to the evolution of the huntaway, the two surnames associated with that story are very important. Over several generations the Mead family has made a huge contribution to the huntaway and its development, by demonstrating its ability on stations in both islands and on the trial ground. Rex Mead won two island hunt titles and a New Zealand in 1949 and 1950 with a Rag descendant, Rome. The last of the human line to figure that prominently with a huntaway was Kevin Mead in 1993 and 1994, winning island and national titles with Reno. Many more members of the Mead clan have been placed both before and since those dates.

The original source of that Rag story, Bob Pollock, is better known for his Old Clyde line. This was established in the early 1890s when he was head shepherd on Craigieburn Station, east of Arthur's Pass. According to Donald Manson, who worked for Pollock and later became Craigieburn's head shepherd, Clyde was a big black and tan fellow, and slightly grizzled (stiff whiskers). No one knows how Clyde was bred but his importance arose through his considerable working ability and the success of several crosses with bitches of the Meads' Rag line. Either Clyde or his sons were also put over bitches belonging to a shepherd on a neighbouring station, Castle Hill. This was none other than W. V. McIntyre who, much later, bred and competed with a dog now known as Old Bruce who was a great-great-great-great-grandson of Pollock's Old Clyde, on both sides. Incidentally, all these dogs with 'Old' in their name weren't old at the time. In fact they wouldn't have got 'Old' until they were well and truly history. Time would then have allowed their deeds to become legendary, and their importance as a sire or dam fully recognised. This, in human terms, is a form of beatification, but you'd never call a dog a saint, just 'Old', with a hint of respect in your voice. And to hark back to another matter, as Old Bruce is a four-time great-grandson of Old Clyde, this makes Ian Sinclair's Tadpole (born 1948) a ten-time great-grandson of Old Clyde, whose blood will be traceable from several different branches of the tree.

Many of those early shepherds covered a fair bit of the country and their noisy dogs went with them. By 1905 McIntyre had moved from inland Canterbury to the top of the island. In all probability this would have been his first contact with the Meads and their dogs, which he recalled in a letter written in 1935. 'I was mustering on Hillersden Station in Marlborough (220,000 acres, 55,000 Merinos, 60 miles from the homestead to the back, 22 teams of dogs), where they were well established, where they were originally bred and where they were known as "the Rag breed" from the original of 50 or 60 years ago.' By 1910, two of the Meads and W.V. McIntyre had arrived in the North Island, around East Cape. From then on, those men and their dogs would have a very beneficial effect on the North Island's huntaways. Another great influence was a blue beardie bitch called Rangi, who was Poverty Bay born (in 1902), and sent to a W.G. Saxby, who was shepherding in the Wairarapa. Saxby and Rangi returned to Gisborne some time later, but left behind a pup out of Rangi, called Help. Taking on a job that he found required more dog power, Saxby called for Help. Help finally arrived after three months at sea, travelling up and down our coastline, plus at least one return trip to Australia. The ship's cook, who was Help's self-appointed guardian, finally parted with him on the Gisborne wharf when Saxby managed to convince him that he really was the dog's owner. Not only was Help a very good dog, as was his mother, Rangi, but his other major claim to fame came from being the sire of W.V. McIntyre's Bruce.

When Bruce was going to trials — he wasn't 'Old' then — he was the huntaway to beat. In the North Island Championships at Weber in 1919, he was the last to run and faced an impossible task as earlier competitors had put up some all but perfect runs. If W.V. and Bruce were to win they needed a perfect, penalty-free run, and that's exactly what they did. The stud book doesn't have the scores but A.R. Mills, in his book *Huntaway*, states that it was perfect which, back then, would have meant 45 out of 45. 'He never let the sheep feel the full force of the dog until it was needed.' W.V. and Bruce had been runners-up in 1918 and successfully defended their 1919 title the following year. In dog trialling, winning consecutive championships happens about as often as hens get toothache. During their heyday, McIntyre and Bruce didn't have a lot to fear from their opposition, though there was one combination they recognised as a threat: Bill Bonis and Billy. Billy was a first-generation cross from a dog which Bonis's uncle had brought back for him from a trip to Ireland. Alan Box, writing in the *Farmer* in the late 1960s, described the import ('his name was Bob') as 'a rather unusual colour, smoky grey body with tan head and legs'. In time, this vigorous dog's hunter type blood joined up with the Meads' Rag line. The Rag family also had a strong influence in another East Coast strain, the Alf Johnson breed. It's thought that Johnson's original beardie bitch was a sister to McIntyre's Bruce and, therefore, by Saxby's Help. What is for certain is that the Johnson strain were known for their fire, grit and stamina and that line has been carried on to the present day by Dudley Buscke and his son Ross. Both of them have won New Zealand titles working fiery little bundles of bristling indignation: Joe Savoldi and Wag.

Of all the original bloodlines that featured in the huntaway's early development, the beardie type probably had the greatest influence, especially the Scottish half-beardie, which arrived in the 1880s. This dog can be traced as the progenitor of the Rag, Ede's Maid, and Clown breeds and, therefore, to the Buscke and Calder strains of today, and many more. The breeding of Pollock's Clyde isn't known, but as an outcross to the other three early breeds, he, too, was important. In time, though, his blood became intermingled with everything else. In fact,

I'm sure that if you wanted to claim a famous dog of the past as part of the genealogy of any of today's good lines, you would simply follow each branch of that tree until you found what you were looking for. What you won't discover is any official mention of other distinct breeds, such as the Labrador, golden retriever, Gordon setter, Great Dane, German shepherd or Old English foxhound. Those sporting breeds have contributed a tremendous amount to the huntaway world, especially by way of folklore, supposition and anecdote. It has always been thought that at least two breeds made an appearance in the breeding of the Poverty Bay and East Coast huntaways. It's well established that the Meads put the Gordon setter over some of their bitches and that's where the big, upstanding, deep chocolate-coloured dogs with mid-tan points and eyebrows came from. The most obvious of this type to compete at the top level was Bill Donaldson's Big King, who steadily marched and barked his way to a North Island hunt title in 1972. His longish, wavy, black coat, lengthy floppy ears, tan on his legs and beetle eyebrows all said Gordon setter. His breeding? Well, it goes back to the East Coast, and the name Mead pops up more than once.

The very big, loose-jowled, black and tan, or black, tan and liver, dogs that appeared in the huntaway lines of the same region are the result of an infusion of bloodhound. This type of dog didn't become obvious until the early years of the Poverty Bay Hunt Club. The nucleus of their pack of hounds were imported but, because they had no central kennels of their own, the hounds were farmed out. Deducing what happened next isn't difficult, nor was it then, especially when the progeny got on a trial ground and opened up with blood-curdling howls at the beginning of a run. Whether some of these matings were planned or not, no one's saying, but you can be pretty sure that it did happen. Especially as a bit of extra-curricular activity of that nature matches English foxhound breeder Nick Wheeler's description of both the breed and Conservative MPs: 'As long as they hunt, eat, sleep and have sex, they are happy'. For Ian Sinclair, his conviction that the foxhound had been involved was confirmed a few years ago when he visited the Puckeridge Hunt, between London and Cambridge. 'In a huge cage full of hounds I saw one outstanding big tri-coloured hound, which looked a dead ringer for many of our black & tan hunt-aways. I asked the huntsman about him and he said that he was what they called an "Old English Hound".' The very distinctive looking, and sounding, progeny of the early crosses have gone now, but the markings and the big flat paws that were made for steady plodding can still be seen. You may also come across a dog of that type, beginning a run with its head right back, baying as if there were a full moon up there, not three sheep wondering if their end was nigh.

The most significant huntaways of the foxhound variety were Eric Rodger's Rogue, and his sons, Pluto and York. By all accounts, they and others weren't very easy to work, as their brakes were difficult to apply from any sort of distance. Another observation was that, though they worked well in the heat, they weren't big on stock sense. Another breed which made an appearance, then faded away, was the Great Dane. In the late 1940s Kingi Lambert, then shepherding on Siberia, west of Taihape, bred a strain which Ian Sinclair describes as 'HUGE. At one Mataroa trial I asked Kingi "What the hell have you got in those dogs of yours — Great Dane or something?" Kingi, as ever with the perfect answer, said "Boy! When you get them from the Pa, you don't know what they've got in them".' Apparently they had a cream body and dark head with two other Great Dane traits: blunt jawline and prick ears. They, too, disappeared from the scene because although they had quite good stock-handling ability they lacked the aggression and noise many triallists like to see in a huntaway. Kingi was no exception, since King, with whom he won the New Zealand zigzag in 1949, didn't seem to have any Great Dane in him.

The matter of whether the Labrador has also been involved in the huntaway's development seems to be a very vexed question indeed. Those who have a good-looking, solidly framed, black dog, with a bark reminiscent of a Newfoundland sporting breed, deny that their dog is anything other than huntaway through and through. The best reply to that is, what is a huntaway? Since it's a dog which shifts sheep with purposeful noise, after that — as discussed — anything goes. There have been some very good, jet black, and vivid gold, huntaway strains, particularly since the Second World War. The most famous line, known as the Takapau All Blacks, stemmed from Storm, a dog owned by Bill McSporran of Takapau. Storm was out of Bess, a black bitch owned by the Speedy family from the southern Hawke's Bay coast. She had been given to Bill to work during the war as her two previous owners, the brothers Speedy, were serving overseas. When they returned, Bess went back to them, and was put in pup to another Speedy dog, Roy. Bill McSporran, being a great fan of Bess, wanted one of the litter and was given a big raw-boned creature, which Alan Speedy considered 'too ugly to sell'. There has always been a certain amount of contention over who the sire of that litter really was since Storm, in the eyes of many observers, was extremely Labrador, though Bill McSporran certainly didn't think so. What no one could argue about was Storm's ability to hunt sheep, which he confirmed by winning the North Island zigzag in 1954, coming fourth in the straight hunt and gaining a third placing two years later.

If there is one certainty in trialling, it's that if a dog wins in the big time he'll be in demand for stud purposes. Charlie Anderton was one of those who took a bitch, his Rose, to Storm and that's how the Takapau All Blacks were born. They certainly became as successful as a good football team, despite, or because of, the cloudy pedigree on the father's side. It's a subject that still brings a wry smile to trialling stalwart Charlie Anderton's face. 'She had eight pups, just the one bitch. Now they were all black, jet black. Of course Bill McSporran's Storm was half Lab. Now you wouldn't want to say that to Bill, but where he got Storm from they had a big black Lab dog as a house pet. No matter how many dogs you put over the huntaway bitch, it didn't matter, the Lab was there first! You can only fertilise eggs once. Ooh, that was a great litter [the Storm-Rose cross], all top dogs.' Nearly all of them ended up in a championship run off, and some were in several. The most famous was Dick Schaw's Guy, described by Peter Newton as 'that *real* huntaway …' This was after Guy had come under Bill McSporran's wing and won a New Zealand hunt title in 1965. So were Guy and his fellow Takapau All Blacks one-quarter Labrador? Charlie Anderton thinks so; Bill McSporran certainly didn't and the

Speedy family shares that view. Conversely, many who saw Storm reckon that he looked just like a Labrador. Whatever the real facts, and the mists of time have done a good job of obscuring them, it's a good story and very much part of huntaway folklore. Just the same, and despite cases of individual denial, there is no doubt that infusions of black and gold Labrador bloodlines have found their way into the huntaway and done a lot of good.

I remember being told in a lecture room, many years ago, that there are more variations within a breed than between breeds. So we shouldn't be too surprised when we see various lookalikes among our huntaways, especially in a breed lacking any criteria for colour and conformation. Looking at the top dogs of the last twenty years, you can see all manner of types that could suggest outside parentage. Tony Sheild's Wag was a very golden dog, and not only because he won an island title in 1977, and Jim Hay's Doug looked like so much like a German shepherd that Mrs Hay called him the 'the Alsatian'. Despite that, he won one New Zealand and three island titles and, to give this tale yet another twist, Doug was a great-grandson of Bill McSporran's big, black Storm. Bill Donaldson's Big King looked very Gordon setter, and those big, liver, black and tan huntaways from the East Coast must owe a trait or two to the hunt club's hounds. I remember once describing Anthony Shrubsall's huge huntaway, Cougar, as a cross between a mastiff and Great Dane. From the more conventional side of the tree, the input of the Smithfield, German collie and Border collie shouldn't be forgotten either. This is especially the case in the southern half of the South Island, where plenty of black and white huntaways, who put their barks in very clever places, are still working and winning. The list of contributors is endless, including a white beardie who, to a couple of Christchurch ladies, resembled a polar bear.

One point is inescapable: whatever planned outcrosses or unusual accidents occurred, they have been well and truly watered down by now. More importantly, those incursions have in no way diluted the objective set by last century's shepherds, to create dogs to work stock with noise. Remarkably, that basic objective was attained in a very short period of time, with all the dog trial clubs that were founded last century having hunt courses in action before 1900. In my opinion, one of the main reasons why the huntaway was fixed so quickly was because most of the earliest parent stock from Britain wasn't firmly fixed either and possessed a wide range of genetic traits. Selecting from that source, and others, for the ability to work with noise, speeded up the process, especially when coupled with Darwin's theory: the heretability of characteristics adopted through training and environment. All of this shows what can happen when practical people select generation after generation with a specific purpose in mind. To that end the evolution of the huntaway is a direct parallel to the development and refinement of the British Border collie, as outlined by Herries McCulloch in the previous chapter.

The end result of 140 years of breeding is the most exciting working dog you will see anywhere. Watching a good huntaway peel sheep off a broad face on a muster, effortlessly leaping and backing in the yards or, in full song, marching a trial trio uphill, is to see a dog doing exactly what it was bred for. What is also very obvious, especially if you take note of the wag of its upright tail, keeping perfect time with its chorus, is that huntaways just love to hunt.

6
NAMING RITES

Peter Newton called them 'tripehounds', Ian Sinclair 'meat converters' and W.V. McIntyre 'an economic necessity'. To the rest of us they are sheep dogs, though the word 'dog' can be preceded by an adjective that has a direct relationship with either a recent incident or a whole series of them. And none of these prefixes needs to be derogatory. The canine follower that's won five of its last eight starts will certainly be, at the very least, a 'good dog'. Others with better than average records will probably be described as 'quite good', 'promising' or 'useful'. The downhill journey between 'useful' and 'useless' can be quite a quick one, particularly if the mishap that sparked the change occurred in public, just five minutes ago! There are plenty of other descriptions that can be applied to various of our working dogs, especially those with attributes other than those of a specialist huntaway or heading dog.

The best-known New Zealand variation is the handy dog, which heads and hunts. This variety can have a down side, through an undesirable strain which will do little more than hunt for food and head for home. Another of that ilk would be the 'turner', which simply turns good food into something far less desirable. While we're dealing with the lesser lights of the working dog world there is also the 'sooner', a slack and useless critter which would sooner lie in the shade. Another is the 'Sunday dog', a deeply religious animal which treats everyday as the Sabbath and, therefore, won't work. Not everyone accepts that definition. Some Southerners believe that a Sunday dog is a very biddable

creature which, even when spoken to quietly, always does as it's told —
first time and with no further fuss. These attributes remove the need
for shouting and anger, which make such a dog the ideal mate for
working on the Sunday morning following a rugged Saturday night.

The common source of the handy dog is a cross between a huntaway
and a heading dog, known as a shandygaff. The term's original meaning is a beer spiked with lemonade or ginger beer which, to many
New Zealand shepherds, would be a terrible mistake. So, too, for many
stockmen, any cross between our two working types would also be an
error, though they do happen. Some hunt-head crosses have been
planned and some of those which weren't arranged became so successful that they could never be described as an error. The best-known
of these was Wattie Ross's Shandy, as in shandygaff, who won New
Zealand hunt titles in 1953 and 1954. Although the mating may have
been an accident, it was freely acknowledged. Not surprisingly, the
owners of both the heading dog sire, Scott, and the huntaway mother,
Meg, had the same surname; they were R. and G. White. By all accounts,
Shandy wasn't the most powerful huntaway to win a national, but with
Wattie Ross at the helm, what noise the dog did have was always delivered in exactly the right place. Wattie is still the only triallist to have
won national titles in each of the four events, taking five in all. Shandy
was also aptly named for reasons other than his background. He had a
full coat, which was the light, reddish brown colour you'd expect of a
heavy draught beer, diluted with fizzy drink.

One of the handiest dogs I've ever seen at a dog trial was a regular
performer at Wairarapa trials in the 1980s. Bruce Caswell's Spook was
the result of a planned huntaway mating and the sire was a top dog,
Merv Utting's Wag. Yet, to see little black Spook on a heading course,
he looked to be bred for the work. Conversely, when he was on a hunt
course you'd also think that he was born for that. He was, too, it was
just that he was ambidextrous. Above all, Spook was a sheep dog and
happy to work with or without noise, whatever was required. In 1983,
when he and Bruce made their annual visit to Martinborough, they
competed on all five courses; in those days we had a special, show ring
course for heading dogs, as well as the four standard events. The duo

were placed in the short head maiden, were third in the open straight hunt and earned more than 90 points on each of the five courses, a feat that has never been bettered (and never will be either, as we no longer have a special).

Regardless of breed or working type, what you actually call a dog — its real name, not the description you're currently applying — can be arrived at in a number of ways. For a working dog, the first requirement is that its title is short, distinct and easy to call, which eliminates the three- or four-word combinations that still occur with a wide range of other animals. This was also the case with our early imported heading dogs and their direct descendants. The Trotter family of North Otago had several with names like sentences: Storm of Ben Lichen, Lass of Arran and May of Lint Hills. Out on the hill when the work was being done, though, they would have been nothing more than Storm, Lass and May. The full, treble-barrelled names were obviously designed to look good on pedigree papers, as were others from the turn of the century trial: Little Jack Bob, Orphan Boy, Wee McGregor, Armstrong's Sweep, Thora Dust and Southern Cross. A more recent double-barrelled example would be Dudley Buscke's Joe Savoldi, who won a New Zealand hunt in 1974. I'm pretty sure, though, that when he was in action, there would only have been time to call him Joe. The need for brevity means that most sheep dogs, whether they get to a trial or not, have three- to six-letter names, such as Fly, Tip, Kip, Scot, Ben, Moss, Maid, Tess, Gay, Jan and Gyp. All can be delivered very quickly, without giving the caller cause to splutter or creating any confusion for the dog. I have heard of one called Spud, who can't have been a top dog. After a day of working him, his owner got very sore lips with constant, loud repetition of the plosive and spluttery 'Spud!'

Looking over the 28 place-getters at the last three New Zealand meetings (1995 to 1997), the dog with the longest name, Howie Gardner's Trounce, had seven letters, but could still be pronounced very easily, as could another very popular name in the prize lists, Prince. The most awkward to deliver would be Allan Lower's Crumpy. One early trend that has nearly disappeared is using the same name through several generations. Invariably this was because the first with the name was very good and won a lot. A good example is Bob Wilson's Mac, with whom he won his first trial in 1924. In his wake or memory, Bob had a Mac I, Mac Again, Sergeant Mac and Miss Mac. All of these, you can be sure, would have been plain Mac when they were being worked. The Waitaki Valley's John Anderson, Ginger's grandfather, had a dog called Toby, who was followed by a Toby Again, Toby Senior, Toby Junior and at least another Toby Again. Ian Sinclair did something similar recently when he named a son of his heading dog Cap, Recap. Ian also, I have discovered from his writings of 35 years ago, created the first Spice girl, calling a young heading bitch Spice back in 1971.

A recent trend is to follow a theme down through a line. An early example would be Wattie Ross's Kaiser, who sired Fritz, the father of Barry Joblin's Rommel. Barry also had a heading bitch called Fly, whose daughter Barry christened Zip — which wasn't at all the way the old Scots shepherds would have intended the name to go. To them, Fly meant knowing and sharp or smart. All dogs start off as pups and are called 'pup', 'pup-pup' or 'puppy', until their permanent handle is affixed. At least one of Barry Joblin's dogs slipped through the naming net and, even when it was eight or nine, and still winning open hunts, he called it Puppy Dog. The best-known naming pattern these days belongs to Lloyd Smith's line of barking trees. Huntaways all, the first was Oak, then came Bud (as in oakbud) Birch, Larch, Teak and Spar. I once had a pup of the line and named it Bark — he did too. I must admit to a preference for themes of this kind; after Peg came daughter Clip, who begat Tai and Hook who, in turn, produced Catch. Alf Boynton's Chief was the head of a North American Indian line, which included Apache, Tribe, Cree and a bitch someone else named Squaw.

Other triallists have been known to create a pattern of similarity through always having rather unusual and, therefore, very distinctive names. John Bartlett is a good example with Booze, Gonz, Hinkle, Judkins, Ra, Pedro, Coast, Jose and his most recent creation, Geek. Peter Atkins is another with a penchant for colourful titles with, among many, Beast, Tootsie, Terror, Wicked, Shadow, Sting and Paris, whose last litter produced a bitch called Tango — last Tango in Paris!

He also had a bitch called Loot, with a son, Heist. Within the realms of good taste, all that matters, of course, is that a dog recognises its name and responds to it, no matter how odd it may sound to others. There has even been a dog called Odd, christened by Merton Leslie, who is both a veteran dog triallist and an esteemed Holstein Friesian breeder. His heading dogs' smooth coats were always in the pattern of his black and white cattle until along came a very white dog of the line, which had a bit of black round the head and, heaven forbid, some tan! It was a tri-colour which, as he'd never bred one before, Merton thought rather odd, and Odd it became. But when it came to winning sheep dog trials, its behaviour wasn't at all odd.

There are thousands of other dogs who also owe the inspiration for their names to the colour or pattern of their coats. Patch (over one eye) would have to be one of the most prevalent of this form, along with Dot or Spot (usually on the head), Tip (of the tail), Brin (brindled coat of any combination), Blaze or Flash (of white running from forehead to nose), Speck (generally on the legs) and Paint (looking as if it has gone head first into a bucket of white). A dog with a completely white head and neck can also be called Baldy. I was once commentating a show ring run off, where one of the finalists was called Baldy and, unfortunately, I remembered that the human side of the operation was also rather bald. While discussing the dog's name, I suggested that if the triallist took his broad-brimmed hat off, we would see they were a matching pair! Being a sport, he doffed his hat, and the crowd enjoyed the joke. He did, however, give me a very old-fashioned look at the excellent boot lunch that always follows the Hawke's Bay Show's dog trial final. Of all the names motivated by colour, Blue must be the most popular; there'll often be more Blues on a trial ground than in an Australian footy team. Black is another regular as are offshoots such as Dark, Darkie, Nigger (no longer popular), Night, Nugget and Sin (black as). There are plenty of Snows, none more famous than Ginger Anderson's, who not only won some 60 open heading events, but also had a song written about him. Other coat colours with names to match include Grey, Rust, Red, Smoke, Sandy, Brown, Bronze and Tan, along with the already discussed Pink.

Other physical characteristics are also adapted for naming purposes. A huntaway with big feet can be called Boots or, more recently, the Sir Richard Hadlee-inspired Paddles. There's been at least one very large dog called Stretch and another big bony fellow named Horse. At the other end of that scale there's Shorty, a huntaway, of whom more will be heard later. Some heading dogs can be quite tiny and that's what they're called, or alternatives such as Midge or Skeeter (mosquito). The other physical characteristic that often suggests a name is a set of very alert, permanently pricked ears. It won't be called Prick (out loud) but, very probably, Sharp. I saw a dog once with one very upstanding, prick ear, but on the other side it had a lug which, though cut from the same pattern, was only two-thirds successful in standing at attention. Accordingly, it was called Flop. As a word, Flop is short and succinct to call, but it does mean failure and that, I reckon, is tempting fate. In this case, fate won, as the dog was a flop at everything, bar sitting on its haunches and, with head tilted to one side, staring at you as if it was auditioning for a role in a Disney dog movie.

Of the other names that push their luck, Crash would have to be the best — or worst. There has been at least one with that moniker, and every time this huntaway ran at a trial, he crashed. Three years ago I thought Deirdre Bartlett was throwing caution to the wind when she named her young huntaway Smash, though, under her tutelage, all Smash has broken is other competitors' hopes. The huntaway her husband, John, brought out in the 1997 season was one of the best named I've come across for a long time — Talk. She's a good talker too — that's why she got the name in the first place — qualifying for the New Zealand Championships at her first open trial and coming fifth at that event. Of Talk's pups, the two the Bartletts kept were duly named Song and Chats. The latter's handle was doubly apt, having a mother called Talk and a father, Bully, owned by Gary Chatterton.

Some years ago I came across what would have to be the best example of the wrong name for the right dog. I was judging a hunt at the Rewanui shepherds' trial, when a young fellow came by the truck from which I was working and said that his dog's name was Bolt. He and Bolt then walked into the quad and, once the sheep were released, I called 'time'. The competitor immediately started the dog by uttering his name, which he lived up to in every sense of the word. He completely ignored the sheep and disappeared over the left-hand horizon. It was some 20 minutes before he was recaptured and the trial could start again. In a way the dog can't be blamed as it quite literally proved that it was both intelligent and obedient. After all, his boss did say 'bolt'! The opposite to that approach is giving a dog a very positive name that you want it to live up to. Bernard Murphy certainly did that when he gave the name Dream to a young heading bitch of his. Early in her first season, and barely two years old, Dream won three open events in four days. The dream run continued for many years, as she and Bernard won championships, were placed in many more and represented New Zealand in test matches against Australia. There are many other names that reflect attitudes or actions, and often sum up a dog's main strengths. Good heading dog examples would be Nudge, Boss, Speed, Smart, Swift, Guile, Style, Slick, Strong, Spy, Faith, Hope and Calm — and the greatest of these last three is Hope, as she and Stuart Millar have been placed in several championships. Some huntaway names reflect the attributes necessary for the job: Drum, Punch, Bully, Boxer, Butch, Boom, Bold, Rowdy, Sound, Slam, Steel, Major, Toff and Glee. All of them are in direct contrast to a very useful huntaway bitch called Grace, who had the good manners (grace) to ask sheep to go in a certain direction and, what's more, they usually went.

Two of the most traditional sources for sheep dog's names have been royalty and the aristocracy. The stud book and result sheets over the years have listed more Kings, Queens and Princes than Europe's ever had. Equally, there have been plenty of Lords and Ladies, a few Squires, several Knights, and hundreds of huntaways called Duke. There's been a Duchess too, who, even when she was old enough to be a Dowager Duchess, was still winning hunt events. Maori names are also very popular, especially as they are succinct, easy to call and there are plenty of good ones in the three- and four-letter bracket: Tika, Tui, Tahi, Tangi, Rangi, Moki, Mana, Rua, Rohi, Iwi, Koro, Waka, Puke (hill) and Poi.

There are as many different motivations or associations as there are names or incidents that can lead to the creation of new ones. A dog belonging to Toot Lincoln from Poverty Bay was born around the time of the devastating cyclone that hit the East Coast in early 1988; accordingly it was called Bola and, unlike its namesake, this Bola wasn't a disaster. Alf Boynton's current heading dog, Spoke, was so named because, as a pup in transit to Alf's, he got his head jammed in a bicycle wheel. Around the time of the Iraqi invasion of Kuwait, triallist Doug Collins was doing his best to break in an extremely quick young heading dog who was proving very difficult to steer. So much so that, while giving a rueful look and shaking his head from side to side, he'd describe it as 'an unguided missile'. After some control had been introduced, and elements of sense applied to its direction, the missile analogy led to the dog being christened with the name of the most publicised armament of that time, Scud. And Scud, like the missile, became quite a menace, but only on the trial grounds of Hawke's Bay.

Having given a youngster a name, the next stage in its life is training. There are plenty of ways of doing this and since there have been several books written on the subject — from William Whyte's in 1919 to Les Knight's in 1984 — I do not intend to follow in their footsteps. Of all the methods I've read about, seen demonstrated and tried, I've learnt one thing — the simpler the process that's used, the better it is for both teacher and pupil. The heading dog method Les explains in his publication, *A Guide to Training Sheep Dogs in New Zealand*, I first saw used by his old friend, Mervyn Wadsworth of Marlborough. This capitalises on the dog's natural balance to teach it its all important left and right commands or sides. A keen adolescent with some real promise will always look to be at 12 o'clock on one side of a small mob, to the boss's 6 o'clock, over on the other. By the trainer then moving a few metres to his right, the dog will quickly do the same to maintain its grip. As it moves to that point, what is destined to be its right command will be given at the same time. An identical technique will be used for the left and then, to make it more fun and get some distance, this will progress into what Les calls the 'merry-go-round'. The dog is then encouraged to run round the mob on a particular side's whistle or command and come back behind the trainer, and round again. By increasing the distance from the sheep and adding a kick out to go round an obstacle or through a fence, training for the all-important run out has also begun.

Whatever the method, the most important attribute a successful tri-allist or good shepherd wants to pass on to the dog is confidence. This comes from encouragement and consistency and is very important for a young huntaway, which needs to be able to develop its noise on sheep before too many limitations are introduced. The prime aim after that is to have the dog facing the sheep, in front of the boss and, from that position, with guidance that could be as basic as a gentle nudge with the knee, it begins to learn its sides. For either type of dog, some triallists use a harness literally to steer the dog into remembering its key commands. Others use a rope, or a pole attached to its collar or shoulder saddle, to achieve similar results. There are, however, quite a few very good triallists and trainers who don't have the temperament to be attached to a promising youngster. For them in particular, the merry-go-round is ideal. Whatever the system, training a responsive, keen and energetic youngster to do what it was born to do is one of the most rewarding things I know. It gets even more rewarding when the dog you've trained starts getting its name in the results. Long before that, though, it will have gained a lot of experience and proved itself, doing everyday stock work at home on the farm. That, after all, is why we have dogs in the first place and working together on a daily basis is how the great mustering and competitive parnerships have been developed.

7

REAL DOGS AT HOME AND AWAY

The basic idea behind sheep dog trialling is to provide a fair and practical test, for competitor and dog alike, which will allow them to exhibit their skill, or lack of it. To me, this means an event which can measure the ability that breed of working dog would need to show at home. Judging standards are also based on the principles of good stockmanship. Aah, if only it were that simple! The practical side of things isn't too difficult to arrange: the right type of country and some commonsense course design. After all, trialling involves down-to-earth people, who aren't interested in courses that have them and their dogs performing bloody circus tricks. The ingredient that can always be relied on to be uncertain, even unfair, is, of course, those woolly dream destroyers, the sheep. It is impossible to use the same ones all the time, as they'd either end up better trained than the dog or just dig their hoofs in and become an immovable feast, not to put too fine a point on it. The aim is fresh sheep for each competitor and all from the same mob. Under normal management that also assumes they will be off the same farm and of the same breed, age and gender — or lack of it.

Being consistent with the sheep put up for an event would seem to be easy enough to achieve, but in certain parts of the country, where dairying, beef production or intensive cropping have become increasingly important, it can be hard to manage. Clubs do try, especially if they want competitors to return on an annual basis. Even so, some of us have been known to say that the Andersons, Boyntons, Brysons and

Murphys of this world get the good sheep, and we don't! It's always the sheep, you know, it couldn't possibly be the dog or, heaven forbid, a competitor's error. To hear some of us after a calamity, you would certainly believe that only the woolly terrorists could be at fault. That is, if you hadn't seen the run yourself. If so, then you wouldn't have an understanding ear which, in one way, is unfortunate, because you'd miss out on a shout. By tradition, it's in the bar where the best and most creative tales of woe are told.

All of this has been the case since trialling began, but the big difference today is the courses themselves, as there have been a lot of changes since the 1880s. Reading of those days, though, it appears that it wouldn't have mattered what the course was like; the sheep weren't interested in participating and that was that. At some of the original gatherings, the judges literally had to grasp at straws to find a winner; as at Omarama's first trial in 1915. 'The open hunt was won by George McAughtrie's fabulous "Brandy". He was the only dog to complete and even he missed the top set — only to recover and complete.' At other times, such was the chaos that, after picking a winner, the judges gave up. In 1908 at Methven: 'Class III (Huntaway and Slew). Only first prize was awarded in this class as the work done by the second and third place getters was not considered satisfactory'. Earlier I described heading events where the dog would run out with great gusto, only to arrive where the sheep should have been. Today, the judge would call the dog off and give a re-run a couple of runs later, when the dog had regained its breath and the triallist had stopped muttering, 'That would have been her best head this season.'

At some early trials, heading dog competitors were required to work two different mobs, then join them up or separate them or put them in a yard or … goodness knows what. At other events, anything from two to twelve sheep were put on the mark up to half a mile away, and the dog had to bring them down to a marked area or ring. There they had to be either held still or manoeuvred about to prove that everything was under control. On a hunt course, as many as ten or a dozen sheep were to be hunted between two widely spaced gates, which could also be half a mile distant. As trialling became established and the numbers of competitors increased, they soon worked out that ten or twelve sheep at a time would pose some long-term problems. Not the least was the number of sheep that would be required, especially if they were all to be from the same mob. It was soon realised that three sheep were sufficient to provide a good test. Even in a trio there's enough variation to find a tearaway (who needs leg irons), a vague and indecisive soul (requiring a counsellor) and one who faints at the mere sight of a dog and could do with a stretcher.

Having a threesome allows a loner to stand out, yet leaves the other two with company. All the triallist has to do is marry them up again, if possible! When there's two, even three, of an independent nature, the dog has to be in three places at once, which is impossible. Getting three unmanageable beggars at once is known as the luck of the draw, and when your draw has been that unlucky, a wise competitor gives the judge a wave of 'thank you' and disappears to the bar. After all, trialling has been described as 'a game of skill, infused with a slight element of luck — a good dog, usually makes its own luck.' On a huntaway hill, good luck can come from drawing one sheep with a dominant streak, since this will make her a strong leader, who wants to do nothing more than march uphill. Her partners, having weaker minds and lungs, should follow, though probably at a lesser pace, opening a gap between what will become two separate units. It's at about this time that the luck runs out, as the dog's job of steering the front one from one side, then ducking back to urge the others on, becomes rather difficult. The challenge will increase markedly when one of the rear duo runs out of steam and lags behind with a bad case of jellied knees. If you do anything other than stand the dog absolutely still, the sheep will fall over. Keep doing nothing and you'll have three mobs. Both situations add up to the same thing — go to the bar. In this case you would have some justification for blaming the sheep. That is if you hadn't hooled the dog on at the start and forced the delicate one to use up all its available oxygen in the first 20 metres.

In commentaries I used to say, 'There's one in every mob, no matter how small it is.' What I meant was that, when sheep are put to the test, there'll always be one whose sole aim is to be awkward. As generations of triallists will testify, that sort of creature will show up more readily among three sheep than it will in a mob of 20 or 30. This is because, in a trio, all three are equally aware of the dog's presence and pressure, which gives both competitor and dog a chance to make or condition their sheep, right from the start. But in a bigger mob a really spooky creature can hide among her mates and only show out when the pressure comes on at an obstacle or the yard. By then it's probably too late to condition her, as she's already made a big enough dent in your points tally to make waiting around for the results a waste of time.

Other comments I regularly delivered when I was behind the microphone referred to sheep's relative intelligence. In fact I didn't credit them with any grey matter at all: 'If she had another brain it'd be lonely'; 'Three mobile morons on manoeuvre ... total IQ, ten'; 'It's not that she's stupid, it's just that she hasn't a clue!' I uttered that nonsense both in the name of entertainment, which was one of the programme's roles, and to blame the sheep for a problem created by either the competitor or the dog. In the early days especially, I felt that it was most unfair to put triallists on national television and then criticise them in front of over a million viewers. Instead, I picked on the sheep, which was convenient, but unfair. Sheep are not dumb and always possessed enough tactical cunning to outwit any man and dog team who made a mistake or left a gap for them to depart through. What's more, sheep have very good memories. When they've found a gap round a obstacle, or discovered a certain weakness in a dog, they'll keep trying to exploit that chink in their armour. Very often this will create a stalemate and many a run will come to grief at that point. The sheep, one, triallist, nil.

I keep referring to dog trial sheep as she, because at many trials we work with female stock: lambs, hoggets, two-tooths and even mixed-age ewes. There are rare exceptions where entire males are worked, though only as ram lambs, and the bolshie little buggers have a lot more fun than the competitors, especially at the yard! Ewe lambs of five to eight months of age are a very regular challenge. Small and innocent-looking they may be, but looks, as always, are deceiving. They're too naive and have no real personality or confidence of their own and, too often, all three will lack the boldness necessary to become a leader. Having a lamb with an independent streak gives a competitor a chance of coaxing it in the right direction, so that the other two can be encouraged to trot along behind it. Unfortunately, the regular scene at an obstacle has three fidgety adolescents going nowhere in slow circles; playing their traditional roles in an ongoing drama of indecision.

LAMB ONE: What do we do now?

LAMB TWO: I don't know.

LAMB THREE: One of us is supposed to be a leader.

LAMB ONE: What's a leader?

LAMB TWO: I don't know.

LAMB THREE: One of us does something, and the others follow.

LAMB ONE: How do you know?

LAMB TWO: I don't.

LAMB THREE: My mother told me ... she won lots of dog trials.

LAMB ONE: How?

LAMB THREE: By just standing here.

LAMB TWO: Don't we move at all?

LAMB THREE: You can, but only in little circles and *(inclines head towards yard)* you're not supposed to let them push you towards that.

LAMB TWO: Shouldn't we go in there at all?

LAMB THREE: Not if you can help it!

LAMB ONE: And if we stay here, what happens then?

LAMB THREE: Eventually they just get sick of it.

LAMB TWO: That's good. Then what?

LAMB THREE: We'll be sent back to our paddock.

LAMB ONE: How will we know when that is?

LAMB THREE: The man in that hut yells out 'time' or something and these ones *(nods towards triallist and dog)* have to go away and take us with them.

LAMB TWO: And what do we do then?

LAMB THREE: Everything they want us to do.

LAMB ONE: But you said we weren't to help them.

LAMB THREE: Only when they wanted to get us in there (*refers to yard*). Once that man calls out, it's all over and we'll have won!
LAMB TWO: And we're to be good?
LAMB THREE: That's what my mother said. It really annoys them when we're well behaved, and it doesn't matter!

Watching that kind of charade in real life, just before working lambs from the same mob, is not a lot of fun. I remember one such occasion when a whole group of us fell silent as each realised what we would soon have to deal with. A general description of the gathering's mood would be collective depression. After a while, Charlie Anderton, a very experienced and capable triallist, broke the silence: 'You know, it's watching this sort of thing that makes me think of judges at a diving competition, and how they give extra points for the degree of difficulty. My word, you'd get quite a few extra for these!'

When there were big mobs of Merino wethers in the South Island High Country, they were used regularly on hunt courses and very successfully. That's when they weren't debilitated by drought or from having to share their meagre diet with thousands of rabbits. In good condition, they'd have the energy and inclination to walk up steep hills like the gentlemen they were never allowed to become. Peter Newton was a great fan of hunting wethers, Merino or half-bred: 'The hunt hill at Oxford was as steep as a hen's face, but those Woodstock [Station] wethers would climb it like stags.' He judged there one year and the sheep were so good, there was no need for a dog. 'One young competitor struck three cracker sheep that set their compass straight uphill. Although he didn't do any real harm, this bloke's dog persisted in interfering with them until finally I was moved to remark to the time-keeper:"If that bloke would tie his dog up, he'd get a good run"!' The modern alternative to wethers are cryptorchids. These are ram lambs whose malehood hasn't been removed but, with the aid of a rubber ring, the testes aren't able to descend into the scrotum, preventing them from mating successfully. They do develop a male carcass, which is what they'll become before they're much older. Generally these are Romneys or Romney cross, and they often test both the dog's determination and the competitor's patience. Unlike some classes of stock, though, they stay around to see if they have to move, rather than taking to their scrapers as soon as they see a dog. Having sheep that face up and challenge is an important part of dog trialling's test because they're asking the dog, 'Are you good enough to shift me?' If the answer is yes — and they're moved with subtle strength, not a rash dive — then there's a great chance of the trio coming under the dog's spell, and a good run eventuating. If the answer is no, go to the bar!

Making every effort to be as fair as possible to each competitor has given trialling a degree of structured uniformity. Over the years, this has led to criticism from some farmers and runholders who don't compete and regard trial courses as impractical. They also say that handling a mere trio doesn't provide a true test for a *real* farm dog, lacking the challenges it would meet if it had to work a *real* mob on *their* property. With the exception of those belonging to semi-retired people or others, like myself, who aren't full-time on the land, trial dogs are, first and foremost, farm dogs. Anyway, criticism of dog trialling's relevance to everyday stock work is as old as the sport itself. William Whyte first dealt with it at Waipukurau in 1903. 'I issued a challenge to a spectator who was denouncing trial winners in general as useless for work other than on three sheep. I had just won the two heading events and offered to wager the sum of £50 that with this dog I would complete the same two courses within the maximum time allowed, with 300 sheep, provided the obstacles were enlarged proportionately.' Whyte also said that with the same dog (Boy I, I assume) and size of mob, he would then complete the huntaway course. In the end, no money changed hands. 'He [the sceptic] refused to accept the challenge on the grounds that the dog was a phenomenal exception.' Ten years later, Dannevirke's Charlie Hay was challenged to a similar contest. Hay had just won the North Island hunt title with Tweed, a son of Whyte's Boy (yes, father headed, son hunted) and an anonymous correspondent made similar accusations. These, too, disappeared before Hay and Tweed had the opportunity to prove the critic wrong.

After sheep, the element that always differs between each course of the same kind is the country it's run on. Although the design and guideline dimensions of each of the four standard courses — two for heading, two for hunting — are exactly the same on paper, those plans tend to fly out the window when applied to the lie, or lean, of a particular piece of land. Shorter, longer, wider, flatter, steeper, tussocked, riven with slips, or pock marked with sheep rubs, each has an appearance all of its own. Some are more awkward, with blind spots where the dog, with or without the sheep, is out of view. Others have potholes that seemingly swallow dog and sheep, only to spit them out again, in the wrong place. Each has its own tricks or traps, which is why attending a trial for the first time is so interesting and, after misreading the country, so educational. This lack of natural uniformity is a good thing too, since every paddock on every farm is different, as is every mustering beat.

Adjusting to different country is one thing, coping with what's growing on it is another. I know of one heading course where, if a dog takes a certain line on the run out, neither competitor nor judge sees it for almost half the journey. This is because mature, broad-leafed poplars cover most of the hill and, naturally, the trial is held early enough in the autumn to ensure that none of the foliage has begun to fall. In those situations you stand at the foot of the hill and wonder what's happening; hoping like hell that the dog appears in the right place. If you're the judge, and the dog appears in the wrong place, you make the most of it, since what the eye can't see, the pencil can't deduct. On other courses, shorter plants, such as thistles, can be a problem for dogs with tender feet. The first huntaway I trialled with, name of Shorty, hated prickly plants of any kind, to the immediate detriment of stock control. No matter how well she had a trio marching uphill, if there were thistles in the way, madam's prime interest was where her paws could be painlessly put. On a good day, Shorty would do her best to navigate her way through these Scots and Californian forests, by strutting about with her forelegs out in front, in the pointy-toed fashion of a true prima donna. At the same time, what noise she did make could only be described as a harmless falsetto. The sheep realised they were no longer the focus of her attention and did their own thing, while I stood at the foot of the hill, wishing I could do … something!

THREE SHEEP AND A DOG

Shorty's best, or worst, demonstration of this habit was at the 1991 South Island Championships at Omarama. Our run on the zigzag course was early on the first day and it seemed that everyone who wasn't involved on another course, had come to watch — friends, sponsors, dog trialling's hierarchy, the lot. The course there is a big one with all the tussock, rock and upland groundcover you'd expect of a true High Country course. Three good sheep (Merino ewe lambs) were put on a flattish apron of clear ground in front of us. Shorty was duly set alight, and she fired up with all her customary vigour and purpose. The trio

were quickly shifted about 15 metres on to the hill proper and, keeping pace with them, Shorty marched on to this great slab of High Country landscape. No sooner had she done so, than she let out a couple off squeaks — not a thistle in sight either — and went all pointytoed. From there to the top of this tall course, her total output, larynx and limb, was, at best, no more than 50 percent. Shorty's main focus, as I found out later, was a low-growing, slightly prickly burr, which covered most of the hill. If she had been suffering from worn-down or raw pads her ultra-sensitivity would have been understandable and, what's more, I would have been disqualified from the whole meeting. There were no foot problems, it was just Madam drawing the line at the class of country she reckoned she should run on. Throughout the week, Shorty was the only dog out of 180 who put on that sort of performance. In many ways, and most of them were positives, Shorty was a very special kind of dog!

She and I had a much better run a couple of days later on the burrfree straight hunt course. Not a top run, you understand, though it could have been quite useful if the human side of the operation hadn't hesitated, just below the finishing pegs, and let the sheep slide off the course. At least it showed that, when it suited her, Shorty was a real huntaway. The only problem was, hardly anyone saw it. One embarrassing run and we had lost our following! The main point about the variations that occur from course to course, and the range of contour and groundcover they're set on, is that trialling is not just a matter of steering dog and sheep through a few markers or obstacles. In any run, the country's there to be read, as are the sheep, and then their respective quirks have to be translated into tactics. The dog itself also needs to be considered, especially if it has problems with certain classes of country or sheep. All this adds up to the fact that sensible triallists tend to go to trials with contours and stock that suit them and their dogs.

For some, the most suitable conditions may be found well away from regular trial grounds, where competitive concoctions have been dreamed up that would put many of the old timers' layouts to shame. These have been designed in the name of entertainment, and I would have to take part of the blame for some of the prototypes. In drawing

public attention to the versatility of shepherd and dog, these events —
for two-man and dog teams, even — have their place. But the backbone of sheep dog trialling in New Zealand, both cultural and competitive, is built around the four standard courses competed on at 165
open club trials throughout the country. From February to May each
year, heading dogs compete in the long head and short head and yard,
and huntaways sing their way up the zigzag and straight hunt courses.
It is only by being placed in the open classes of these events, that a dog
can qualify for New Zealand and island championships. The winner of
an open gains five qualifying points and this diminishes by a point a
place, down to one for fifth. Six are needed to qualify for the nationals and five for an island, so as the season wears on some competitors
start travelling a long way from home: 'I only need one point'. For
some, the sheep, course and judge are in their favour and they qualify;
others don't. After that initial disappointment, they start thinking about
next season and the training will begin. And this isn't difficult to
arrange, since it's farm work. After all, any dog who can handle that on
a daily basis will cope with the challenges any livestock can offer, at
home and away.

8

OF COURSE

Of the four different events or courses, Event I, the long head, is probably the most traditional and the best test of shepherding's most basic skills. This entails simply sending your dog up a good-sized hill to head sheep (go round and arrive behind them), lift them (get them moving) and pull (bring) them down, as directly as possible. It ends with the hold: sheep at a standstill in a 20-metre ring and held there, with the dog and triallist balanced on either side. As with any test, the so-called straightforward ones provide the greatest opportunity for error. The three sheep stand waiting up to 800 metres away, in the liberation area, which is also known as the hook or 'the strings'. This is a makeshift fence that holds the sheep, as near as possible, to the same spot for each competitor. To enable the dog to bring them out of there, without having to carry wire cutters or kid the trio into doing some hurdling, the hook is wide open on the downhill side. Once the judge has said 'time' in basso profundo tones the dog runs directly to the hill to head them. It should be said that if one of the country's four women judges were officiating, the call, 'time', would be closer to the contralto end of the scale. As a rule the hill will be a big one, or even very big. This is because, as Peter Newton once said, 'A big hill is the only place where a dog can really prove its worth.' Testing dog and shepherd on a good hill is what separates New Zealand trialling from all the other countries where trials of one sort or another are held.

On flatter country, a course stretches away and, visually at least, you feel as if you're losing contact with it. The further it goes, the more its perspective is diminished, and separations, such as the dog's distance from the sheep, become harder to estimate. By contrast, a hill is slap bang in front of you and dog, triallist and judge alike get a fair chance to see what's important. On no course is the challenge more obvious than the long head or long pull. To run a big hill, a dog needs plenty of natural drive and has to be fit. Dogs with faltering legs and wheezing lungs are inclined to deafness at critical moments and take shortcuts. Waikato triallist Bill Silvera once described this condition by referring to his dog immediately after a strenuous run. 'Look at her, she's that unfit she's standing on her tongue! Did you know that when their tongues go out like that, their brains go right out to the end of it? They don't think very well with the brain out there!' The other essential element for heading is having good steering gear, so the dog will go where you want it to. By responding to its remote-controlled rudder, the dog will veer to the left or right, which is known as 'taking its sides'. It will take these if plenty of solid homework has been put in before the pair went trialling.

The run out begins in the same 20-metre ring as it will finish and the competitor stays within it until either the dog returns with the sheep, the triallist decides that all is vain and retires, or the judge calls 'time'. That means you've run out of it and, as my favourite long head marshal, Jack Brown of Tinui, has been known to say to reluctant finishers, 'You've had a fair go ... on yer bike.' The outrun or head is judged out of 48 points, which we think we should receive far more often than we actually do. Judging, however, is best done from behind the ring, not within it. The head should begin with the dog running at, then onto the hill, not ballooning out and wasting effort. It then angles to one side — invariably the right — to run as directly as is practical on that country, to the shoulder of the head. This is the widest part of the outrun, where the dog is adjacent to the sheep, though a safe 40 to 60 metres or more away. From here the dog keeps climbing, to cut out a non-threatening arc and come round to stop behind the trio, some 10 to 20 metres away. If all this were achieved by a dog who looked as if it wanted to get to its trio as quickly and purposefully as possible, then it would have to be a 48-pointer — especially if it were my run! I use the possessive quite deliberately too. It is impossible to stand on the flat and not be with the dog every stride of the way. You urge, direct, cajole and even warn the dog as it runs your errand. Above all, though, you encourage, because you really want it to get there. This means that when the dog does arrive, and in style, calling out 'good dog', right there and then, is the least you can do.

In each section of our standard courses there are all sorts of incidents and anecdotes I can use to illustrate some of the great and not so great moments that have occurred in the past. A good run out, though, is exactly that, with no apparent drama; the potential for conflict with the woolly ones is still to come. The best description of an ideal head is to compare it with the outline of half a pear, with its bottom uppermost. That's particularly the case as the dog makes a safe and wide arc round the top, and finishes by coming downhill a little, towards the sheep. By approaching them at the finish of the run, both dog and triallist, whose urgent whistles will coax it forward, have shown they're in complete control. There are times when the dog is arriving at the 12 o'clock mark, well above the sheep and the boss takes a deep breath and blows a stop whistle big enough to halt an express train. Not surprisingly, the dog drops to the ground as if the whistle were a rifle and it had just been shot. In many instances, while the dog may be dead in line (12 o'clock) with the sheep and the whistle-blower away below, it's out of sight behind a brow and has no idea where the sheep are. That is heading the hill; we're supposed to be heading the sheep.

Though it is the dog who does the running, heading makes plenty of demands on the triallist, even when working an experienced and confident dog. Anxious moments will usually occur as the dog approaches a critical point, such as a rock, tree, fern or slip, which it should pass above in order to get sufficient height to then put a good top on the head. As the dog nears the landmark, the number, volume and authority of the whistles will increase, especially if the dog looks to be wavering towards a shortcut. If there are any spoken commands, the tension in them will be obvious. To find out whether the dog went past the critical point on the right side, watching isn't necessary. Failure usually brings a long silence, followed by a low growl and resigned whistling or a verbal message such as, 'I'll get you my boy!' If it were successful, the urgency will have disappeared but there'll still be plenty of commands. By now the boss will have realised that he or she is on to a hot one and will be all out to capitalise on potential that can be seen, but hasn't yet been secured.

Before a run, even a quick look at some really big long head courses is enough to throw doubt into all but the most assured minds. Time after time, when judging, you'll hear competitors volunteer various, down-payment excuses on their way to the ring: 'Hasn't been running out very well lately' or 'Just a young dog, but I'll give it a go … only way it'll learn.' My favourite doubting Thomas story comes from Christine Wright's history of the Methven club, *Whistles in the Wind*, describing an early competitor sharing his fears with the judge: 'If I cast to the right the dog will get McClennan's cows, and if I cast him to the left, he'll get Harrison's bitch!' There's another form of worrier, who looks for the slightest thing that could possibly distract the dog. Spotting something on the horizon they'll say to the judge or course marshal, 'Those sheep over on that ridge there, my dog can see them.' The concern is that the dog might traverse half the district and fetch the distant mob, instead of the trio in the strings. There are times when you reach for the binoculars so you can see what's causing all the worry. Competitors' fears are often very valid, as there's nothing worse than a good run ruined by another trio emerging from the scrub or tussock. The dog that runs out for three and comes home with six doesn't get double points; it receives a re-run. When strays from another course or an earlier run are spotted, the countryside gets an ear-shattering straggle muster from a competent huntaway. Hunt exponents love clearing up around heading courses, just to remind the 'pointy shoe people' who run 'sneakers' (heading dogs) what a real dog can do!

At the other end of the scale is the very experienced competitor with a championship title or two who walks out with an older dog following him. They've been a team for years and won plenty of trials at every level. Yet he, too, may utter an aside: 'She's getting a bit old for this sort of thing. Still fit, though. Might as well give her a run, eh?' You call 'time', the dog doesn't wait for the boss's starting command and goes immediately, swift and true across the flat, soars up the hill to curve round from the shoulder and scamper over the steep benches near the top. She hardly breaks her stride as she crosses the broken country over a rough ridge, and drops down on to the brow above the sheep. There she halts, to give the sheep a steady stare, a moment or two before the sound of the boss's stop whistle would have floated up to her. That, in a nutshell, is a fair description of Barney Strong's and thirteen-year-old Bonny's run on the long head at the 1997 Waikato Centre Championships. It wasn't a 48, as she over-headed, which means she went past noon on the clock and landed at 11.

Stopped behind the trio, the dog catches its breath, and the triallist does the opposite and heaves a sigh of relief. Next comes the lift, which isn't judged separately, as it's the beginning of the pull and, without doubt, the most important part of it. Lifting sheep — not to be confused with sheep stealing — could be described as the gentle art of getting animals to move, before they realise that they're already in motion, and under another creature's control. This is the getting-to-know-you phase, during which the dog mustn't make sudden or aggressive moves and unsettle the sheep. The cliché 'fist of steel in a velvet glove' certainly applies here, as dogs need a kind but strong approach — 'I'm in charge, don't be frightened. All you have to do is what you're told.' Obviously, thousands of sheep have been handled insensitively, and still are. That's why, on a bad day, trio after trio can bolt down or across the hill. When sheep don't take instant offence, and wait to see what the dog will do, the likelihood of a winning run increases. That's my view, but Rupert Sharpe's is a touch more cavalier. 'To win an event a header must run out, just right. Round the sheep he must pause and pretend he is waiting for orders from his handler. Whether he can hear or not, he will start his pull, after standing for a while with a self-satisfied smirk on his face.' Sharpe, lucky man, obviously had confident dogs following him. When a dog's working 600 to 800 metres away, the more self-assured it is, the more it can be left to get on with it.

Three Sheep and a Dog

While liberating sheep on my club, Martinborough's long head, I've seen some marvellous work from only 20 metres away, especially Bob Bryson's great bitch, Queen, who won a New Zealand title and was placed in several others. On one of the many occasions Queen competed at our trial, the sheep's behaviour at the time she ran is best described as spooky. An unsettling sou'-easterly breeze was sneaking through the saddle where the hook is, and the dog's appearance was usually sufficient excuse for the sheep to decamp and disappear round the side of the hill. Because of the subtlety of her arrival, Queen's trio didn't do a runner and they dug in at one corner of the hook and up against the netting. Naturally, Queen was on the top side and crept slowly to within 10 centimetres of the boss sheep's nose — only the wire separated them. By this time Queen was poised on three paws, with her head angled to her right, as if she knew that the pressure of a full-on stare would be too much. There, as a breathing replica of the Lake Tekapo sheep dog memorial, she stayed for well over two minutes. Bob didn't say a word, just stood in the ring 700 metres away and left her to it, which required as much self-control as Queen's stationary pose. Her nose-to-nose confrontation took place near the end of the liberation set-up, leaving a very open side door for the sheep to make a dash for it. They never considered it. The calm, binding effect Queen always had on sheep welded them to the spot, as did her alert stance, best described as 'anything you can do, I can do quicker'. The spell was finally broken when the front sheep conceded and took a tiny shuffle backwards. At that point, Queen calmly moved her head from right to left and, as one, the trio turned to their left to walk downhill. Her Majesty followed, dipping her head regally to pass under the netting, then took up the balance behind them. With the odd adjustment for the sake of progress and direction, and occasional advice from Bob, the procession stayed that way as they walked to the ring. Queen and Bob won, of course, by winning round one at the top of the hill.

Another of the legendary runs on Martinborough's long head is often recounted with great relish by club president David Harris. It's all about the performance of a dog we'll call Spot. 'After he headed, he stopped a few yards back behind the sheep, and eyed them. Head

112

stretched forward staring, tail straight out the back and one front paw just off the ground … oh, he looked the part. The bloke working him said, "Up Spot," so he lifted his paw — the one that was already in the air — about half an inch and stood stock still. So the bloke said, "Up Spot" and again the dog just lifted its paw a fraction. "Up Spot", another bit. After a while the man was starting to get a bit frustrated, "Up Spot … *up Spot!*" Again, just another flicker of the paw, upwards. Well, this went on for a fair while and finished up with the dog holding his paw well above his ear. So this bloke took a really deep breath and let out a great big "*Up Spot!*" Spot just launched himself in the air. He cleared the netting and grabbed the nearest sheep and hung on while it gave him free ride to the foot of the hill and they ended up in the ditch, with the dog still hanging on. The man left the ring and came tearing across the flat yelling, "Get out of that, Spot, get out of that, Spot!" I'm pretty sure that was the only time he ran that dog here.'

A top pull is built on a master (triallist), master-servant (dog) and servant (sheep) relationship: the dog's boss, the boss of the sheep, which are supposed to be subservient. This works only when the dog has the balance and strength to play the part of master. The same invisible thread of control that good huntaways create with their noise can also be created by a heading dog's quiet strength. In a controlled pull the sheep will virtually lean back on to the dog and adjust their moves as a direct response to its control. If the dog's forced to sit down, or is sent where it and the sheep lose sight of each other, the thread has just been broken. The dog's next move or unexpected appearance could easily spur them into actions that will haunt the triallist for weeks to come. The accident was probably caused by the triallist forcing the dog to do something it didn't want to do, and the dog was right. As with the lift, the dog is often in a better position to make judgements, no matter how obvious it is to the boss what the dog's next position should be.

I well remember having a useful run on very difficult sheep which, all day, had performed a quick Houdini to their right two-thirds of the way down the hill and escaped at speed. In our run, Clip anticipated this with a quick block, and kept pulling them on a good line. It was the last run of the day and the judge, Peter Boyce, and I chatted about it afterwards. He made special reference to Clip's run-saving block, to which I readily agreed. 'Yes,' he said, while giving me a knowing look, 'and just before that you told her to sit down!' At which I managed to look sheepish and said 'Mmmm' — only a fool argues with a judge after a handy run. I left at this point as the trio had lined themselves up on the bank of a very swift, full creek, and were preparing to dive in. They really were curious creatures, just not interested in responding to a dog. They were a cross of one of the newer imported breeds, the Texel. I believe they look good on a meat hook and are very tasty on a plate, but they certainly don't have a place in dog trialling. They had the last word that day, as two of them did take a dive, and what a bloody performance that led to! If nothing else, trialling is a great leveller — high and dry one minute, down and damp the next.

During the pull section of the Barney Strong and Bonny run I mentioned before, the sheep seemed to be leaning to their left, like every trio before them. Usually, if given the slightest opportunity, they'd disappear in that direction at a gallop. Barney asked Bonny to go to her left to cover; she ignored him. The sheep kept coming straight, though they were still looking to their left, but the old lady stayed tucked in behind them and Barney, still concerned about that wide open door to the side, gave her another left command. Once more, Bonny carried on as if nothing had been said. At this stage, Barney, with hands on hips, growled and gave her what's known in cricket circles as 'the teapot'. Though I was behind him, I could well imagine the look she was getting — not that Bonny looked! Barney didn't say another word. Sheep and dog came down the hill another few metres, and then the trio finally made their move — but to their right. And guess who was right beside them stopping them from going more than a metre? Bonny. At which point Barney threw his arms in the air and called out, 'All right, so you know everything!' At which point he walked round in a little circle, shaking his head and muttering to himself. For those lucky enough to be there, this was one of those incidents that add spice to a day's trialling. It was also one of the best examples you'd ever see of a working relationship between a top shepherd and an instinctively good dog.

As with the head, there are 48 points up for grabs in the pull, but as there are other factors involved, like sheep, getting a full-pointed pull is as rare as finding teeth in an eight-year-old ewe's mouth. The likes of 46 or 47 are very good scores indeed and if competitor and dog have achieved that, then the last section, the hold, should be a breeze. This is when the sheep walk into the 20-metre ring and need to finish, facing the dog, with the triallist balanced on the other side, arms out, appealing for the hold. This is not a matter of leaping about and pleading to trialling's equivalent of a cricket umpire, but a competitor's silent signal that he or she thinks they've got a hold. It's then up to the judge who, if all three parties are stationary, will voice agreement by calling 'right'. The hold is designed to prove that the sheep were well enough handled to be able to finish standing calmly at hand. That's not always possible. I can recall many trios hurtling across the flat, straight at me, as if they'd had me in their sights since I sent the dog up to fetch them down. It didn't take long to work out that trying to stop them is futile, and I soon learned to step aside, watch them go in the front and, a quick 20 metres later, come out the back, then stop. Doing my best to look composed and unconcerned, I would then collect them with the dog and put them in the spent pen (for used sheep). Although they'd looked totally unmanageable a few seconds ago, this isn't difficult. You see, sheep know when they've dashed your hopes, and that there's no need to waste any more breath and effort. That's why, after they've rushed through the ring, they'll take a couple more paces, halt, look round, and laugh at you. They know when the show's over.

What can be even more humiliating is when a course marshal decides that you and your dog aren't up to it and, with a faintly patronising air, quietly puts his dog round the trio and they obediently amble into the yard and join their mates. And outsiders wonder why we sometimes get cross and walk back to the ute muttering under our breath, about everything in general or the dog in particular, that supposedly well-trained miscreant who, panting with all the effort, has returned faithfully to your side. Not too close, though, just outside drop-kick range! After all, the run was going well until she got bored with the calmness of it all, and flicked in and whipped the nerviest member of the trio into a gallop. As you'd expect, verbal and physical violence is not allowed on or near any trial ground, and any transgressions are dealt with immediately by the judge or a judicial committee. And don't be misled by my comments about bolting and uncontrollable sheep. Clubs go to a lot of trouble to put up stock which will allow a fair chance. Changeable weather and the normal patterns of the day have their effect on sheep behaviour, but nothing unsettles them more than a rash dog or an irrational shepherd.

If ever there was going to be a perfect run, it would have to be without sheep, dog or human and, therefore, would need to take place in the mind. Not long after the television series first associated me with trialling I attended, as a rural journalist, a Federated Farmers' function in Wellington. During the course of the evening the federation's treasurer, Ken Reid, called me over. The Reids are from the hard rolling hills and craggy rocks of the Lee Stream area in Otago and have a well-earned reputation as sheep men, shepherds and triallists. Ken's station, Horsehoof, was named after the family's original brand, registered in the 1870s. 'Now John,' he said, shifting over for me to sit beside him, 'I want to tell you about my run when I won the long pull at the 1944 South Island Championships.' He then looked away from me with his alert stockman's eyes focused into the distance and the memory of it all. 'It was one of those clear sunny mornings you get near the mountains, and when I walked out from the tents to the ring, you could see everything as clear as bell … quite a bit to see too. It was a huge hill, with a fair bit of rubble over it, and some really big, bare rocks near the top. They called time and I sent the bitch away, one of our breed. She ran well too, and it was pretty rough going over what flat there was, but she hit the hill in the right place, and began to climb. Ooh, what a climb. No grass to speak of, bits of a kind of briar in places, that's all. And steep! She never hesitated, kept going all the way. I kicked her out below the rocks and she responded and cut out above them, just lovely, then brought her round — she was blind to the sheep — so she was well above the hook. After that I called her on, to stop on a bit of a ledge above them — it was all rock you know and terribly hard on the dog. Even so, it was the best out run I ever had, John', as he turned back to look me straight in the eye. 'Had to be a 48 … had to be.

'The sheep were Merino wethers, and touchy, especially on that country. I just kept bringing her on to them, as they were so strong that if you stopped the dog, they'd turn and walk straight up to it. We got them away quite well and they came straight down, except for some of the bigger boulders that were in the road. Walked them all the way too. Didn't need to give her any sides either, just the steady, to give the wethers time to pick a track through the rubble and stuff. Down at the bottom I got the two-minute call [two minutes left] but it wasn't a worry as the ring was quite close. They came into it with no problems, and I swung the dog round and bang, she stopped them first time. They were facing her at about 6 o'clock and I was pretty close to 12 o'clock. Must have been perfect, and the call "right" came immediately — and a lot of applause, as a fair crowd had built up during the run. I'd never had one as good as that before nor, I'm sorry to say, have I since. But it was the winning run, the only championship I ever won.'

If you were to search the archives for confirmation of Ken Reid's win with Fly (I think), you wouldn't find it. The only mention of a 1944 South Island Championship is a note that none was held between 1942 and 1944. Yet when Ken was reliving that run, to look into his eyes, bright with the sheer joy of those moments, you knew that memory had happened all right and, when it did, his spirit was among southern hills and rocks, as were the dog and the sheep. The venue wasn't. It was Italy, near Monte Cassino. At a time when the New Zealand Division was standing down from the battle, Ken got up one morning, walked from his tent and did what he loved to do at home: run a dog on a big hill. On this occasion it was also a championship final. The right time to have what Ken Reid reckoned was 'the best run I ever had'.

There are four points for the hold which, with the two 48s, comes to a possible of 100. Once there were six points for the work in the ring, but for a much more complicated manoeuvre. When the sheep entered the circle, the triallist needed to be in the centre, with the dog on the outside and the sheep between them. They then had to be driven a full revolution one way, then a full turn the other way, to finish at a standstill. Fortunately, this unnecessary demonstration has been replaced by the hold. Some would have us believe that a perfect hold happens only when the competitor is at 12 o'clock, at the top of the ring, the sheep somewhere near the axis of the hands and the dog below them at 6 o'clock, with sheep and dog staring at each other. Competitors can do their level best to choreograph this, but such precision isn't necessary. All that's required is to show that triallist and dog are on balance and have a grip of the sheep. One of the country's leading triallists, Paul Sorenson, tells a story about the first time he ran on a long head when Les Knight was judge. This was after Paul had made a few visits to Les's farm for tuition on the finer points of trialling. 'After fiddling about in the ring with lots of flourishes and a great show of confidence I was looking for a four-point hold, you see. Then there was this low growl from the judge's box: "For God's sake, stop showing off and finish the bloody job!"'

I saw only half of one of my most memorable long head runs. This was at the 1980 New Zealand Championships at Mararoa, in northern Southland. I got to the natural grandstand — a small hill opposite a much bigger, tussock-clad one — as Geoff Allison's Fay finished her head. The experts already assembled on the knoll all agreed that the head was a good one and so was the rest. I described it all in my report in the *Farmer* as '… the gentlest of lifts and a perfectly straight pull home. Fay has a knack of making sheep like her, so by the time she ushered them into the ring, they were as happy as cats on cream.' Which was my way of describing how the four of them, Fay and the sheep, just seemed to walk down the hill together, grinning at each other for a total of 97.5. Runs like Geoff and Fay's make the job look so easy that you could begin to think that the only human requirement is to stand there while the dog does the rest. If the dog did do it all unbidden, the competitor would have to take a lot of credit for training the dog so well, then trusting it. According to Bob Guthrie, there has been at least one run where complete handler silence was achieved. 'In the North Island champs at Gisborne, in 1939, Ray Twoomey went to the mark in the long head with Spark. Without a word of a lie, from the moment that dog left him, till he had the sheep down, the hold, everything, old Ray didn't say a word; not a command, nor a whistle. Headed them, pulled them, nary a whisper … great run, they were just out of a place!'

On another occasion of complete silence, the reasons that caused it were bottled ones. 'There was one island run off [championship final] where this bloke went out to run, and he was dead drunk. Got into the ring for the long head, and just sat down and went straight to sleep. The judge called "time" for the run to start, and that was enough for the dog; away he went. Lovely head, good lift, and pull as straight as a die. The trouble was, his boss was sound asleep the whole time! Then the dog brought them into the ring for the hold and just held them there … on perfect balance to the man. If he'd just got up and put his arms out to get the hold, it would have been a winner.' Unless a competitor has a dispensation from the judge for assistance, to overcome a more than passing disability, such as failing sight, there can be no outside assistance or interference during a run; including yelling, 'Wake up!' After the run, though, whatever is necessary to keep the trial running can be said and done. 'In the end they had to wake him up to get him out of the ring for the next competitor!' Having a bar on most grounds can cause problems for competitors who have over-wet their whistle. Some years ago at Otairi-Pukeroa, near Hunterville, a local farmer was having a brilliant run on the long head. Suddenly, to everyone's absolute amazement, he called his dog off and walked away. Back in the bar he was asked why on earth he had pulled out when his dog was doing so well? 'Because I couldn't decide which of the blighters to work!'

There are other reasons for not seeing sheep or dog so clearly; failing sight does afflict a few, generally older, competitors. It would be silly of me to say that this isn't a handicap, but it need not be the reason for withdrawing from competition. Failing sight is progressive, and the first sign of a competitor having difficulty is when he uses binoculars for the top of the head and the lift. In the case of William Whyte, his difficulties were made more obvious because he would tie a white handkerchief to the dog's collar, to make it easier to follow. Failing sight usually means that the sheep at the top of a long head can't be seen, nor can the latter part of the run out and the beginning of the pull. In these areas, the competitor is allowed a spotter who tells them what's happening and can also make some pertinent suggestions about what commands to give, especially when a dog is running at full tilt on the head. 'Give him a right ... another ... keep him going [meaning the run whistle] ... he's hit the shoulder, hold him out ... good, bring him round ... 3 o'clock ... 1 o'clock ... bring him up, you're behind them, stop! ... well done.' For the competitor, converting that information into instant commands which the dog obviously obeys takes a tremendous amount of ability.

The first spotter-competitor combination I saw in action was in the long head at the Mangamahu nationals in 1983. Ian Anderson was competing, as he had at every New Zealand since 1936, and his son Ginger was the spotter. Ian wasn't placed but he was well qualified, with points to spare, and there's always a large number of fully sighted people who don't manage that. For many years — with one exception, over 20 years ago — that was the case for Ohingaiti's John Marshall, both when he first took up trialling and as his sight began to diminish. For some years now he and his spotter, Bruce Christie, have stood together at the foot of various heading courses and worked two of the fastest running out dogs in the business. You might think they wouldn't be ideal for this type of delayed situation, but they really want to run, and all that's needed is some steering. For a season or two that facet of the operation was a problem but in 1997, at the age of 86, John Marshall qualified both his dogs to compete at the New Zealand Championships. He did not win but, by earning the right to compete there, he gave a lot of people, and himself, a tremendous amount of pleasure.

The other disadvantage some competitors have to overcome is a lack of mobility. Farming, the main occupation of about 95 percent of all triallists, is not only a physical job, but one that often requires working in wet and cold conditions. It's pretty hard on knees and hips and it would be unusual to go to a trial where there wasn't one person who was about to, or had recently had, a replacement joint of some kind or another. Walking with sheep in the drives on a short head and yard course is particularly difficult for such a competitor. It's even more awkward if the sheep want you to run alongside them in their rush to get to the yard. I remember Gary Brennan having a difficult time after his hip operation; he said that if the sheep ran, he just walked off. Even with two sticks, the way his last good dog, Paddy, worked, and was worked, meant that Gary walked off very few courses.

For many years Merton Leslie of Reperoa competed with the aid of two sticks and did very well. On at least one occasion when I saw him walking behind sheep during a run, he was concentrating so hard on holding the balance that neither stick seemed to touch the ground. Some years later, a further reduction in mobility meant that he became a long head specialist. I last saw Merton, aged 86, run his excellent bitch, Lace, at the Tux Waikato Championships in 1997. Once he got in the ring ready for his run, he sat on a shooting stick and didn't need to move again until, after a very good head and pull, the sheep came quietly into the ring for the hold. Lace had the trio in such a calm and obedient state that, as soon as they saw Merton, they stopped. His inability to move quickly to the point of balance was a half-point disadvantage, but not a disaster. With a total of 96.75, Merton and Lace were placed second, a remarkable achievement for a man who was first placed in a New Zealand Championship 51 years earlier, with third and fourth in the short head. Unlike many pursuits, dog trialling does not restrict the participation of people with at least some disabilities. After all, it's not a test of how well the triallist runs a good big hill; that's the dog's job, if it has a competent driver.

9

THE OBSTACLE COURSE

The short head and yard is the second of the standard heading courses and, true to name, starts with a head and pull, each carrying a possible 22 points. They're less than half the value of the longer event, because the sheep are usually half the distance away. The run ends at a 2-metre-square yard; sometimes the sheep are in it, other times they're all around it. A lot of bright hopes have ended here and some have succumbed completely. 'Old Jack dropped dead running his dog at Rangiwahia; hand on the gate, yarding … nearly had them in. You know, he used to say to us, "It's my wish that I die on a trial ground, having a run. And if I ever get my wish, you buggers rush out and in the back pocket of my trousers you'll find a bloody fiver. Get it and go and shout for the boys".' When telling me that story, Doug Cochrane stopped, thought for a moment and said, 'You know, when it did happen, I can't remember whether we got the fiver out of his back pocket or not!' There's no doubt that closing the gate on a very good run and faultless yard is a little like going to some sort of triallist's heaven. First, though, you have to get them off the hill, and one aspect I didn't mention earlier was the wrong way to head sheep.

The worst and most penalty prone method is known as cross heading. This happens when the dog starts from the competitor's right, but at some stage crosses the direct line between sheep and shepherd, and heads them from the left. Immediately the judge does a perfectly dreadful thing and divides the heading points by two. Then, like a true sadist, he or she carries on and subtracts the penalties for the indiscretions that led to the head being crossed. The one thing you can be sure of, when this happens, is that you won't be involved in the prize-giving. I know, Peg was very good at crossed heads. So good that, in my first season, I was inclined to forget what damage this could do to the final tally. Running on the tall-tussocked long head at Lumsden, in Southland, I had a pretty useful pull and quite a good hold in the ring which, for once, didn't seem too small and I managed to keep out of the sheep's way. I was rather pleased with this and chattered on about it to Dereck Haines, later to become national president. After a while he found he had to stop giving noncommittal 'mmms' in response to my building up hopes of a mention in the minor dispatches — the maiden. He slowly turned his gaze from the run we were watching and raised an eyebrow in my direction — 'Yes, but you did cross your head!' I then fell silent.

After a crossed head, the next most point-destroying indiscretion is what some call a snooker head. As the name suggests, the dog leaves the triallist like ball from a cue and speeds over country that's nothing like a felt-topped table, straight at the sheep. With no thought of a natural swing out, and completely deaf to the loud pleadings from below, the dog can hit the trio from beneath. This shatters them apart as the cue ball would a triangle of reds. At this point there's a temptation to try a cover-up and desperately call, 'Divide!' Don't, it only draws more attention to the tragedy. Often, though, in the final seconds of what appears to be a sure-fire snooker head, the dog will make a last-minute concession to its heading forefathers, and flick out as it gets close to the sheep. This may be little more than whipping round behind them, with all the width of a small fish-hook, to give them a fair old nudge from behind. As a result, the sheep never stop running until they've got a very long way away. The best trick of all that a dog can pull on a run out is a slashed or headless head. In terms of the effect this can have on the competitor, this is best executed by the dog when it has done everything perfectly and looks to be on a winner. That is, until it gets to the shoulder — the widest part of the head — and looks 90° to its left and says, 'Aah, there they are'. To this point, the triallist's been happy about the job and, silly person, starting to get confident. A good operator, though, would have noticed the dog's quick inward look at the sheep, and started to go on red alert. Alas, before he or she could even decide whether to disengage the lips for a yell, or purse them for a whistle, the dog's taken a hard left and zipped straight across the hill to arrive right beside the hind hoofs of the rear sheep. That's the last time those legs will be stationary for quite a while.

In the short head and yard, triallist and dog assemble in the quad, which is 20 metres wide, and face the hill. The dog leaves from there and must bring the sheep back through the front door, between the poles closest to the hill on either side of the quad. Squeezing sheep through a gap the width of a cricket pitch can be harder than you'd think. Some trios become quite touchy as they draw closer to the competitor, who is probably getting a bit noisy, which makes the sheep want to veer away even more, which makes the triallist get a little noisier, which makes …! To take the pressure off, there can be a distinct temptation to step out of the quad, which can't happen if the run is to continue. In these situations the compromise will have the competitor trying to look as thin as possible, jammed by the marker on one side, and the dog exerting enough pressure on the sheep for them to wipe the paintwork on the inside of the marker over on the other side. Where the work on the hill has been good, with calmness reigning all the way to the quad, they'll come through the centre and it will all look far too easy. Apparent ease, though, is the hallmark of quality work and nowhere can this be better shown than on the flat sections of the short head.

Once the sheep are in the quad, the 30- to 50-metre first drive begins. Also 20 metres wide, this can be on the same line as the pull or take an abrupt right-angled turn from the front door of the quad. It can also veer away on a lesser angle or even wind round in a semi-circle; whatever works best within the local landforms. The other fit, crucial to any chance of success, is that of the three mobile parties within the drive area. The competitor mustn't leave it — unless there's been a decision to take an early smoko — the sheep shouldn't, and the dog, within reason, is pretty much a free agent. If it were to get right in front of the sheep, and take the lead off, it would be penalised, as it would be for sitting back and watching the boss do all the work, but it can take up the balance and work outside the marked area. The most important don'ts in driving are the competitor not going past the shoulder of the front sheep, and not walking backwards. If the sheep break back behind you, reversing to help is a very natural thing to do. The dog has to do that, while the triallist stands there wishing that the problem hadn't occurred in the first place.

Generally, the dog will be on one side, competitor on the other, while the sheep walk calmly down the middle. When there's even the slightest list to port or starboard, and the sheep start leaning over to your side of the course, you find yourself walking a little quicker to hold the line. They increase their speed, so do you. Imperceptibly they move into a slow trot, you do too. Effortlessly they move up a cog to a fast trot, and you respond, while they angle closer and closer to the edge of your side of the drive. After that the pace lifts to a canter, then a gallop — and all this time you've never been able to improve your position beyond fourth place! By now they're well away from the designated driving area — you just managed to stop inside it — and then something goes click in the memory bank. You remember that you did bring a dog today. Yes! That'll be the one you accused of pushing the sheep on to you and bellowed at: 'Siddown ... SIT!' There it is, 40 metres away, still sitting, tongue hanging out, drooling and grinning at you. In fact, it's probably splitting its sides, but has too many brains to show it. Called into action, the dog needs to head the escapees and bring them back to the next section, the hurdles, which they shot past at great speed.

On a good day, which we all have and store in our memory cells to cherish for ever, driving sheep is one of the most satisfying things you can do with stock. As the sheep walk along they're well aware that, with each taking their respective side, shepherd and dog are in control. As they look to lean left or right, you adjust the dog's or your own position accordingly. Sedate driving such as this not only feels good, but it usually means that negotiating the hurdles should be a breeze. Generally the hurdles are 3 metres long, and are set 3 metres apart, to run parallel to each other in the line of the drive. There are no wings to them, other than the dog and the competitor on either flank, and when sheep play up here, they can take quite a bit of flanking. Ten metres out from this obstacle the triallist steps into a free working area, and can move around to help the dog, but not replace it. Just the same, it's amazing how instantly nimble some people can become, despite the number of their years or the width of their girth. This is especially so when the trio appears to be walking briskly to pass through the hurdles and, in a thrice, dart off to dive down the outside of the woodwork,

on the competitor's side. Suddenly you see side-steps, agrarian ballet movements and slip fielding of a calibre you would never have believed possible. When reflecting on incidents when you weren't quick enough to save the day, you realise how instinctively quick dogs are, and appreciate how much human effort and energy they save.

Not all of every dog's moves are necessary, though younger dogs, in particular, have an innate fear of losing their sheep and hate the thought of them getting any distance away. This can mean that, no sooner has a youngster done sterling work putting sheep through the hurdles than quick as a flash, she's whipped round and stopped them from coming out the other side. At her first trial or two, Clip, my current heading dog, could head hurdles in the blink of an eye. Although flicking round and holding sheep on to me was natural for her, I did not enjoy standing in the mouth of the hurdles trying to fend off sheep who wanted to shoot out of the gap they'd just been put through. At the same time I was busy kidding a young and slightly dis-oriented dog to come back round to help get everything going forward again. In that direction is another drive of 30 to 50 metres and then the final obstacle, the yard. As with the hurdles, 10 metres in front of it are pegs that mark a line the competitor can't cross until sheep number three has crossed with hoof number four. Go over the line too soon and you might as well go to the bar. Once the sheep have cleared the 10-metre mark, the competitor goes to the head of the gate and grips and opens it out by 90°. This cannot be let go until the sheep are yarded, time runs out or, fearing a heart attack or a nervous break-down, the competitor throws in the towel and departs.

Closing the gate on a well-yarded trio is very satisfying since it's the same as getting the sheep in on time for drafting or shearing. It's also the final test not just of your ability and that of your dog, but also of the latter's strength. When sheep first arrive at the 2-metre-square yard they usually try to duck and dive away from the yard mouth, and a good dog will always block them, making escape impossible. Accordingly, they will then move on to plan B, which is to turn and face the dog in the ultimate challenge. This in-your-face confrontation was a major part of what success … *a Dog's Show* had as a television series. The tension created by close-up shots of dog and sheep, nose to nose, glowering at each other, transfixed viewers and got their hearts racing. What do think it's like for the triallist? One sweaty palm's welded to the gate, the other's strangling the crook, and every fibre of your body is willing the sheep in. At the same time, you're quietly encouraging your little dog into reversing three intimidating sheep into the yard. And the woollies have long since worked that the only way out of this enclosed space is the very same opening through which they're being forced to enter. Therefore, they may well ask, why bother going in, in the first place?

The best example I've ever seen of a dog taking on three sheep in full confrontation mode was in the final of ... *a Dog's Show* in 1978. Rex Berkahn's Laddie faced up to three Drysdale ewes, about 5 metres from the yard. This breed are renowned for their stubbornness and can take some shifting, not that Laddie was concerned about such things. With calm confidence he walked straight up to them and, without any hesitation, and in a dead straight line, reversed them right into the pen. In my commentary at the time I compared Laddie's power to that of a tractor relentlessly ploughing uphill. That yard ensured that Rex, Prince and Laddie won the title. There have been other times, on and off television, when apparently top dogs have been simply shoved out of the way by very determined sheep. These creatures have an acute sixth sense for quickly recognising when a dog might be starting to lose its resolve. The slightest twitch of a dog's head, backward shuffle or edge to the side is enough for strong sheep to gain the confidence to bear down and begin to reverse the dog. At this point, a wise competitor quickly calls the dog off, thanks the judge and disappears.

There are times when the dog is standing its ground and the most belligerent of the three sheep decides, 'Well, if it won't walk back, I'll just shove it out of the road.' Then the bolshie beggar just leans back a little and charges straight at a creature that's about a quarter to a third of its size and weight. In this situation the dog has only one form of positive self-defence, its teeth. Despite all the disapproving 'oohs' and 'aahs' you might hear when the ivories are involved, a dog can use its teeth, but only as a last resort. Doing so gives the dog a chance of holding its ground. It does not, however, mean clamping on to the sheep's jaw and wrestling it to the ground, or flying around wool classing, leaving telltale fibres hanging from its teeth. For the dog, use of the teeth should have only one outcome: to show the sheep who's boss. To achieve that, blood does not need to be drawn, but it happens and when it does, jumping to the conclusion that the dog is a 'dirty beggar' can be unfair. As W.V. McIntyre once said, 'A dog's no good to you until it knows the value of its teeth', which I think means that a dog will become more confident and assured when it knows it has a last line of defence. Conversely, if the dog takes the initiative and dives in with teeth bared and grabs a flank, neck or rump, this is the sign of a weak, irrational animal and penalty points will drop like poplar leaves in May. When dogs don't let go or return for a second helping, the judge will quickly appear, with a loud and definite 'thank you'. This is trial-speak for 'get that bloody creature out of here, *now*!'

There is another way a dog can push sheep into a yard, other than

with powerful and balanced use of eye and the threat of teeth. This involves a paw and was first seen by the wider public at the 1918 North Island Championships, and duly reported by the press. 'A remarkable incident occurred in the run of Mr Whyte's Boy. The sheep … were a bit stubborn, and gave the dog some trouble. He was backing them in inch by inch until they stood with only their noses out of the gateway. He then slowly and quietly moved up until he could touch them, and putting up his paw, gently pushed one sheep back, and the yarding was complete.' Not only was it completed, it was the winning run. For Whyte and Boy it was the second leg of the double, as they had already won the long head title.

The most novel of all yarding techniques would have to be one Bernard Murphy witnessed as judge at a show ring event in Taranaki. The competitor was Lou McCracken, the dog Hardgraves, and the sheep were the usual anonymous trio, firmly dug in at the mouth of the yard. They stood there defiantly facing the dog, waiting to see what it would do next. Hardgraves was to do a very unusual thing; a manoeuvre you could expect only from a dog as well versed in obedience work as he was in sheep dog trialling. In other words, Lou had trained his dog to be competitively ambidextrous and, for once, made full use of this versatility. Realising that the run was at an impasse, Lou in his precise way, said, 'Hardgraves, roll!' Still facing the sheep, Hardgraves bent at the knees, went on to his side, rolled over on his back and got up on all four feet again, still staring at the sheep. They were mightily impressed. So much so that they did a roll of their own and turned and walked straight into the yard. At which point Lou would have closed the gate and, typically, said 'Good boy, Hardgraves,' and given him a well-earned pat. The only other person whose opinion mattered was Bernard Murphy, who was faced with a rather novel incident on which to pass judgement. Bernard is now our national patron, and has seen more runs than a mobile canteen can serve hot dinners so, after due thought, he put Lou and Hardgraves in first place.

In such a tense head-to-head confrontation, only a charge from sheep or dog would have changed the situation. In performing his side roll, the dog dissolved that tension by switching the sheep's attention to something completely different. As a result, and in an entirely different frame of mind, the trio enjoyed the change and in they went. Had Hardgraves' roll meant that he turned his back on the sheep or yielded ground to them, he and Lou wouldn't even have got fifth. In most circumstances the only canine turn you'd see under pressure at the yard would be a 'turn-tail'. This occurs when a dog can't take the pressure any longer and literally goes into a spin — though staying on its feet — momentarily presenting its tail to the sheep. In the heading world, after indiscriminate biting and cross heading, turning tail would be the next most frowned on fault. Whenever a dog has executed a pirouette or two of this kind, a sensible handler will call it off. Spinning can be the result of an inherent weakness but in younger animals it can be caused by confusion and a lack of confidence or experience, and the problem can be cured.

The line sheep must cross before the judge calls 'right' and the gate can be shut is the point where the gate would hang, were it closed. Aside from the rare feats that Boy and Hardgraves performed, trios go in only as a result of canine pressure, which can be from an outside source. In his book, *The View From the Brothers*, North Canterbury farmer Ben Rutherford recalled the day he came third at the Hawarden A&P Show's dog trial. When the results came out, Bob Wilson had him surrounded, by coming first, second and fourth. Rutherford was also running a Wilson-bred dog, which he had thought might not get the sheep into the pen. 'Just as I had almost come to the conclusion that I was not going to yard, my sister-in-law's white Bull Terrier, which had a lurid black eye, escaped from the pet dog section and came over to help. One look at him and the sheep bolted into the yard. I did not accept the judge's suggestion and claim another run because of interference!'

Other ingredients can also lead to confusion round the yard, especially after a well-lubricated drive on a very hot, February day in the Taranaki hinterland. This was the background to the run of the then national short head and yard title holder when he got to the yard on Tututawa's grounds near Stratford. After a bit of fumbling, he got the gate open, after a bit foxing from the sheep and some very good covering from his bitch, Pearl — who, like all good dogs, was teetotal — the sheep got to the mouth of the yard. Pearl edged them all the way in, and the judge duly called 'right' to close the gate. Swinging (even slamming) it shut is usually done very quickly lest the sheep escape. When a body's reflexes have been somewhat dulled, closing can take a while and, amidst a fair bit of kerfuffle, it certainly did on this occasion. When our intrepid triallist finally blocked the opening, it put the seal on a very full yard, which included the sheep, along with the dog … and the man! They didn't get a bonus for the extra bodies in the pen, but I do believe they got a place.

Shutting the gate on touchy sheep is something that most do quickly, never more so than when a trial is nearing its conclusion and competitors know that very few trios have been corralled. By then they're well aware that yarding would give them a fair chance of a prize, and qualifying points. The down side is that they often hang around too long, hoping that they just might fluke it, while sheep and dog wear themselves out going round and round the pen. I was part of one such occasion, working a pencil, not a dog. The action round the yard had always been fast and often furious. The sheep were getting more and more frazzled and always in their wake was a little dog whose tongue was hanging low enough to skim grass grub. Early in the piece the tones from the general at the end of the gate had been bass to bass-baritone; his voice now had a distinct soprano edge to it. This routine had been going on for nigh on four minutes when, all of a sudden, the dog hit the critical point of balance — some wished it had been the leading troublemaker — and straight into the yard the sheep went. The judge (me) stopped mouthing fish imitations and croaked a disbelieving 'right?' Instantly, the gate was slammed with the force and echoing crash you'd expect from a door closed by the loser of a two-hour argument. The shock waves this created added wings to the heels of the leader and she flew straight over the back of the yard and out to freedom. Frozen to the spot as the escapee tore across the flat, the triallist nervously turned his head in my direction and, in querulous tones, enquired, 'What do I do now?' 'Get rid of them,' I replied, 'you've got your yard.'

The rule book has plenty to say about sheep going through the gateway and also gives guidance on what to do when they pop back out again before the gate's been shut. On the matter of a sheep going in the front gate and immediately hurdling the back railing, it says nothing. The only requirement is to get them through the main entrance and, once the gate's closed, the run's over. All hell can then break loose — and it did — but it won't change the fact that the yard has been completed. There have been plenty of occasions when one or more sheep have leapt past the gate as it was being closed. If they get by, then you have to start again. If the sheep had quite clearly been in and you were able to parry one or all of them back with the gate, to say nothing of a touch of knee and forearm, then the yard will stand. This means that the run's points tally will be boosted by the automatic ten-point bonus accorded to all full yards. As well, the work is judged out of 22, so a top yarding effort can yield as many as 32 points, close to a third of the total of 100. That's why competitors who don't yard never have much personal interest in the final results.

One thing worse than not yarding would be actually doing the job and not having it recognised by the judge. That can happen today, but only where the rules have been broken by a competitor to gain an unfair advantage. They are duly disqualified, and that's how it should be. When trialling was very young, and courses and rules had local twists to them, a judge could ask for a repeat performance. Rule 19, from Methven's programme of 1905: 'The judges not being satisfied with work at yards, may order the sheep out after being penned, and competitor to continue working them to the judge's satisfaction or till time expires'. What we don't know is whether any judge was ever brave or silly enough to demand a repeat performance. I'm sure that if we were to try that on today, the competitor's reaction would be very predictable. Even if you did the sensible thing and put your hands firmly over your ears, you'd still see the signs! I've heard of another instance where Southlander, Mark Kerr, was tempted not to close the gate on a full yard, to end a run in which the dog performed very badly. Despite its behaviour, the sheep, after covering a lot of country at pace, did go in but, as Mark related afterwards, not because of the dog's efforts. 'When they were going in I said to the dog, "I've a good mind not to let you have this yard, you don't deserve it"!' When you've won three New Zealand and ten South Island titles, as Mark had, you've earned the right to be particular.

Of all the desperate, last-second gate closings there have been, the most famous and public would have to be Bob Bryson's second yard in the doubles final of the 1980 series of … a Dog's Show. The doubles involved two dogs and six sheep, which were split into two trios to be yarded separately by each dog. Through eight preliminary runs and another four in the semi-finals, no one had managed to yard both lots within the tight ten-minute time limit. In the closing seconds of the first run in the final, Bob pulled it off. As he went to close the gate he knew two things: first, that if you did get that particular strain of Corriedales in the yard, they loved to bounce straight back out again; second, he was also well aware that his ten minutes must be all but up. Accordingly he swung the gate with great gusto. When Bob and the gate arrived at the fastening post, the foot he was planning to land on hit something quite fresh and slippery, and his lower limbs just kept on going. Naturally enough, he ended up on his backside, with more of the offending material smeared over his best strides. What made matters worse was that, after he had suffered that indignity, and gained 93 hard-earned points, the other finalist, Eric Stringer, with Geordie and Lyn, came out and filled both yards, to win the title with a 95. Bob and his dogged duo, Bruce and Trump, did turn the tables on Eric in the inter-island match and also gained great fame through the climax of his run in the final being screened more times than any other in the series' seventeen-year history. The gate episode was one of those calamitous moments featured in the television commercial with the slogan, 'It's moments like these you need Minties'.

For many others, there have been far worse accidents around the yard than just slipping on to your backside and resulting in a far more bitter pill to swallow than a Mintie. No one realised that more than W.V. McIntyre. His thoughts on the subject of yarding were often related by another trialling character, Bob Guthrie. 'It was at the New Zealand Championships in 1963, one of the last times he competed.

Old Mac had his usual place by the gate, selling pups to young blokes and he was casually watching this guy who couldn't control his sheep. They were going round and round the bloody pen, not doing any use, until time was called. He took his sheep off the course and came back through the gate. Old Mac stopped selling pups and just said, "My God, man, just a minute, come over here. My God, man, I know exactly how you feel. By God, man, don't be downhearted; the territory round that pen is vast, and the ability of those sheep to take advantage of it is truly remarkable." The boy went away as happy as hell. Those were old Mac's exact words too, right off the cuff. The old boy was a great philosopher and made up all his own anecdotes and stories too. Like that one.'

Of all the particular skills an emerging competitive team practises, the off-balance work precision yarding requires is well down the list. After all, there's not a lot of sense in having a dog which can work sheer magic on sheep round the pen if you can't get them off the hill in good condition. When a young team arrives at the yard, with the sheep in a co-operative frame of mind, it can make you weep to see the opportunity slip away through lack of experience. It was at Waitahuna, in West Otago, where I was given my first real chance of closing the gate in a standard yarding event. It has to be said that neither Peg nor I had done a lot to settle the sheep down, but they really wanted to go in; perhaps they'd decided it was the only safe place. The first sheep literally sped past me to get in, the second was right on her heels and the third was navigating her way round the corner the gate closes on to. This was all too much for Peg who, overcome by all this ovine co-operation, tore round the back of the pen and, staring in from between the rails, gave the already resident pair a very toothy grin. Sheep three was almost in but, taking one look at the dog, realised she'd made a dreadful mistake, spun round and bolted — and the others followed. At this point the judge, Eric Stringer, turned to his wife Pauline, who was clerking, and said, 'I see John's decided that he wants to really earn his first yard, not have the sheep just give it to him!'

A year later, with me poised at the end of the gate and Peg glued to three sheep halfway across the yard mouth at Tututawa, I was wishing

I could have those Waitahuna sheep back again. It was a case of both man and dog frozen to the spot, with the mental attitude of an old-time civil servant — too scared to do anything in case it became a mistake. It was almost time to eat and quite a crowd was gathering for the traditional pre-lunch cocktails and mutton salad. The last thing I wanted to do was ruin this hard-earned opportunity, as I'd never hear the end of it. I remember Les Knight calling in a low voice from the hollow by the gents' facilities, 'Cough'. Too frightened, I didn't. Anyway, Peg decided to shift a little and the sheep shuffled back a touch. That's a good idea, I thought, so I suggested she repeat the process; she did, and the trio co-operated. Realising I was on to a good thing, I kept Peg coming on, and the sheep kept walking back, until the magic call from the judge, 'right!' The gate was slammed with complete relief, Peg was patted and from the bar, cookhouse and car park came a cheer that I'll never forget. I'm sure the crowd's verbal salute reflected their relief as much as mine when I closed the gate. After all, though it's not easy being an indecisive tyro on the end of the gate, it's even more frustrating giving him advice that he neither hears nor heeds. If the yarding process goes on long enough, some spectators can become just as involved as the competitor, and you can be abused for not being good enough to complete the job on the gallery's behalf.

On at least the one occasion that I've been told of, the gallery has provided more than verbal assistance. Many years ago at Martinborough, they didn't have a conventional short head and yard but a drive and yard course. This consisted of a couple of sets of hurdles and the customary 6-foot-square box to end it all, but no head and pull. The course was set right in front of the cookshop and provided plenty of entertainment for the women who worked within. The year that the sheep were at their worst — according to some, that could make it any one of a number of years — the women became quite sorry for the competitors, as they watched entrant after entrant being led a merry dance around the yard. In time their sympathy turned into action, when one of their favourites, Jack Harris, father of today's president, Dave, was having a hell of a time with three delinquents at the pen. Jack was concentrating on his dog, the sheep and the open space he was trying to coax them through, when he suddenly realised he wasn't alone. Looking up, he saw the entire cookshop staff encircling the business side of the yard. Edging slowly in, with their aprons flapping in the wind, the women cornered the sheep, which realised they were well and truly beaten and went in. Everyone thought this was very funny, including the judge who, despite his sense of humour, disqualified the run for over-assistance at the yard. That's the way the rule book would have it too, but I do think Jack Harris should have got some points for being so popular.

From the different individual approaches to yarding, the style that appeals most to me was created by playwright Roger Hall. He wrote the dialogue for the musical *Footrot Flats*, based on Murray Ball's definitive New Zealand cartoon strip. In the course of the story Wal and Dog compete at a dog trial. The scene for this was established through the use of the *Dog's Show* theme and using me as the commentator.

Alas, true theatrical fame eluded me, as I was shielded from the foot-lights of the world stage by being a mere voice on tape. As with any good dog trial, the stage was set with hurdles, a yard and three sheep. Female actors all, they had a lot to say, and very long eyelashes, which had little effect on Wal and his mate. At the yard, the production faith-fully replicated the traditional eye-to-eye confrontation, which the sheep seemed to be winning. That is until Dog stepped aside to let Wal try his powers on what the commentator had described as 'a bunch of petulant prima donnas', drawing the reply, 'Ooh, fame at last, my dears'. As you'd expect, Wal's technique wasn't drawn from the dog trial handbook. He leant over and whispered in each ear, 'Freezing works, freezing works, freezing works.' They went in, too, but with a little extra physical assistance from man and dog.

Since then, whenever I'm trying to yard three toughies who are defying my dog with arrogance and agility, I think, 'Freezing works, freezing works, freezing works!' This hasn't lifted my batting average at the yard, but it's a useful outlet for pent-up frustration as I walk away, a beaten man. For a consolation prize, there's something very satisfying about telling sheep where you think they should go. When certain classes of sheep are proving troublesome, their value at a slaughterhouse would be far greater than on the trial ground. Not so long ago I judged an event where the sheep were quite good in patch-es and just appalling at other times. During one of their awful phases a disgruntled competitor, who'd never had a chance with them, stomped past me and said, 'You wouldn't think these bloody things were worth $60 each, would you?'

'No, you would not,' I replied, 'but they have to be killed and on a hook for that money.'

He stopped, nodded reflectively, 'Yeah'. Then looked at me with growing enthusiasm — 'Do you want a hand?'

10

THE SOUNDEST COURSE

Running a huntaway at a dog trial is very different from working a heading dog. During the latter's run there can be periods, such as the lift and calmly controlled sections of the pull, where little needs to be said, or reacted to. When it comes to running a huntaway with fire in its belly, and steam in the air (yours), there are no built-in tea breaks — it's all go. Not surprising really, as the dog was designed to exert instinctive pressure on stock with noise, vigour and an outgoing personality. And this means that, to be obeyed by a top barker, you need a fair dose of those attributes yourself. There's one other gift an aspiring huntaway competitor needs: the ability to think like a sheep, yet be able to go to the bar and drink out of a glass, not a trough, and sit down at the cookshop table and eat with a knife and fork. Good operators have both perfect table manners and an instinct that allows them to predict what sheep are going to do next. Such a talent is quite uncanny, really, and means that the gap through which the trio were about to escape is no longer there because the move was anticipated and the dog put in place to cover it. By then, the energy the sheep would have used to make a dash for it has been harnessed to take them further up the hill, without realising that they're doing exactly what was required.

Good huntaways have a similar sense of anticipation and, like good heading dogs, have the ability to ignore instructions, and be proved right. On other occasions they'll cover a move no one else could predict. Of all the top huntaways I've seen, the one I'll remember best is Bob Barris's Quin. A very big black and tan dog, he had a personal public address system that allowed him to march up to 20 metres away from sheep and still have them under perfect command. I was lucky enough to see Bob and Quin chalk up point five from paradise (99.5) on three different occasions, while winning national and island titles. One of those runs won the New Zealand Straight Hunt in 1983, despite the fact that, when the trio were nearing the top of the hill, they seemed to be considering a swing to their right. Quin was asked to cover that side but just kept underneath, marching and singing, showing a strength of purpose that forced the sheep to ignore their right-wing leanings and keep on the straight and narrow, all the way to the finish. As Bob said afterwards, 'I asked him to go twice [cover the right] and he ignored me, so I thought, all right, you're the man on the spot, and left him to it. And he was right.'

There are two standard huntaway events, the zigzag, which I often describe as the one with the bends in it, and the straight, which has no intended corners. The whole idea behind a huntaway event is to have

the dog pick up its sheep at the foot of the hill and march them all the way to the top. Unlike the Grand Old Duke of York, you don't get to march them down again; that's someone else's problem at the end of the trial. The course for the zigzag hunt can be longer than 400 metres, with three sets of markers or flags (drum lids), 20 metres apart, to steer the sheep through. Each pair of markers is offset from the previous one so that, once the sheep pass through one set, the dog has to angle or swing them towards the next set, which is known as a slew. The course needs to be set on country that may be very steep in parts, but with natural and practical leads that sheep can follow. This means that, because our hills weren't laid out by landscape architects, the uphill distance between each set's markers will vary, but the points available for them doesn't. There's 33 for each of the first two sets and, to round it off to 100, 34 for the third or top set. In all dog trial events, judging is a matter of removal; you start off with 100 and, for every imperfection, another point or so is removed.

A perfect run on the zigzag would see three sheep walking steadily up the centre of the course to pass, in a nicely compact group, through the middle of each set. After some four or six minutes of this stately progress, they would then climb out through the top set, brushing their hocks against the little peg that marks the centre line of the finish. By this time, everyone on the ground would have tears in their eyes and lumps in their throats, because they'd realise that they had either just died and gone to heaven or witnessed a miracle — for the average dog triallist, it would amount to the same thing. Even if the dog were an angel in canine drag, though, the sheep wouldn't allow this to happen. There have been perfect scores in hunt events, but very, very few. One of the reasons is that, even if the sheep did follow a precise line throughout, other factors can bring the judge's pencil into play — none more so than penalising certain traits exhibited by the poor beggar doing all the work. These are called dog faults and, on certain occasions, they can be the scourge of a huntaway competitor's life. If a dog doesn't bark by the time the sheep pass the first set, it's called off; obviously its owner was confused and entered the wrong dog on the wrong course.

A completely silent dog is an extreme example of a lapse in larynx and lung power. Much more likely would be a dog swinging under the sheep, from one side to the other, to put in a block or create a slew, and not using its noise as it travelled. Another regular fault is when the dog's firing out some really impressive noise but not directing it at the sheep. Instead, passing seagulls, nearby tussocks and distant mountains are being given the message. As they say in the South, 'You bark at sheep, not Mount Cook … you'll never get it to shift.' The worst example is a dog which has been trained with hand signals and turns round repeatedly to see what's required next, and will sometimes just stand there, barking downhill at the boss. Judges don't like that at all, and neither do triallists, especially when they realise that they're to blame. Along with not barking at all, the other serious misdemeanours are turning tail, seeking and finding things of interest to the nasal passages — and going to the toilet — in other words, any action not directly related to facing up to sheep and shifting them with good noise. Sniffing is a bad fault as the dog will often stop and concentrate entirely on an interesting smell or seek one out. As with the other lapses in attention, this all adds up to a double penalty: the judge's deduction and a break in control, which will let the sheep off the hook and allow them to make, and execute, some plans of their own.

My first huntaway good enough for serious trialling was Shorty, the kind and characterful brown and yellow bitch with the sensitive feet, whom I've already mentioned. The first open trial she and I ran at was Taumarunui, where the courses, sheep and facilities are good enough to be used for New Zealand Championships, and are. Running on the straight, we got them away well and up and up the trio climbed, with Shorty providing both the impetus and the direction, along with the odd suggestion from me. About two-thirds of the way up, a frightening thought occurred to me: 'Hell, this could be a good run!' The sheep and Shorty were getting on just fine, and had become so much of a unit that you could have thrown a blanket over the lot of them as they marched steadily towards the top, and glory. Accordingly, I reacted in the only way I then knew — I panicked, throwing in a big stop whistle to give me more time to work out what stupid thing I'd do next. Fortunately, I didn't get the opportunity to come up with any-thing of my own because, in low tones from the rear, came the author-ititive suggestion, 'Hunt her on.' I hesitated, and did nothing, except wonder whose voice it was. The message was repeated in more insis-tent tones, 'Hunt her on!' It was then that I came to two important conclusions: one, the advice was coming from none other than the judge, Alf Boynton, and, two, it was very good advice.

I hunted her on, and on and on, until the sheep were about 20 metres from the top markers and showing signs of tiring and starting to spread a little. 'Give her a right,' said the voice. No hesitation this time and Shorty's right whistle hit the air waves. Worked too, but not well enough for Alf; 'Give her another one.' I did. Almost immediately, there was a sight I never expected to see on my first day out hunting with the grown-ups — three sheep just below the top markers and climbing beautifully. It all seemed too easy. The only blemish would have been just before that, when Shorty headed off towards some rushes, as if she were searching for something, though a quick whistle had brought her back on line. Moments later I realised what she'd been looking for — the ladies' loo. On her second brief search, she found it — right in the middle of the course! Not only did madam stop about 8 metres below the finish and give full and silent concentration to the evacuation of an earlier meal, she even turned round and had her back to the sheep. This meant that she could look down from beneath the brow and torment me with a big toothy grin. While this was going on, the sheep, who obviously thought a lot of Shorty, very kindly stopped and waited for her. To this day, I wish they hadn't, as they were about half a metre — maybe even less — below the finish. I remember turn-ing in despair and asking Alf if they were over since, if that was so, Shorty's current activities wouldn't harm the points. 'No, they're still in,' came the reply.

After Shorty finished her personal business to turn and, with great style and aplomb, hunt the trio the few centimetres necessary to finish the run, I called her off. Shaking my head at what might have been, I walked past the judge's hut. 'Do you want to see what points you had until that business at the top?' 'No thank you,' I replied and carried on half a step more before turning back to look. We would have got 97, which would have given us second place. Sufficient points were removed to ensure that we weren't placed at all, as a dog that pauses to piddle or poo in the middle of a run doesn't get its name on the results sheet. It should be said that it isn't normal for a judge to work competitor and dog while driving a pencil. Some do, especially when they see a newcomer about to blow a big chance. Alf certainly does and so do those of us he has helped over the years.

From a stock handling viewpoint, the principles of running a huntaway are the same as with a heading dog, though the sheep are pushed up, not pulled down. The beginning of the run is critical; the equivalent of a heading dog's outrun and lift rolled into one. The dog has to approach from the right direction, introduce itself with positive yet polite authority, then coax or cajole the trio into taking the right line. This all happens just a few metres from the competitor, which may not be an advantage. It certainly isn't a plus if the competitor is standing in the wrong place, throwing everything off kilter and putting unnecessary pressure on the dog. For example, when triallist and dog are both covering the line to the right of the sheep, no one should be surprised if the sheep do a runner in a lefterly direction, despite what the triallist thought would happen. Many competitors are influenced by the runs before them, especially if the sheep have all been tearing off to the right and the dog hasn't had a show of getting them away well, if at all. 'Ah ha,' you think, 'time for a big block on the right.' That's put in place and the sheep think, 'Ah ha, time for a big bolt on the left', and leave, very quickly. That's dog trialling!

Officially, there's a 20-metre-square quad at the foot of the hill in which the triallist has to be at the start, at the end and in between times. The dog begins there, too, but with matters more pressing elsewhere, doesn't stay for long. From a yard and release set-up, to the rear or round the side of the quad, three sheep are walked towards a common area or reference point. This could be a rock, thistle, rush or stump — something that's marked down in the judge's mind — and the liberators do their best to walk each trio to the same place. Every effort is also made to let the competitor have the sheep when they're walking or, at the very least, facing uphill. If everything is right and as fair as possible, the judge calls 'time'. A command is given to the dog, who has been watching with quivering concentration, and then it seems as if all hell has broken loose. In fact, though, the dog is releasing some pent-up emotion and stamping its authority on proceedings by saying to the sheep, 'Hello, I'm in charge'. At this stage the dog is kept back as much as possible, so as not to waste the distance between the parties, since the extra pressure from moving in is a useful weapon further up the hill. Small balancing moves are best, to move slowly towards the sheep, to get them walking. This strategy will always be much more successful than a howler who goes straight at the trio, yodelling rashly, and suddenly has three distraught mobs of one littering the hill. To the person responsible for the dog this is not a good feeling. Often there are bits of scrub, tussocks or rushes around the base of hunt courses, though, in my experience, they're never tall enough!

I looked for their shelter on several occasions when running Shorty. She, it must be said, though blessed with plenty of personality and stock sense, did not do well out of her christening ceremony. Shorty wasn't a great title for a proper lady, but it was a considerable improvement on the original name it stemmed from, owing to her being the runt of her litter. Madam, or Granny as I often called her, was given to me as a four-year-old, fully working proposition by one of the most unselfish people ever to be involved in trialling, John Bartlett. He and his wife Deirdre are top competitors and twice have supplied me with lively, barking machinery who brightened most days, darkened a few and always shifted sheep in a very perfunctory manner. Too much so, at times, though often under mitigating circumstances. A decade ago, after being away with the dogs for a well over a fortnight, I managed to detour to Marlborough's Wairau Valley trial, while heading for the inter-island ferry. The previous week the dogs had spent most of the time tied up by the commentary caravan while the 1987 series of … *a Dog's Show* was recorded, so they were raring to go, especially Shorty. I remember walking briskly up the gully to Wairau's excellent matagouri and tussock fringed, zigzag course, with Shorty, eyes gleaming in anticipation, bouncing along beside me.

Three half-bred hoggets were put in front of us, Jerry Roborgh, the judge, called 'time' and Shorty leapt into the air, yelling, with all four legs rotating, ready to go forward. When she descended and her paws engaged, the sheep had heard and seen enough, and were already absent. They did take the right course, though, straight up, with Shorty in hot pursuit. After about 50 metres she caught up with them, hurled a few orders in their ears and got an immediate response. I too, had been engaged delivering instructions, on my rural whistle-phone, but Shorty's receiver was off the hook. There was no doubt, however, that she was transmitting very effectively. The end result of 200 decibels of canine music at 50 kilometres an hour was that, about halfway up the steep course, our once tightly knit trio were now confetti. One had bolted and was quickly disappearing into distant tussock. Another had branched off and dived under the nearest matagouri bush, trying to hide, but Madam was right alongside, dancing on the spot singing, 'I can see you, I can see you', or barks to that effect. Sheep number three had literally fainted, mid-course, and there she lay, traumatised, with her jaw flat on the ground as if she couldn't be seen. Quickly summing up the situation, I turned to Jerry to indicate I was retiring, thanked him and hastily stepped out of the quad. He looked up, after making a very final-looking flourish on his judging pad, and said, with a wry grin, 'There's plenty of time. You've only used a minute, there's eleven to go.'

The best advice Shorty and I were ever given came from Bernard Murphy, who once suggested that, a couple of times in every run, 'You should both stop and count to five … to give the sheep a rest.' To be fair to Shorty, in the matter of the Wairau Valley débâcle, her owner should have found a way of releasing some of her steam before unleashing her on three innocent sheep and an unsuspecting judge. At the start of any hunt, subtlety is the only really constructive approach and there are different ways of ensuring that, some of them not entirely kosher. One gentleman I know used to run a very strong and wilful huntaway who was difficult to hold and the only real opportunity for exercising any restraining influence was when the dog was nearby — at the start. This technique was built around reminding the dog of devices used in training, especially various metallic things he carried in his pockets. He would enter the quad with hands thrust deep inside his trousers and after the start would rattle some loose change, which the dog associated with something and steadied down a little. Not for long, though, and as it started to hit its stride again, a pair of nail scissors would be clicked, to coincide with the first stop or steady command. This would check the dog slightly, but it would soon be back to full strength to be given another stop, accompanied by another metallic sound. None of this could be officially heard by the judge, and it really didn't matter, because when a dog needs this amount of attention, it's not too hard to work out what the end result will be. The final lifeline thrown out to rescue the run sounded suspiciously like the trigger mechanism of an unloaded starting pistol. This certainly got the dog's attention for a few more metres, but after that he had the course to himself and enjoyed his freedom to the full.

A friend of this triallist had a similar technique, though a different weapon. His was a .22 calibre pistol, left over from a war he'd been to, which he used to fire noisy blanks during training sessions to reinforce commands that his dogs may have wanted to ignore. At times, to activate the dog's memory cells, he, too, would pocket his unloaded firearm and take it on a dog trial trip. Before the run, and some distance from the judge, stewards and starting area, he would look at the dog and sternly utter the critical command while, with his hand deep in his pocket, he clicked the trigger. The last time he did this he was the next to run and, out of sight, quickly took the dog through its drill. Unfortunately, his preparation hadn't been as thorough as usual since the pistol was loaded and went off with a rather loud bang. Even more unfortunate than the report, which did attract a fair amount of attention, was the painful fact that the bullet had not been blank, but was light birdshot. Under normal circumstances this is pretty harmless stuff but, point blank and within the pocketed confines of a decent pair of cavalry twill trousers, it can create quite a mess. Straight-backed, though clutching his upper thigh, our old soldier marched past the judge and announced that he wouldn't be having his run right now, but would take it later in the day. He walked a hundred metres to his ute, loaded the dog, got in and drove some distance up country to visit an acquaintance with medical knowledge. As promised, he returned by mid-afternoon to have his run. I doubt that he was placed.

Under the rules those techniques are not allowed, and nor are firearms or any other training devices permitted anywhere near a trial ground. Rather than being too officious, except where a dog's well-being is at risk, some officials believe in hesitating a little, to allow natural justice to take its course; it usually does. The point about trials, and the dogs who are regularly taken to them, is that it's not too long before they work out that trial grounds are discipline free areas and, understandably, some take advantage of this. For a competitor this can be extraordinarily annoying, to the extent that some look for ways in which they can put a check on proceedings and remind their dog that, even though it is a dog trial, it's not a sheep hooler's free-for-all.

At the start of a huntaway run there can still be a place for the dog to do a bit of hooling, despite the fact that care is needed to get a nicely controlled lift. A feisty dog, well aware of the noise it possesses, will often clear its throat in spectacular fashion. Some will even rear up on their hind legs and perform a very arresting canine chorus. After the dog has got that out of its system, and ensured it has both the sheep's and the judge's full attention, the lift can get under way. If the dog is a good shepherd, and being supervised by someone of similar ilk, it will be watching its sheep very carefully and looking to move them on to the hill proper. Each trio is a little different from the rest, and no two dogs are alike, so these variables remove any risk of boredom setting in. Just the same, there are times when, after a succession of useful dogs and average sheep, you can be lulled into a sense of sameness. Then, all of a sudden, some promising young huntaway will come along and, with an attention-grabbing opening salvo, will be saying, 'Watch me, I'm dynamite.' Don't worry, son, they will, especially as runs involving highly volatile youngsters can blow up in a very spectacular fashion.

When a newcomer makes a first appearance at a trial and, by virtue of his dog, makes an immediate impression, questions will be asked. Every district has at least one old timer who will be a retired liberator and marshal and can still be found at the foot of the hill in the line of observers. It's characters like this who are very good at finding out about new arrivals — mainly because they're nosy beggars who won't shut up until they've learnt all they can. With an appallingly filthy canvas hat or cockie's potae rammed well down his forehead, the enquirer's eyes, well recessed beneath the rim, will never leave the run as it progresses up the hill. Not that such focusing will impede research in to other matters.

'Who's he?'

'Young chap Mckenzie, Steven, though, the boys call him Borax.'

'Eh?' The light of realisation dawns in his eyes. 'I suppose he's poking it at them all the time. Working round here, then?'

'Yes, on Wharekauri. They had a big cleanout when the new manager came in, he's one of the replacements.'

'Where's he from?'

'Down South, worked on a few big places … from town originally, Timaru, I think.' At this point the dog does something quite flash and attracts a nod of approval from the local interrogator who, with a tilt of his head in the hill's direction asks, 'What's the dog?'

'By Simpson's Jock out of a Quin-Bess bitch.' Our man's eyes open a millimetre wider than their normal hill-watching squint. 'How did he get one of them?'

'Simpson's his uncle.'

'Lucky for some. Works him well.'

'Yep. Won the straight at Whanga' last week.'

'Did he?' At that point the sheep climb through the top flags. 'He'll probably win this one too.'

The run over, his gaze can now leave the hill and concentrate on the fountain of knowledge he's been tapping. 'How come you know so much about him?'

'He's engaged to my daughter.'

An answer that leaves the nosy one speechless, albeit momentarily. Long enough, though, for the source to disappear and go in search of his prospective son-in-law. After congratulating him on his run, he then began discussions on a very important matter. A fair swap, in fact — a daughter for a pup!

Conversations at the foot of a hunt hill are usually fragmented and spasmodic, ideal for filling the duller moments during and between runs. The participants will be either clustered round, leaning on a ute, or standing at rural ease — legs apart and knees slightly bent. Often, one leg will be bent more than the other, to favour a crook hip, with the boot beneath the good hip parked closest to the hill. No matter where the trial is or who's attending, you can rely on hearing the same range of topics being discussed in a time-honoured way. One of the favourite subjects will involve a fairly well-known dog, who's been around for a while. Not long after it's begun to run, one of the line will turn to a mate, two or three along and ask, 'How old would this dog be now?' Invariably, he'll have asked the wrong person and the query will pass, in desultory fashion, from one to another. After several 'wouldn't knows', a 'Bob'll know' and a couple of 'ask Stan or Mike' comments, an eavesdropper from a nearby group will lean in their direction and come to the rescue. 'He's an Oak dog, isn't he?' This means that Oak is the father; to which everyone nods their agreement. Not that some would know, but any form of association with a dog of that class is sure to get a nod of approval. 'I'm pretty sure he was one of the Kate litter, which would make him eight. I got one of them … didn't turn out like him though,' as he inclines his head in the dog's direction.

It goes without saying that if it really were necessary to know the dog's age, all they needed to do was wait till after the run and ask the owner. But that would not only be far too practical, it would reduce the chances of sharing the casual, offhand companionship that's nearly as important as trialling itself. Some hunt courses are ideally set up for relaxing as you watch the day go by. At Tututawa, there's a quite tall knoll behind and above the start and the club have tacked some old slabs on top of low-set fenceposts as seats. It's a superb view, and you can hear some interesting things too. A typical comment, as the gallery watches a dog doing a great job of getting offside with its sheep, would be, 'Good sheep'.

Which, in time, will draw the reply, 'Yeah … shame about the dog!' Just occasionally you'll hear something juicy enough to flick your eyes off the hill. That's usually when either dog or sheep do something quite dramatic and everyone underlines the incident by going 'Oooh'. Immediately you turn back to the hill but, too late, the sniff, turn tail or quick sheep break is over, and you have to rely on someone else's description. That's hunting, though, the quick and the dead. Certain things have to be reacted to very quickly, which is why it's essential that competitors can see everything.

From within the confines of a 20-metre-square quad, following all the on-course action is not always possible. On some very steep hills, or those with an awkward brow and a depression or dip behind them, competitors can't see enough and are allowed to walk backwards. With some courses that can mean reversing a considerable distance. In short, the higher the run goes, the further back you walk — in reverse. I remember one zigzag course, no longer used, where the liberation pen was jammed under a tree, on a narrow strip between a road fence and a small creek. The trios were released via a bridge over the creek. The dog would follow them and, quite often, the competitor would too. Once the run was under way, they didn't stay for long, because the first set pitched and angled away very steeply from the start. That was followed by a difficult to gauge dead spot in the second set, then a tempting side door escape route for the sheep and an awkward shoulder towards the top. This meant that, as sheep and dog went forward and upwards, the competitor was in reverse for most of the run.

Looking and concentrating in one direction, while physically going backwards, can be a rather hazardous business. In this instance, after shuffling back across a narrow bridge, you then negotiated the release pens, came through a 4-metre gateway and reached the lank cocksfoot and cooch cover on the verge at the side of the road. Stepping over, then down, from this was tricky, especially the inevitable Achilles heel jolt as the verge finished and the narrow gravel road began. This was always expected but very rarely did anyone accurately predict where the step-down was.

By this time, the sheep would be finishing the first set and a right-hand slew had to be applied to line them up for the second set. Concentrating on that greatly increased the chances of catching a heel on the verge at the other side of the road, and finding yourself on your backside, with your whistle suddenly sitting alongside your tonsils. Less predictable obstacles also existed in this vicinity: competitors waiting their turn and a few spectators. Backing into someone was bad enough, but you'd shoulder them out of the way and battle on. The greatest danger, though, was a dog running loose. The average hunt-away is around knee height so, if you reversed into one, your legs folded up like a pocket knife and you ended up lying parallel to the paddock, with at least one hand in an odiferous blend of last night's dog biscuits.

If you were still on your feet, by the time you'd reached the fence at the other side of the second verge, the sheep were nearing the area where they and the dog were hardest to follow. The best place to see that was a bit further back, in the paddock on the other side of the roadside fence. Getting there meant locating and negotiating a gateway little more than a metre wide. Through that, not only did you have a great view of everything but, finally, the obstacle course was behind you. Breathing a sigh of relief at making safe ground, you relaxed a little, only to come back to earth with a thud, realising that one of the trio had skipped round the outside of the right-hand flag on the second set, and the run was over. All that for nothing! Well, not really for nothing; it's always fun facing a double challenge and, as you say, 'I've still got my straight [hunt] to come.' When differences are created by local landforms or structures, trial officials often brush off any criticism of the irregularity with: 'It's the same for everyone.' Rubbish! If it's supposed to be the same for all of us, why don't the others fall over?

Much of the above is a personal view of the Ohingaiti club's zigzag course of a year or two ago, before a couple of major slips changed both the shape and surface of the course. Even when all the hindrances existed, you could still see some unforgettable work there, especially a 98.5 I saw John O'Neale and his wonderful whiskery woofer, Tough, put up. Tough had a bark that came from deep within his belly and on its way out shuddered his shoulders, shook his head with single-minded purpose and shifted sheep very positively. He wasn't nearly as tough-natured as his name might suggest either; in fact, he was quite a character. Never did he look more of a trick than before the final of the 1988 North Island Zigzag at Masterton. Totally unconcerned about anything the afternoon might have in store for him, he sauntered around among the crowd with a large and completely intact cattle beast's cannon bone clamped between his jaws. I suppose the bone served as the canine competitor's equivalent of an Australian cricketer's chewing gum, except that Tough wasn't chewing on it at all; you could have been forgiven for thinking that he was carrying it around for company. Unfortunately he and John were unable to get a similar sort of grip on the the three unco-operative sheep they drew in the run off that followed.

One of the most important factors in working a dog on the zigzag is being aware of the boundaries of the set the sheep are in at the time. Because of the customary slew or change of line, as the trio passes through each set of flags, each section is at a different angle. This is why competitors walk from one side of the quad to another, from set to set, or traverse half the district, backwards! Though it's unmarked, the line between the marker on one set and the corresponding one on the same side of the next is important. As with the drives on a short head course, if the sheep cross that, they have left the course and this incurs a greater penalty than a certain amount of wobbling around within the 20-metre wide working area. Even more critical is missing a marker. By tradition, if you did this in the North Island, you cleared the course of sheep, dog and self, and disappeared. In the South, the judge immediately whipped six points off your tally — plus a few more for the mistake that put the sheep out there — but you were able to battle on until the end. That southern right was lost when the rules were revised a few years ago.

When sheep are lurching close to a set marker and look as if they could go one way or the other, it's the equivalent of a heading dog battling it out at the yard — will they, won't they? It can create as much spectator tension too. Just stand behind a group and keep an eye on them and the sheep at the same time; if the woollies need to lean in a certain direction to keep inside the flags, the onlookers will sway that way too. For those who have limited mobility, movement of any kind at the bottom of a huntaway course is very difficult, which is why I was amazed to see Merton Leslie competing with a huntaway during the 1997 season. It must have been decades since he had been a hunt competitor, but there he was with a young dog he had broken in. It worked well too, obeying commands that came from the same place throughout the run. I saw them compete at Morrinsville, where Merton was driven into the quad, a director's chair was set up and from it he directed proceedings. In trialling almost anything is possible though, for those with failing sight, working a huntaway would not be. Everything happens too quickly for a spotter to be involved, especially during the critical and action-packed moments at the end of the run. For Merton, having a huntaway was ideal since, during training sessions on the hill by his house, it hunts the sheep up, for his heading dogs to run out and bring them home.

At many venues, moving back to see the top of a hunt course is as important as moving from side to side. At Ohingaiti you took a grand tour, at Methven you go back level with a big bush, and at Pio Pio in the King Country there's a bridge over a quite large creek to be negotiated. This course used to be the responsibility of leading competitor, judge and character, Ned Hayes. Once when Ned was releasing sheep there, a bloke who wasn't all that well liked — because he was always looking for an advantage — was getting his run started. As usual, once the sheep and dog were under way the competitor began reversing across the bridge. On this occasion, when the competitor was about halfway, there was a spot of bother on the hill. He stopped to concentrate on the necessary tactics, which required the dog to take a sharp move to one side; this it did, quickly and cleanly. At the same time, in an unwitting reflex action, the man also moved sharply to one side, quickly and cleanly, over the side of the bridge. Completely soaked, he stood up, coughing and spluttering, in the middle of the creek, to find marshal Hayes on the bridge, directly above him. Leaning over with a forceful glare, Ned laid down the challenge: 'I suppose you want a re-run, you lousy beggar'. He did, too, but he didn't get one; it was his fault he fell off.

It's the judge who decides whether you're given another attempt. It may have been the same character who, some years ago at another King Country trial, had great trouble throughout the run with one particularly unco-operative sheep. After the run he went up to the judge, Les Knight and, on the grounds that he reckoned the miscreant had once been a pet lamb, asked for a re-run. There's no doubt that former pets can be a real problem at a trial as they think they're human and, therefore, are extremely arrogant; the last thing they'll consider is taking orders from something as ordinary as a dog. Les was well aware of that, but in this case he wasn't convinced that the claim and subsequent request were in order. So he merely replied; 'If you can get it to walk up to you and suck your finger, I'll give you a re-run.' At that point, the discussion came to a halt. Not only did the dog not get a second go, but the locals missed out on what would have been an unforgettable sight: a fully grown man, with one finger extended, following three sheep uphill while calling encouragingly 'lamb-a-lamb-a-lamb-a-lamb'.

11

THE STRAIGHTEST COURSE

Of all sheep dog trialling's tests, the straight hunt looks the least complicated, and the easiest to achieve. As the name suggests, all you have to do is pick up three sheep at the foot of the hill and hunt them straight up to finish between the markers at the top. This is dog trialling's most recent standard event; it was only added to the championship calendar in 1947 and, on a couple of early occasions, replaced the zigzag. From 1949 on, though, huntaways could finally go to major meetings on a par with their heading colleagues and run on two different courses. For newcomers, the straight hunt looks a lot less daunting than the zigzag, because it lacks the complication of the extra markers and changes in direction. Very often, the finish will appear to be rather close, adding to the impression of simplicity. At this point it's worth noting that the reason it seems so close is that the course is very steep. Some country can also be very deceiving and fade away in the middle much more than it appears to. Often you hear a competitor who's just worked a course for the first time return to his mates and say: 'There's a lot more country in there than you'd think'. These are factors well worth considering, along with the sheep that are on offer. They probably won't be closely related to the mountain goat type animal that would be best suited to skipping up a steep face. Some sheep, try as they might, will falter near the top, especially if they've been given too much curry early on.

The most physically testing country for sheep and dog is a reasonably steep hill striped with benches running across it, all the way up. Each of these steps is a short, but almost vertical climb of its own. As more and more of them are tackled, gaps begin to appear between each of the sheep in the trio. Not long after that, the back sheep's front legs will fail to make firm contact with the top of a bench and it stops, while the other two soldier on. It tries again, fails and slithers back a little to subside on to one of its hips, lower its head in sorrow and throw in the towel. Sooner, rather than later, the competitor does too. The finest run I've seen, on a hill best described as the natural equivalent of Parliament's front steps, was on the straight at Geraldine. There, a series of tussock-clad benches continue all the way to the crest and, as an added difficulty, the sheep were Drysdales, a breed with a rather unyielding attitude. Despite this or because of it, they can be very good on heading courses, especially when there are television cameras around. In the two series for which we used them on … *a Dog's Show*, their foot stamping and arrogant stares ensured good entertainment and — most of the time — they worked well for competitors with strong dogs.

On a huntaway hill, though, Drysdales are very difficult. Each time the dog throws a salvo in their direction, they about turn, as if to check where the noise is coming from. Achieving even a semblance of uphill progress, let alone a steady flow, is damn near impossible. Those were the conditions facing Ron Christie and Bess when they ran and won at Geraldine in 1980. Ron was one of those competitors who, when required, could think like a sheep, but still had perfect table manners. He and Bess won two New Zealand titles but I'm sure neither of them had to work harder than they did that day. It was as if each of the benches were another hunt course to be started and finished. Once they got under way, though, every time the leader looked to turn and make a challenge, little black Bess would be directly under the sheep telling it to 'face the front' and 'get a move on'. As soon as it obeyed, Bess would swing back under the tail sheep and tell it to 'keep up'. It was very clever work, which continued all the way up and in the straight line the course demands. It was one of those runs which, because of the constant battle with the sheep and the terrain, just drew you in. The only distraction was a little voice at the back of your head saying, 'This can't last, these sheep won't play ball all the way to the top.' They did. While

Bess and the Drysdales were battling it out, there was absolute silence, as the few of us who were there savoured something well worth remembering.

The various challenges that exist on every hunt course are often increased in bad weather. This is especially the case on steep North Island courses, which can become very slippery and create extra difficulties, through no fault of the triallist, dog or sheep. This was certainly the case in a situation that Jim Hay faced as a judge. Dubby Power from Pongoroa was in action and, despite the weather, he was having a hot run. 'They were up near the top and it was so wet that the back sheep slipped back downhill a few yards and stopped just in front of the dog. Dubby shut the dog up and kept him dead still. Then the ewe slowly picked herself up, looked round, saw her mates — they were stopped up above, waiting for her — and then carefully picked her way uphill and joined them. Then Dubby got the dog to open up again and they hunted through the top. He won — 98.5. I didn't touch him for that slippery ewe … it was such good stockmanship and control.'

The other climatic factor that can change the course of a run is wind. Not only can a really good gust blow away a critical command — an excuse I've used more than once — but it can also pick the dog up and carry it to the side of the course. That happened at the 1988 island championships at Masterton, where a dog in action near the top of the straight hunt was plucked off the hill and deposited some 6 or 7 metres away. At the same time, a gentleman who was enthroned in a small tin structure on skids suddenly found that he and his hut were both lying on their sides. This particular structure was of the 'long drop' variety, which was very fortunate. Had it been one of those fancy models with a bucket, the incumbent would have got a lot more than just a fright.

Masterton was Jim Hay's club for over 40 years. It was there that he became established as a top administrator and competitor, as well as judging at three New Zealand Championships. Among the many good dogs he ran was a three-legged header called Ike. Despite having just the one front leg, Ike gained fourth place in the 1966 New Zealand long head, and was the only dog to have a full-pointed head (48) in both runs. Despite that, it's Jim's achievements as a huntaway competitor that will be remembered best, especially during the 1970s when he ran Doug. This dog looked more like a German shepherd than a New Zealand huntaway, but it was one of the cleverest animals I've ever seen work sheep. Doug and Jim had an amazing working relationship, and were so inseparable that, more than once, I talked about Doug Hay and Jim in commentary. A variation on that was 'any moment now Doug will whistle Jim to the right, to hold that side …' Neither of those descriptions impressed Jim very much! He is a rather pragmatic man and you're always well aware of where you stand with him. If your position, in his opinion, is in the wrong place or you're offering a questionable attitude or argument, you don't have to wait very long to get his thoughts on the matter. That's why, in the no-nonsense world of dog trialling, he became one of its most respected administrators, judges and competitors.

During the 1970s, dog trialling's Wairarapa Southern Hawke's Bay Centre produced three top huntaways, all of whom won a New Zealand title and a host of open events. Two of them, Jim Blinkhorne's Bloke, and Arthur Harrison's Rock, each won 28 open trials, a total of 56. So did Doug, on his own! Bloke was a lovely coated dog with good noise who got on well with sheep. Rock bristled with power and, when he got sheep marching, they marched. But Doug was something else again. To see and hear him start a run gave you a prickling sensation up the back of your neck. He'd simply rise up on his back legs and introduce himself with a series of sounds that could only be described as a cross between a howl and a roar. Fully aware of the sheep, he would come down on to his front legs and start moving towards them. Jim never said much at this stage; he knew what Doug was doing and the dog knew what was required. At times it appeared as if that's the way it was all the way up the hill.

In the straight hunt run off at East Coast's ninetieth jubilee, Doug and the sheep were getting on so well that Jim took a stride or two to his left to relax against an elderly totara strainer post. With his left elbow resting on the top, hip against the side and legs crossed, Jim was very comfortable, thank you. A bit over halfway up the face, there was an old overgrown slip, with a reasonably deep pothole beside it. If sheep got close to this it became a right-angled escape route to the left. When his charges were nearing this Doug was on automatic and, maybe, getting bored with the classy exhibition the run had become. Still relaxed on his leaning post, Jim suggested a little left to cover the track leading to the risky area. This, Doug decided, was too mundane so he flicked to the right. With a few extra barks to hurry things up, he literally chased the trio into the slip. Jim got out of casual mode just as quickly and, marching determinedly towards the hill, told his champion huntaway exactly what he thought of the situation, and what had to be done to rectify it. Unlike any other dog who'd been in those circumstances, Doug had the trio popping back out of the pothole, like corks from bubbly bottles. The run then continued straight up to the top and, calm and controlled as the finish was, Jim never relaxed sufficiently to return to his leaning post. That gave Doug two victories that day: the jubilee hunt and one over the boss. Mind you, there were plenty of other occasions when he liked being left alone.

Early each year at Rewanui, on the Wairarapa's Castlepoint road, a shepherds' trial is held to introduce young people to dog trials, and to give young dogs an outing before the main season starts. At lunchtime the centre's top heading dog and huntaway give demonstrations. For many years that meant Jim and Doug, with what became a fairly set routine. Jim would set Doug alight under three sheep, which he would nurse across the flat — it was the long head course — and on to the hill. By then Jim would have turned his back to the action and started addressing the crowd about working a huntaway. Occasionally Jim would refer to Doug and the sheep but each just concentrated on his own job, without troubling the other. The dog was probably working at around 60 percent effort, but always in total control of the sheep and their direction. In short, it was an excellent example of how a real sheep dog can look after stock. About three-quarters of the way up the hill, Jim would turn round and quietly give a little whistle which, by Doug's reaction to it, could only mean 'let's do the business'. That's certainly what the dog did and, in a second, a gentle piece of shepherding had all the noise, balance and intensity you'd expect of a top competitive run. It would end with the sheep being steered into the heading course liberation area, ready for the next demonstration. There, Doug would rest them against the netting, put in a couple more barks to remind them not to move and, while Jim was answering questions, amble downhill. It was as if he did the same thing every day — and, in a way, he did.

Both man and dog were closely involved with … *a Dog's Show*, winning in 1979 and 1980, and Jim organised the North Island eliminations for the first series. There wasn't a hunt that year, but even so, while we were setting up the doubles course, Doug showed a few of us how he could yard sheep as well as hunt them. A few years later, Jim was the national co-ordinator for the series, replacing Cyril Perry, who competed that year. To increase the challenge and lift viewer interest, we didn't have the standard 20-metre apart markers up at the finish, but two candy-striped gates 8 to 10 metres apart. In placing these with Jim, I was keen to have them closer than he first suggested. I'd expected an argument but, not hearing any, I quickly hammered in the necessary standards, tied the woodwork to them and set off downhill. I recall commenting to Frank Torley that narrowing the gap was easier than I expected, as Jim didn't offer any real objections. I should also add that this was a year before I began competing with a huntaway. We had a very successful hunt competition in that series, and hardly anyone didn't make it through the top. With a certain amount of smugness I pointed this out to Jim on the last night. 'Yes,' he agreed, 'it did work well. But I have to tell you that the morning after we set it up, I went to the grounds while you were having breakfast, walked up the hill and pulled the gates out to where I reckoned they should be. You jokers never noticed … worked well too.' Game, set and match to the master!

There's no flexibility with standard huntaway courses. Not being set up in the name of entertainment, they're practical to begin with. As with the zigzag, at the top of the straight, halfway between the flags, there's a small centre peg, to help the judge define the true line across the finish. Away below, in the quad, I have nervously watched the end of a useful run as the first two sheep strode past the centre peg. Unfortunately, the third sheep had all the shaky-legged symptoms of an uphill journey that had been just a bit too progressive for her. She wobbled to the peg, sniffed it, took half a pace forward and slumped to the ground. As she was sitting right on the peg, she didn't find it very comfortable and, courageously, summoned enough strength to get to her feet, and take another shaky half-step. Silently I, the judge, onlookers and the dog — who'd long since been told to be quiet — willed her forward but no, her half-step was to the side and there she slumped again — with one side of her belly literally wrapped around the peg. She still hadn't cleared the line, which dashed all hopes of even a minor placing, let alone a win.

When the sheep have completely cleared the line, the judge calls 'right' and everyone immediately relaxes; very often, that includes the dog. Some, hearing far more casual commands from the boss, celebrate the reduction in discipline by giving the now redundant sheep a real hool-up. This usually ensures that not only are the sheep right off the course, they're halfway out of the district as well. The South Island equivalent would have the sheep parked just below the snowline and badly out of breath. The dog — if it's not too far away to see — is sitting on its backside, tongue falling from one side of its jaw, looking downhill with an idiotic grin. When a dog completely takes over in these circumstances, it is very difficult not to tremble with frustrated rage, and scream threats and promises. Drover Sonny Osborne had to do something similar when he was trying to stop a hard-nosed individual called Chum. Without any invitation at all, Chum would just take off in full voice, and at top speed tear across a paddock towards sheep. 'A dog trial neighbour of mine noticed this. "Won't he stop for a whistle?" I replied, "Well, not exactly, but if I scream and rave, jump up and down and tear out handfuls of grass, he sometimes slows down a bit!"'

I've always reckoned that some huntaways have actually been trained to react in a certain way, as soon as they hear the call 'right' spoken in authoritative tones. Time after time you see the sheep cross the finish, hear 'right', and there's the dog, dipping its backside, going to the toilet. At that point, this does not harm the run, though it may not do much for the hillside. Once the judge indicates that a run's over, no more points can be deducted. Some dogs know the relationship between sheep passing through the top markers and the end of the run so well that they anticipate the moment of relief. That can lead to disaster. I've seen a trio finishing a very good run, by marching in Indian file across the finish. Obviously the dog reckoned that the job was over, and began a more personal task. Alas, the hind sheep decided to check out the centre peg and stopped to give a good long sniff. Without any call from the judge, the run was still in progress and the dog was, quite literally, caught with its pants down. The competitor was also caught unawares and had to adjust quickly to the fact that what looked certain to be the winning run, had just turned to …!

Trotting out examples of what can go wrong with courses, sheep and dogs allows us to attribute blame and therefore offer all sorts of reasons why a particular run, or several, failed. What can be even harder to bear is when you have no excuses and you and your dog have done your absolute best and still not got a mention. One year at Martinborough, Shorty and I had a useful run on each hunt course and, with a day to go, I left to go up-country to a judging job. It was towards the end of the season and we only needed one more point to qualify for the championships. Being in the call — the top five — on each course was a big boost and, mentally, I had our bags well and truly packed. To digress for a moment, one of the most annoying things about dog trialling is that the gun operators, with in-form dogs, always wait till the last day of a two- or three-day meeting before they put in an appearance. On the other hand, their holding back allows lesser lights to experience a bout of euphoria for 24 hours or so. On that occasion, a touch of the euphorics was all Shorty and I got. Although 95.75 and 96.5 were useful scores, all they earned us was a fifth and a fourth equal — with three others — in the local listings. Mind you, perseverence will bring its rewards. Three years later, we ran on the first day of three, and had a useful run with a trio that were a bit awkward at the start, but okay after that. During the next two days, the sheep got worse and worse and forced gun after gun to fire blanks. The result was that our useful run, which turned out to be another 96.5, won the open. I was working through the nights at that time editing … *a Dog's Show* and the ring I got the morning after the trial ended was the best wake-up call of my life. A by now aging and one-eyed Shorty — one was removed after a very serious infection — also got a wake-up call, from a bloke in gumboots and a dressing gown, wanting to give her a pat.

The best 'we did everything possible and still missed out' story belongs to Bob Guthrie. He walked up to me at Takapau's grounds where they've not only had a tradition of canine All Blacks but also very good hunt courses and sheep. He pointed to a dry, autumn-toned hill behind us, its face dotted with the appropriate markers. 'I ran here on the zigzag in 1959, got 98.75 and got sixth … out of the money.' Dick Schaw's Guy, son of McSporran's Storm, won with 100 and the other four placegetters — most, if not all, Takapau All Blacks — were separated by quarter points. This meant that the dog on 99 was a mere fifth, but still ahead of Bob and his barker, McHardy. Their hard luck was to continue: 'The next week we went to Taradale and scored another 98.75, and got another sixth — Ned Dahm's Tangi won with 100. The two best runs of my life and not a place! Sometimes you wonder what you have to do.' At which he turned and walked away, shaking his head. Three years later, Bob and McHardy won the New Zealand straight hunt title.

The partnership who gained perfect points at the Taradale trial, Ned Dahm and Tangi, were both pocket-sized editions of their kind but won, among a host of other events, a couple of New Zealand hunt titles. The second of these was at Masterton in 1963, when Tangi was a teenager and Ned certainly wasn't young either. He was also, as his brother Joe recalls, recovering from a severe heart attack and a stroke. 'Tangi seemed to know that this was to be the swansong of the great partnership between her and Ned. She did a near perfect run [98], and even though Ned made several errors of judgement (due to his state of health) she completely ignored them, and went on to win the championship.' The then governor general, Sir Bernard Fergusson, was in the audience and had a good chat to Ned at trophy time, as Joe recalled. 'He congratulated Ned on the wonderful recovery Tangi had done when the sheep suddenly veered off line. "That smart piece of work must have earned Tangi a lot of extra points."

'"Like hell," said Ned, "I was bloody lucky the judge didn't dock some points off for that."

'"Well, well," said Sir Bernard, "if I'd been the judge I certainly would have given Tangi a lot of extra points for that."

"'Right," replied Ned, "you're a man after my own heart," and, patting the governor gently on the shoulder, added, "I'm going to put your name forward to be the judge of the next championships." It was then the governor's turn to pat Ned on the back — an unforgettable sight, Ned and the governor general laughing like a pair of kookaburras, and patting each other on the back.

"'You oughta be ashamed of yourself, taking liberties with the governor like that,' said Peg [Ned's wife] as she tore a strip off him afterwards.'

It's worth noting that the dog who was second behind Tangi at that championship was the Takapau 100-point winner of some four years earlier, Dick Schaw's Guy. He was another natural shepherd who just carried on with the job, regardless of his instructions. He was out of Charlie Anderton's Rose and no one remembers Guy better than Charlie. 'He was so brainy. I remember one time when he was going to the mark and John Lowes [he had a litter brother, Roy] was standing beside me and said: "Now you watch this — Dick will start him on the right, and the dog will go there, but then move to the left, with no indication from the sheep." Sure enough, Dick put him to the right and Guy put in a couple of barks and then off he went to the left, picked up the balance and away they all went. The left was the place ... Dick didn't know that when he started, no way of telling, but Guy did, he just had that bit extra. Dick wasn't a great general, you know ... didn't need to be with Guy doing the work.'

Of huntaways that haven't required a lot of supervision when they've been performing, the most recent independent operator to attract attention would be Bill Hinchey's Ben, one of an Eric Stringer's Chum litter. At least three of Ben's brothers competed at championships and all were long-limbed, though not heavily built, with the black and white markings you'd expect of the Southern strain. Ben also had a fair bit of tan, and all the eye and concentration of a natural shepherd. Right from the time the liberators started walking the sheep out, he'd be firmly fixed on them, stretched forward and frozen in a pointer's pose. The freeze quickly thawed as soon as Ben got the word from the judge. He certainly didn't wait for Bill to say anything, but that's not the way it was with them. A tall, loose-limbed, laconic man, Bill neither wasted words nor over-projected those he did utter. When he and Ben were in action, such was their understanding that there was no need to shout, especially as many of the decisions were made by a dog who could be trusted. Their best year was 1986, when they won a North Island championship and were runner-up to national and South Island titles. At those nationals, Bill and Ben's non-verbal relationship drew a lot of attention, to the extent that a triallist, leaving before the meeting ended, advised Hinchey's mates, 'If Ben gets into the run off, give Bill a pie and a paper so he has something to do.' To which another character added, 'And tell him to hang on to the paper after the run, as Ben will want to read it too … he's clever enough.'

There are some trial grounds where competitors have to be a touch clever too, especially those where both hunt events are run on the same hill, but not at the same time. In most cases the one set of top markers will end each course, though some clubs have different coloured markers, a bit to one side or another. It can be that the centre peg for the straight is actually the left-hand marker for the zigzag or vice versa. The most important thing for a competitor is finding out from a reliable source what course is being judged at the time. Some clubs have the same person judge both events, so looking to see who's got the pencil is little help. Professed ignorance immediately after a shoddy run is a technique some of us have tried. Several times I've started out on the straight and, by poor steering coupled with a demonstration of how much I needed to reline my dog's brakes, have turned in a useful zigzag. Once, when that happened, I turned round and called in the general direction of the judge's hut, 'You do realise that was my zigzag run?' Echoing from the corrugated iron depths came the quick reply: 'It was not! You had it before and it was too straight. Show your bitch the programme before you run, she'll work it out!' She could have, too, but even those with far better track records can find that the problem with the straightest course is that it can also be very narrow.

12

ANOTHER DAWN, ANOTHER DOG TRIAL

Between Northland's Mangonui Sheep Dog Trial Club and the Waimahaka Collie Club in Southland there are some 170 clubs affiliated to the New Zealand Association. That figure can vary a little, give or take a club or two in recess, the ominous march of forestry and, in other areas, the expansion of dairying and beef production. Over the last 120 years, trialling has withstood greater threats than any current trend can impose, and has done so because of our nationwide network of local clubs and their committees. All but half a dozen of these run open events on all four standard courses, and attract a following from outside their district, with the visitors looking for championship qualifying points, the simpler pleasure of a companionable day at a decent trial or both. If you're good enough or sufficiently relaxed, either, or both, can be arranged.

Each club has its own quirks, traditions, architectural gems and distinctive personalities. As well as ensuring that no two trials are the same, this makes going to events, other than your own, much more interesting. Not only are the sheep and the individual courses all different, but so, too, is the food at the cookshop, the demeanour of the barman, the sense of humour, or lack of it, of some stewards and the whole ambience surrounding the event. During any trial, that atmosphere is liable to change, owing to the usual variables: sheep behaviour, an erratic climate and whether some visiting triallists are having any success. As with all events run by volunteers, club trials are rather fickle things and subject to a few ups and downs, but they always triumph in the end. They're run on a shoestring too, and with facilities that have stood the test of time, though some look as if their time may run out at any moment! To me, that appearance of rustic impermanence is an important part of the attraction, and visually complements the timeless procedures that trialling represents. Nestling under an elderly macrocarpa shelter belt, there's a rusty-roofed, weather-boarded secretary's shack or a cluster of unpainted huts on a valley floor or upland shelf. In either case, they'll mark the end of a gravel track and the beginning of a day's trialling.

Any club's human resources are equally significant, especially those who've relied on one or two well-known competitors to provide leadership over the years. They're the people who've always travelled to other club's events, with considerable success, and done their best to provide a good trial for those who return the compliment. To outsiders, these leading figures are inseparable from their home trial, to the extent that trialling friends ignore its official title and attach an individual's name to the event. Hence, to many of us, Whangamomona is Bernard Murphy's trial, Kapiti-West Coast, Alf Boynton's, Wainui Valley, Bob Bryson's, and Maungakaramea the preserve of several adult Childs. The Omarama trial has always been associated with the Anderson name — at present that means Ginger — and Kyeburn with the Crutchley and Stringer families which, these days, means David and Eric, respectively. None of these nationally established names, however, could run their trial alone, nor would they want to. They're surrounded by local supporters and helpers, whose sole annual contact with trialling will be working at their local trial. For clubs that have big stations in the parish, these have always been a reliable source of labour, especially when the owner or manager is either sympathetic to trialling or a very accomplished competitor himself. With managers, in particular, trialling excellence is not unusual. A station's goodwill usually guarantees a good supply of competent people for liberating, a home for a fair percentage of the local and maiden prizes, and at least one rowdy night in the bar.

The opposite to clubs that have been able to build and exploit a tradition of experience are those in predominantly dairy or cropping districts, which no longer have any serious triallists in their ranks. Fortunately, keeping their trial going has become a matter of district pride and, although they may not do everything by the book, they're trying to, and putting on an event for others to compete in. At these trials, it's a very stupid visiting competitor or judge who criticises a couple of blokes wearing white gumboots and waving lengths of alka-thene as they hustle difficult sheep to the mark for the next run. In many clubs the human core will consist of half a dozen families, who have ensured that their event is a success, and that certain traditions are upheld. Some of these local regularities can be, in the eyes of the pedantic, very irregular. Most of the time, that really doesn't matter; those variations are the quirks that make each trial special, and are the reason why competing at the club level is worth celebrating.

There are very few other events of any kind that have such uncomplicated basic requirements: a mob of sheep, stakes, standards, netting and gates, a wood stove, gas ring or copper, a couple of huts, two or three horse floats, and bread, mutton, whisky and beer. It's not always that simple but, in every club's recipe for success, if you don't find those exact ingredients, you'll come across their equivalent. Not that you would be expected to visit them all, though at least one man, Bill Pullen of Hunterville, may actually gain that distinction. An ardent and very capable hunt competitor with two New Zealand titles, Bill managed a property up north for some years, did a lot of droving on the East Coast and spent some seasons mustering throughout the South Island. He won his first open in his original centre, King Country, as a teenager and since then it's obvious that, no matter where he's been working, if he's had any spare time in the autumn, he's gone trialling. The number of trials he needs to attend to complete a full tally of all our clubs would be in single figures. I haven't even got to half of them yet, but I've certainly seen enough to write chapter after chapter on the variations — human, geographic and structural — that exist. I won't try, especially as it's much more interesting observing a club trial from within.

Though the world immediately surrounding the vehicle was pitch black, a quick glance in the rear vision mirror confirmed that a new day was on the horizon, albeit a distant orange glimmer over the eastern hills. All the public roads were a distance behind now as James Martin, president of the Mana Hills Collie Club, wended his way up a farm track in an effort to be the first at his club's annual trial. James was a local farmer, in his mid-thirties and a keen trial supporter and local competitor. He had only recently become president, as his predecessor, Craig Taylor, had moved out of the district. Craig had phoned last night to wish him and the club well and to give James some very basic advice. 'The first six hours are the worst. Survive them and you and the trial will go the distance,' he said, adding with his customary loud laugh, 'with a fair bit of help from the secretary.' According to tradition, a big factor in James's early survival was complying with what the rank and file regarded as 'our leader's' most important daily task. This meant he was expected on the grounds at first light, with the cookshop copper lit and boiling, so everyone could have a cuppa before work began. At this stage he was sure he'd be first as he was on the narrowest part of the track and there was no way anyone could pass him. Just as well, too, as the old Land Rover wasn't up to racing; in fact it probably wasn't even up to getting a warrant. It certainly didn't have one, though, since it was used solely on the farm or for sneaking up side roads in the vicinity, it didn't really matter.

The first time the rover negotiated this track, it was a brand-new 1955 Series One, of the station wagon type, but not with the appearance of today's vehicles in that category. In this instance, 'station wagon' meant it was covered in, with bench seats on either side, over the rear wheels. Back in '55, and for several years to follow, it had been the Martins' family car, when Mana was rather isolated, with only metal roads and several unbridged creeks. Accordingly, there were strict instructions from the house that, under no circumstances, were dogs allowed to ride inside. This meant that, on trial days, the dog team were perched on a two-wheeled trailer, claws at full stretch for better grip on the deck, while being bounced about among scrim, netting, standards and fencing gear. Once he got to the trial grounds, James's father would hastily use those tools and equipment to finish the holding yards and liberation hook on his course, the long head. These days, all that work was carried out at the main working bee, a couple of days before the trial. As time goes on, the organisation improves, and James was the third generation of his line to be part of that process. Members of the fourth generation would get to the grounds much later in the day, if someone remembered to go out to the corner and meet the school bus. This duty had been forgotten once, 27 years ago in fact, an over-sight of which James, then eight, still had vivid memories.

Crossing the cattle stop that led on to the sloping flat under the hills, where the heading sheep were held, brought sharp notice that James wasn't the first on the grounds. Across the track, a tightly knit mob of some 200 sheep were wheeling round and round, as if they were in training for a wool promotion poster. The clag-up had been created by Colin Black, the short head marshal, who was trying to muster and count off a cut for an early start on his course, traditionally the first in action. Going by the bellowing from the far side of the block, Colin obviously had no idea where either sheep or dogs were. Equally appar-ent was the fact that, in every sense, he wasn't enjoying being in the dark! It certainly wasn't worrying his dogs, who were having a won-derful time. James wasn't having much fun either, as he had to organ-ise the rover into a sudden halt. This, owing to poor maintenance and the creek he'd forded two paddocks back, wasn't all that easy. Fortu-nately everything connected in the nick of time and the old girl shud-dered to a standstill, shouldering far enough into the still circling mob to give the front mudguards their best clean in years. The brakes had even worked abruptly enough to fling a young huntaway into mid-air and drop it, with a loud yip, over the diff and gear levers. Low-flying dogs and certain smells were the main drawbacks from allowing the team to share the same compartment as the driver. Ventilation wasn't a problem, though, thanks to an ill-fitting hind door and a couple of missing windows, of the small, squarish variety. The two older dogs, who always claimed fresh air rights through those gaps, had an uncom-fortable neck stretch during the recent emergency stop, but the frames had prevented them from taking a short flight, with a bumpy landing.

Nosing the rover through the sheep, James found Colin bumping his ute across the paddock to catch up with his dogs and sheep. Full of paternal goodwill, which he thought would befit a club president, James greeted Colin with a very cheerful 'Good morning, how're-you-today?' Being really friendly to a taciturn head shepherd, who stayed a couple of jugs too long at the local watering hole the night before, is a waste of time. This was quickly confirmed by Colin's responses of 'Is it?' and 'What are you, a bloody doctor?' Realising that any more discussion would be pointless, and that offering to help could be life threatening, James graunched the gear lever into the first available cog, said, 'See you later' and the rover lurched off to return to the track. After stopping to open and close two gates — you could never be sure whether the next traffic through would be another club member or an escaping sheep — he reached the club's headquarters. For the next three days, this cluster of huts, perched on a shelf above a clear and busy creek, would be the nerve centre of Mana Hills' eighty-seventh annual trial. Pulling up at the back of the corrugated iron cookshop, James got out to rustle up some kindling and get the copper going. His dogs were also intent on getting out but, given a very firm 'get inside', they were shut in. The catering committee always made it plain that dogs were not welcome anywhere near their domain. This attitude was reinforced by a sign round the front of the building though, every year, there were always one or two dogs who couldn't read.

With a mixture of paper, pine needles and cones, the firebox beneath any rural organisation's most traditional and reliable water heater was soon in full flame. Being 4 kilometres from the road, the club regarded putting in a power line as too costly for just a few days a year. As a result, everything was heated the old way, and at either end of the day, the secretary's office and the bar were lit through the efforts of a borrowed generator. Turning away from the copper, James looked down the track at a series of advancing vehicle lights. Even at this hour, at least one set would belong to a team of travelling triallists. With luck, another of the oncoming convoy would be the secretary; otherwise he'd have to stand in for her and take their entries. He never enjoyed that task, as everything had to go in the official receipt book in duplicate, and he had a bad habit of putting the carbon paper in the wrong way up, or between the wrong pages. As it turned out, two of the early vehicles belonged to competitors but Betty Ross, the club secretary, was right behind them. Before the visitors had a chance to form into a rough queue on the verandah of her official premises — an old single man's quarters shifted in from a farm down the road — she'd parked her car, whipped the generator into action and entered her office.

As Betty unloaded the contents of her fibre suitcase on to the ancient kahikatea kitchen table that served as her desk, the light bulb dangling above it flickered into life. Business could begin and, on cue, she sat down, picked up the pink-paged receipt-cum-entry book and, with her customary warm and welcoming smile, dealt with her first customer. 'Hello Bob, what time did you leave home?'

'Three o'clock,' said a man of middle age from away up-country, who quickly added in response to Betty's raised eyebrows, 'but that was yesterday afternoon. I stayed the night at my sister's, up the road.'

Holding out her hand expectantly: 'And how many dogs are you running this year?'

'Three youngsters, that's more than enough.' Said as he shook his head slowly, 'All they've achieved so far this season is age me ten years in ten weeks. But, my word,' he added with a rueful grin, 'they've had a lot of fun!'

As he spoke he handed over his clearance certificate, which stated that his dogs had been treated for *Taenia ovis*, otherwise known as sheep measles, within the last 30 days. Even though regular treatment is no longer a legal requirement, to protect those who provide their land, sheep and a tremendous amount of goodwill, the dog trial movement insists that all dogs be dosed. Without written proof of that, Bob couldn't even let his dogs out of his ute, let alone compete.

As the mid-autumn day dawned properly, the flow of traffic continued its spasmodic pattern. Many of the vehicles carried workers, as club members are known during a trial, and there were a few more competitors as well. Invariably they'd spot the smoke wafting from the copper and make a beeline for James, his teapot and a large tray of

freshly baked scones and home-made raspberry jam. These were supplied every year by the widow of a former triallist and delivered by her
son. The old lady still wanted to be involved in the trial but had no
wish to continue working in the cookshop, and this was her gesture,
three mornings in a row. The early morning crew thought it an excellent arrangement; fresh scones certainly beat the hell out of dry biscuits
or hastily buttered bread — if someone had remembered to pick it up
at the store! By this time there was quite a gathering, particularly of
locals. Most of them were busy talking about their allotted tasks and,
at the same time, leaning casually against the cookshop and drinking
tea. Sooner or later, thought James, all this talk has to be turned into
action. He turned to the huntaway team and asked when they'd be taking their sheep across the creek, as the hunts were on the other side of
the gully. 'Soon,' came the reply, but it didn't come from the marshal.

In fact, as James suddenly realised, he hadn't seen Jack O'Malley, the
senior hunt marshal. 'Where's Jack?'

A shoulder shrugging 'Dunno' was all he got in reply. He decided not
to worry, as the O'Malleys lived at the other end of the district, almost
an hour away.

Part of James's job was making visitors welcome and he took the
teapot to a couple of new faces. He was also taking a mental roll call
of the club's human resources and noted that the crew from the district's largest station, The Tussocks, wasn't to be seen. This was a worry,
since they provided the liberators for the short head; when they did
arrive, though, there would be sheep for them to put in the hook.
Looking into the hill above the flat, which ran along in front of the
buildings, he could see a mob emerging from the scrub and Colin and
his dogs following them. They'd be in their yard in five minutes and
ready for the first run in quarter of an hour. A thought struck him, 'If
there *is* a judge. I haven't seen any!' His stomach took a nasty turn and,
with lengthening stride, James rounded the corner to check with the
secretary that she had confirmed dates and times with the judges. Not
bothering with the steps, he leapt on to the office verandah, side-
stepped a queue of half-a-dozen prospective entrants and began voic-
ing his concern before he was even through the office door. 'I haven't

seen the judges yet, Betty, what time did you tell them to be …?' The secretary just smiled at his concern and, with a mere leftward roll of her eyes, said all that was necessary. Over by the back window were three tidily dressed blokes, also wearing the responsible air judges put on for these occasions. They were sorting out judging cards, and putting the pencils, sharpener, rubber and pads the club provided into their respective old, though new-looking, briefcases.

James was so pleased to see them that his outstretched hand was virtually shaking the nearest one's hand before his feet had started to move in the same direction. 'Welcome! I'm James Martin, the club president, you've had quite a drive.'

'Yeah,' agreed the older and much taller one, 'but we'll do our best to stay awake till it gets dark.' Very much one of the old school, he was well insulated against any chance of rough weather, with a dark blue woollen checked shirt, a mainly red McKenzie tartan tie, and a red and black checked Swanndri. This was topped off with the Australasian stockman's favourite, a broad brimmed Akubra, the brim of which he flicked, just before crushing James's hand with a grip that would have strangled a six-month old calf. 'I'm Tom McKenzie, and this is Ian Magee — he's on the straight.'

A shorter wider chap in less bulky clothing stepped forward, gave James a knowing grin and shook his now numb hand. 'Gidday.'

'And Ken Smith who's on the zigzag.'

'Howdja-do,' said a long, lean character, shambling forward in the slightly awkward manner tall men acquire after spending much of their working life in the saddle. 'I've heard it's a good course.'

'It is,' said James, as he pointed to it out the window, 'especially in a good autumn, as this is, and the sheep have the strength to really climb it. It's a pretty big hill.'

'I'm looking forward to it,' Ken replied, as he looked out the window. With eyes widening, he focused on the top markers, just distinguishable below a sheet of early morning mist: 'Do they need oxygen in the top set?'

'No' said Ian, his mate from the straight, 'just a kind dog and a practical judge.'

'And that's why I didn't bring a dog,' said Ken, as he turned and faced his favourite sparring partner. 'The only hunt I could have here would be on your course. You're too fussy for the likes of me 'n' Mac.' As Ian would be judging the straight at the next New Zealand championships, no one took Ken's banter very seriously.

At this point the president did some very simple arithmetic and, with a puzzled look, turned to Tom McKenzie. 'You're judging the long pull aren't you?' He nodded and James carried on, 'I'll introduce you to your clerk in a minute and he'll take you round there — it's a couple of miles away. But, ah … is the short head judge not with you?' A man of few words, unless he'd just had a really good run, Tom gave a broad smile and nodded in the direction of the door and the yarding course beyond.

'Yes, Mike Doyle, he's walking the course already, that's him halfway up the hill.'

Ken quickly chipped in: 'He'll have already worn out the hinges on the yard gate, making sure it swings properly, and tried to knock over the hurdles, to test their strength. Now he'll be about to get your course marshal to lift the netting in the hook by 3 centimetres, so the dogs can get under.'

'Whether it needs to be lifted or not,' added Ian. 'To be fair, though, it's just his third open judging job and he's dead keen, and thorough … you can't knock that.'

'No,' said James, somewhat relieved that he now had a full muster of pencil pushers.

He then ushered them out of the office and over to the copper, for the early morning smoko they'd certainly earned. They came from two southern clubs and must have been on the road by 4 a.m. to arrive when they did, before 7 a.m. Pointing the judges in the right direction, James did a quick scan of the parking area and was relieved to see the O'Malleys' truck and the man himself letting his dogs out, one-handed. This rang a bell, and explained why their leading huntaway man had just arrived. Jack was an ice-cream addict and, living where he did, there were few opportunities to feed his habit. It was, therefore, part of his pre-trial ritual to stop at the store on the main road for a double-cone triple-scoop. This wasn't possible until the storekeeper emerged at 6.45 a.m. Despite the hour, either storekeeper or customer had been wide enough awake to consider the trial's requirements. Jack was obviously trying to juggle some loaves with his cone-free hand.

A look up the hill confirmed that Colin and his dogs had the short head sheep in their holding yard and, with the judge in tow, were on their way down. On their way up, and about to pass the others, were two shepherds from The Tussocks, ready for half a day's liberating. As Ken Smith had predicted, Mike, the judge, had wanted the netting in the hook lifted but, as Colin related to James over a beer that night, the matter was quickly dealt with. 'All my dogs are trained to go under fences, so I put them under the netting a couple of times and told him, "If my dogs can get bloody under, any other bugger's can … there's nothing flash about my team." That seemed to make him happy and I got him out of there before he got too close to the holding yard up there. It'll fall over one of these days, you know.' James did know, couldn't help but know, as Colin always said the same thing at committee meetings. But, because it was now his responsibility, the rest of the club were waiting for the whole set-up to fall over. Then he would have to stop talking about how bad it was and, at long last, do something about it.

Detouring to the O'Malley dog and bread van, James fetched the last of the loaves from the cab floor, wiped the grime off the bottom ones, thought 'Thank God for plastic bags', and carted them to the cook-shop. There he stayed, to light another fire. This time it was the kitchen stove, so its twin ovens would be hot for the morning tea savouries. This was a big, black Shacklock, rescued from an old station cookhouse in the back country, and over a hundred years old. It even had a water jacket by the firebox with one of those brass lever taps at the front, for hot water. First you needed to fill it, which James did, avoiding criticism from the catering committee, who'd be there in about an hour's time. Going out the back door to the copper, which was situated at the edge of the woodshed, James organised some apparently hesitant workers into living up to their titles, scoffed down the last jam scone and chatted to the huntaway judges. If the noise from the creekbed immediately below them was anything to go by, the sheep for the day were in the process of being shoved from one bank to the other. He then went over to his Land Rover and kidded it into starting, so he could park round the front and let the dogs out. Left in there any longer, they could almost be excused for doing the unpardonable.

Officially parked, he rummaged through the glovebox, to find his binoculars. After using an old rag to spread the dirt spots into an even blur, he focused on the long head hill. By road this course was quite a distance away but not as the crow flew. Just the same, from James's vantage point he could see only the holding yard on the back corner of the hill, as all the competitive action took place on the other side. Nonetheless, it was possible to tell if the course was going by the amount of activity round the yard. In this case, the complete inactivity of the solitary liberator sitting, as usual, on a little camp stool, confirmed that there was no action. Not surprising, thought James, considering that the drive between here and there took at least ten minutes and the judge would be just settling into his box. He smiled to himself as he imagined the sort of look on Tom McKenzie's face when he saw the hut. Big-framed fellow that he was, he may have been tempted to try putting it on like a coat. As it was, he'd have to bend considerably and edge along between the angled writing bench under

the window, and the back wall. The club knew it was too small but built, unsupervised, by a keen clubman, who also donated the materials, there was no way that the president of the time (James's father) could reject it. Anyway, once Tom settled in and saw that the big open window gave him a clear view of one of the best hills in the business, he'd be happy — they always were. Just the same, James made a mental note that, when he visited that course, he'd make sure he was leaving before he asked the customary, 'You're quite comfortable?' Tom would be, too, unless something happened that meant he had to leave in a hurry.

Tucking the binoculars inside his shirt, James turned and saw the short head's first sheep of the day being nursed along the netting race leading to the liberation area. Down on the flat, standing in the quad, was competitor number one, Bob Bullock, the early bird, sizing up the trio that would soon be his. An experienced competitor, he was well aware of the traditional trialling belief that sheep have certain bio-rhythms that can be harnessed. On a heading course this can mean that the first few lots of the day have the potential to be the most co-operative. This is based on the well-established pattern that, when grazing in the hills, sheep come down after dawn and go back up towards sunset. That's why some huntaway competitors can be reluctant to have their runs until later in the day, when climbing into the hill seems very natural to their trios. 'That's never helped me,' thought James as he walked round the far end of the short head course to take his dogs to the creek.

Passing behind the short head judge's box he looked in to make himself known. After they'd worked their way through the standard niceties, it was apparent that Mike Doyle was preoccupied with cutting out a cardboard stencil of the course's outline. When traced around, he explained to James, this would give him a consistent map on which he could follow and mark each run. It was an odd-shaped layout, best described as an L in reverse with the upright — the head and pull — leaning off to the right, like a certain tower in Italy. The sections at the bottom of the L — drives, hurdles and yard — weren't in a straight line, but curved, like a wide soup bowl. The judge's box was a better size than the long head's and was set below the course, in line with the hurdles and yard and on a slight angle to the head and pull, but with a good view of everything.

This wasn't the first time James had seen the type of stencil Mike was preparing; every judge had a system. The main thing was that, whatever the method, it didn't cause constant delays throughout the trial. He was also well aware that the three sheep were in exactly the right place in the hook, and Bob in the quad was making it very obvious that he and his bitch, Sue, were rearing to go. In fact, with all the impatience of the young, Sue had already had two practice starts of her own accord, only to be brought back and made to wait. To show both his readiness and impatience, Bob was rather pointedly looking back in the judge's direction every fifteen seconds or so, but Mike Doyle was too busy to look. Out of the corner of his eye James spotted Colin striding purposefully in their direction, quite obviously to 'see what the hell was going on', as he would also relate at that evening's post-mortem. Quickly deciding to use presidential pressure for the first time, James said, as gently as possible, 'Ah, the sheep and competitor are ready.'

'So am I,' said Doyle as, with his pen, he traced round the stencil on the top page of his pad, headed it up with number 1, turned to the elderly man, Laurie Porter, who was his timekeeper and said, 'Who's this?' That noted, Mike slid the window across, picked up his stopwatch, checked to see that his colleague did the same, looked up at the sheep and, when Bob turned to stare at him again, called 'time'. Sue needed no further bidding and bolted immediately. Bob, though, had been caught a bit wrong-footed and hastily turned to face the hill and a disappearing dog.

Mana Hills' short head was under way and, James noted with a smile that he wisely kept to himself, Colin had been beaten by 5 metres. That was how close he was to the judge's hut when Mike started the run. Colin stood there dead still, thwarted from asking the question that had been welling up inside him as he strode, marshal-like, across the paddock. Above all, though, he was a keen and competent dog man who liked seeing a good dog carve out a hill, and now that 'the bloody job was under way' he was happy to do just that. The president also kept an eye on the course, as he and his dogs finally headed for the creek, and saw a good clean run out that finished up with the dog stopping nicely at 12 o'clock.

When James came back that way, some ten or twelve minutes later, the yard gate was open and Bob Bullock was seemingly frozen to the end of it. Alternating between a stubborn standstill and a fidgety shuffle or two were three cryptorchids just a couple of metres from the open mouth, making the most of fighting Bob and Sue every centimetre of the way. They lost. With twenty seconds left, the first run yarded — a good start to the day.

As James walked past the side of the hut Mike called out, 'Good sheep.'

'Thanks, it's always a relief to see the first man put them in. I hope they do that all day.'

'They won't, the competitors and their dogs'll see to that,' replied Mike, 'but they won't be able to blame the club for putting on crook sheep.'

'Not unless the weather turns nasty and they go out in sympathy,' thought James as he called his dogs in and tied them up under the line of broom that ran down the fence above the creekbed. Walking to the buildings, he then checked that the blackboard on the secretary's verandah had been filled in with the running order for the short head.

This was always the most pressured course and, to eliminate diplomatic disasters, competitors ran in strict order of entry. Keeping it up to date had been James's responsibility for the past few years, and old habits die hard. This was Colin's first year as marshal, which was why he was so tetchy. It also occurred to him that, if Colin got the slightest notion his work was being inspected by his predecessor, he'd become even tetchier. James slipped round the back of the office, past the bar and toilets and headed for the cookhouse. Once again, this was a fire-tending visit, but would be the last for the day as the ladies would soon be taking over.

By 8.30 James was moving among the competitors' cars, greeting familiar faces and introducing himself to new ones. 'So far, so good,' he thought. Both heads in action and the hunt sheep in the holding yards, at the foot of each course. They usually opened the zigzag first, but that wouldn't happen until the club's oldest member, 81-year-old Cyril Barrowclough, had arrived. Cyril's involvement with Mana Hills went back 50 years, when he arrived as a settler on a Second World War rehab block. From then on, the only break in his total involvement with the hunt courses was his eight years as club president in the 1960s. Even then, if the hunt sheep were working well and there were good dogs about, getting him to make the required number of visits to the long and short heads took a bit of doing. Long since retired and living in town, Cyril still saw every run on the zigzag, from the best seat in the house. This was by the judge's side, as his timekeeper or, as Cyril's southern heritage would have him pronouncing it — with the 'e' as an 'e', as 'clerrk'. James's next task was to wait for the old chap and drive him across the creek to his post.

In the meantime he wandered over to the three vehicles unloading trays, boxes and chillybins of food at the cookhouse; the catering committee's advance guard had arrived. In every case their involvement with the club was as wife, partner or mother of a male club member. That's the way it had always been. The only difference these days was that female involvement was no longer restricted to cooking or secretarial work. Three of those on the liberation roster were women and Claire Grant was in her third year as marshal of the straight hunt. What hadn't happened, though, was the obverse: men joining the catering committee. James had heard this was the case elsewhere, but it was probably just a vicious rumour, and guessing the gender of the person who started it wouldn't be too difficult. Another vehicle drew up beside the cookshop but not to deliver food; it was Mary, Cyril Barrowclough's daughter-in-law, with the man himself. Out of the car he popped and, quick as ever, had James by the hand and got the first word in. 'Gidday young fella, what's it like being the boss?'

'Hello Cyril, it doesn't seem any different, everyone still ignores me.' Only in the last few years had 35-year-old James felt able to call Cyril by his first name. 'Did they listen to you?'

'Yes, but it took nearly 30 years … I just wore the buggers down.' That last comment from the short, wiry and still fit-looking Cyril drew a vexed look from Mary. She was busy pulling a rug, two cushions, a heavy coat and a well-weathered satchel off the back seat. James gathered these together to put in the rover. Cyril took one look at the collection and snorted. 'I don't need all that stuff — it's going to be a cracker day, hot as hell, especially in that judge's hut.'

'True enough,' said James 'but with the number here already, the hunts may go late and it could get cold when the sun ducks behind the range. We don't want to have to go looking for another time-keeper halfway through the trial.'

As they reached his wagon, James opened the passenger door and gave Cyril a judicious nudge to help him get his stiff hip over the edge of the seat.

'Thank you, James.' Cyril looked around the interior and gave an knowing sniff, as James tried to find a clean place to store the old chap's gear. 'The first time I rode in this vehicle it reeked of car polish and windowlene, not bloody heading dogs.'

'I've got huntaways too, you know that,' said James, indignantly.

'Yes, but are they any good?'

'You'll find out,' adding with a grin, 'but when I run the young yellow dog, don't blink, or you might miss it.' At this point James gave up trying to find a safe place for Mary Barrowclough's best rug and plonked it and the cushions in the old chap's lap. 'Here, hang on to these. And,' Cyril turned and looked at him enquiringly, 'thanks for coming, it's great to have you.'

Quickly covering any possible display of embarrassment, Cyril brushed the compliment aside. 'You couldn't cope without me. Even if you could, I wouldn't miss it for anything.' At that the engine fired up, the gears clunked and the wagon wandered towards the steep track down to the ford, and the zigzag hunt course on the other side.

Coming out of the creek they headed to the rear of a low-roofed, corrugated iron hut that a judge once christened 'the Shacklock', after surviving three days in it during a heatwave. The rover had barely stopped when Jack O'Malley had the passenger door open and thrust out his hand. It both welcomed Cyril and provided the necessary impetus to have him springing out of the vehicle like a two-year-old. 'Good to see you, Cyril, you well?'

'All the better for seeing you, my boy. Been looking forward to this for weeks.'

'And you're just in time to see the winning run.' Jack's way of saying that he was about to open the course. Going first was not, in James's opinion, necessarily an advantage, probably the opposite, but usually the marshal or another worker led off so everyone could see how the course and its sheep were working. From then on, the dog who opened could be used to clear the course. Parking the Land-Rover away from the hut and quad, James noted that Jack wasn't going to fire his best barrel first. Regular winner and championship performer, Ruff, was still tied up under the nearby scrub. Following Jack as he walked into the quad was Geoffrey, a Ruff son who, they reckoned, would be as big a nuisance as his father in a year or so.

The first run was also important for the judge, Ken Smith, not only to see how the course worked, but also to get a feel for both the release and the liberators. Two of the latter were new and James could hear Ken's suggestions as they walked the sheep towards a small knoll which, as usual, had been designated as the ideal start point for the run. 'Walk up on them a little … keep going … stand still.' That to Simon Collins, a farm manager and new to the district, as he held the balance on the right side. The left was never a problem on this course until the last few metres. Sometimes all that was required of that liberator was to stand up at the critical moment. That's exactly what Gill Collins, Simon's wife, did as soon as the sheep looked to turn to their left. A full-time shepherd on the property Simon managed, she would be stationed out there on the edge of an old slip all day. What's more, that seemingly small contribution would have more effect on facing the sheep straight into hill at the start than anything else. As Gill put one arm out and slowly waved it, to hold the lead sheep's attention and keep them marching on to the knoll, Ken said to her, 'Thank you, that's good ... ah ...,' then muttered quietly to Cyril, 'I've forgotten her name — what is it?'

'Don't know. Never had a woman liberate on this course before!'

With a discreet smile, Ken took a quick breath to increase the decibel level, and called 'time'. Jack quietly gave Geoffrey the word, to start him singing in his well-rounded baritone as he started marching towards the trio.

After a short distance Jack checked the dog, as the sheep had stopped and turned to see what all the fuss was about. One in particular looked very light-headed and fickle, though it also had the potential to turn and climb away, thinking it was escaping. James looked at them closely and wondered what chance he and his yellow tearaway, Rag, would have of getting this lot going. Fifty-fifty, at best, he reckoned. Geoffrey then came forward, like a boxer, dancing on his toes, and delivered a couple of salvoes directly at the nervy one. That literally blew her round to face into the hill and got her into stride. The other two followed and, as in a long-distance running race, the field held its positions till just past the second set, with a tricky 45° right-hand slew to hold their line on the middle of the top set. The toey sheep had obviously been in training and picked up the pace at this point, to go at right angles straight across the course. At the same time, Murphy applied his law of dog trialling, and caused the back sheep to pause to take a breath, then another, and another. Geoffrey, meanwhile, was out wide, underneath the bolter, trying both to check her and turn her up. That more or less achieved, he swung back a little to the breathless one, while the middle sheep hovered between the two camps.

'He won't get this lot together again,' said a visiting triallist, standing near James, 'they're divorced.'

Tempted to offer him a quick bet in support of Jack, James was inclined to agree, but trotted out the old cliché: 'If any team can do it, this pair will.' They did too, and despite losing four or more for the temporary shambles early in the top set, it was still a useful run. To stop Geoffrey gaining a place in the open, another five dogs would have to have very good runs indeed.

Happy that another course was under way, James drove back up the track to park near the office and check on the entries. 'Not counting the locals, we've got 43 heading dogs and 37 huntaways,' said Betty, doing a quick tally. 'And they say there's at least one more car load due from up north, on their way to run at The Plains tomorrow.'

'How many outside heading dogs do we normally get on the first day?'

'It's usually in the mid-thirties,' reckoned Betty who, now into her fifties, had been secretary for at least twenty years and was the most reliable source of impartial advice in the club. 'I don't think Colin will need to look for many locals, to run on his course today.'

'Good,' said James, nodding positively, 'entries may be up overall. If not, at least we'll have a quiet time on the last day.' Pausing for a moment, he continued; 'Make sure, though, that any workers who are only here today get their runs, if it's at all possible.'

'Just the two, I think,' said Betty, 'from The Tussocks. That's the pair liberating now,' pointing at the short head hill. 'Apparently they're needed to bring stock forward for crutching.'

'Right. Will you ask Colin to try and fit them in when they come off the hill, or will I?'

Betty replied with a broad smile, 'You can, I think he's had enough of me. I'm afraid I offended him by telling him off for not spelling competitors' names properly on the blackboard.'

James gave a hearty chuckle. 'And what did he say to that?'

'Not a lot, just, "Hmphff, they know who they are. Got the dogs' names right anyway, that's all that matters," and stomped off the verandah looking for his next competitor.'

'I'll go and find him now.'

'Before you do, Mrs Davison was over before, she wants to see you "as soon as possible".' The last phrase, Betty delivered in the mimicked tones of a duchess.

James laughed, thought 'Oh hell' at the same time and asked, 'Any idea what she wants?'

'Something to do with smoko baskets, I believe. You haven't been making any promises you're about to break, have you?'

'No way. In fact she's going to be very impressed with what's been done.'

As he turned to go, Betty added with a wry and knowledgeable smile, 'Don't get too confident.'

As far as the club, its democratic process and the list of office-bearers printed on the programme were concerned, Mrs Davison was no longer chairwoman of Mana Hills' catering committee. She hadn't been for many years but, for her, titles were important only when they applied to her. All that mattered was strength of personality, the ability to draw oneself up to one's rather imposing full size, and always to look as if you've just left the hairdresser's. In other words, as James's father once said, during his term as president, 'She's not easy, and it's not that she's difficult, it's', as he paused looking for the right words, while sitting at the family meal table, '... it's just that she's bloody impossible!' Recalling the old man's indignant frustration put a hint of a smile on James's face as he mounted the steps to the cookshop. It soon disappeared when he saw that the doorway was blocked, and by whom ... and sidestepping wasn't an option.

'James,' she said imperiously, 'the morning and afternoon tea baskets you promised do not appear to have arrived.'

Game to the last, and knowing he was on safe ground, James merely smiled and said; 'Hello Mrs Davison, nice to see you here ... again.'

She completely ignored his courtesy, suspecting that she was being fobbed off. 'I did expect them to be here, ready to be filled, and they are not.'

'But they are.' James made to get in the door. 'If you'll just excuse me, I'll show you.' Almost reluctantly she moved back and James sidled past others of the catering team, including his wife, Lyn, to whom he gave a confident wink. From a big cupboard under the bench, he started pulling out what looked to be 20-litre drench containers. They were, white ones too, as that had been the product with the freebie James had wanted most last season — an all-weather oilskin waistcoat. The containers were of the US Army, jerry-can style and any sign or smell of anthelmintic (drench) had long since gone. The top of each was now a flap or lid, having been cut horizontally right to the back, which became the hinge. Across the centre was a hooped handle of No. 8 wire, threaded through clear plastic tubing for carrier comfort. Each of these modern smoko baskets had the name of a course painted on it and the number of people to be provided for. Lined up on the bench, James thought they looked quite impressive. 'They'll do the job, don't you think, Mrs Davison?'

Through quite terse lips came a slow, drawn out. 'Yeesss'. A pause, then a quick return to her much more perfunctory persona. 'I suppose we'd better start filling them. I daresay you'll want them soon.' With a fleeting glance and a snappy 'Thank you, James', he was dismissed.

Walking to his next port of call, the short head and Colin, James tried to weigh up Mrs Davison's prickly side against some positive points. She was always there, and even though she must be well into her sixties, worked as hard as anyone. There was another major factor in her favour, which he'd heard Cyril Barrowclough put very succinctly some years ago. The old chap was counselling a liberator who had committed one of trialling's greatest sins: he'd forgotten to return his course's smoko gear at the end of the trial. What made it worse was that both the thermos flasks in that kit belonged to 'Herself'! Not surprisingly, the young shepherd had got an absolute pasting and, in its wake, had taken his wounds to the club's father figure, Cyril. 'Well boy, you might think she's got a brass heart and a lemon tongue, but her cream sponges are the best in the country, you'd never get a better bacon and egg pie anywhere, and those mushroom and mince savouries she makes …' Standing there shaking his head, recalling the wonders of those flavours, Cyril was all but lost for words, but added, 'You've got to balance these things out, son. And,' giving a big grin, 'don't ever try and pinch her thermoses again!' With a loud chuckle he slipped away to another conversation, leaving the lad standing there, lost for words. In time he took the only option open to him in the circumstances; he walked to the bar and got another beer.

After talking to Colin about the entries and the need to try and fit in his current liberators when they came off the hill, James went over to his vehicle to reflect on proceedings so far. He quietly fished a 3B1 notebook out of his hip pocket — the variety course marshals always carry — and studied his checklist. This set out not just the tasks he had to perform but one or two areas he needed to keep an eye on so that any hiccups could be avoided in the nick of time. So far, so good, except that he hadn't seen Bill Graham, the barman, arrive with his refrigerated trailer in tow. This wasn't a worry right now, but later in the day some would be very concerned if Bill and his bottles stayed away. Putting the book back in his pocket, James watched a competitor and dog corner a rather tetchy-looking trio and yard them, at exactly the same time as they got the two-minute call from the judge. As they were being taken away to the spent pen, Colin Black came by on his way to transfer the next few competitors' names from his notebook to the judge's sheet. Without stopping he observed; 'They're good sheep, James. That's six yards out of eight runs so far. And one of the uncompleteds, you couldn't blame the sheep … silly bloody dog kept getting in the way!' Shaking his head in disbelief, Colin disappeared round the back of the judge's hut.

Walking back from his parking spot, James could get a good view of the second and third sets of the zigzag. There was a run in action but with three sheep spread across the course, just below the second set of markers, it didn't look promising. As he turned to get into the rover to collect the smokos, a series of predictably anguished commands came from the gully below, followed by silence. 'There's another hunt run over early,' thought James. The brand-new buckets for the long pull and both hunts were all but ready and, looking out the window, he could see the yarding course's container on its somewhat hesitant way to the judge's box. On either side of it was a four-year-old daughter of catering committee members, who hadn't quite got into the swing of things, and problems with balance and co-ordination were hindering progress. One way or the other, they'd get it there, and be rewarded for doing so. For nearly 30 years Laurie Porter had clerked on this course and, as two generations of club offspring well knew, he had an unlimited supply of large peppermints in his pocket for small people who brought him and his judge their morning and afternoon cuppas. He was also typical of dog trial stalwarts who never ran a dog, but every year, without fail, gave three days of their time to help out. There was an extra cost for Laurie, too; for an adult, there's no such thing as a free lolly.

As James took the last container from the redoubtable Mrs Davison, he heard a conciliatory tone: 'They do seem quite good, James. I think I'll get Donald [her husband] to make one for us to use at the woolshed.' She then added, 'I put an extra cup and savouries in the bucket for the long head — the president usually has his tea with them on the first morning.'

Thanking her for reminding him, James then sat the buckets by the rover's front seat and steadied them against each other. He then looked inside one to see how well everything fitted — it did. Of the two large and durable stainless steel thermoses, one had the name Black painted on it, and the other O'Malley printed on paper and taped on. The tupperware container containing sandwiches said it belonged to Betty Ross, the enamel mugs had blue wool wrapped round each handle and the teaspoons had a dash of green paint on theirs. No one laid claim to the foil wrapped round the hot savouries, or the Marmite jars containing tea bags, sugar and milk. All that, thought James, sums this trial up. Assemble a group of people and their various bits and pieces, nurse it along at the start till they all fit in, then stand back and let it run itself from then on.

By mid-afternoon of the third day, not only was the end of the trial in sight, but James was beginning to feel that his end was nigh as well. If he'd learnt one thing this year it was not to accept responsibilities at both ends of the day. In future he'd delegate his evening duties, but he wouldn't try to get out of his early morning task; he wouldn't be allowed to anyway, that was tradition. He and his wife, Lyn, had also hosted both the heading judges for two nights and, although they were good company, as Lyn said, 'You never really felt as if you'd left the trial grounds. If they weren't talking trialling, then everyone who phoned was!' 'Not that we needed any lengthy conversations on other subjects either,' thought James. He was driving back from the long head where, as well as delivering the workers' lunch, he had run his two heading dogs. To help erase the memory of these events, he ran through his end-of-trial duties. Many of these concerned protocol, such as hosting at the final barbecue the two landowners — the long head was on another property — and the supplier of the hunt sheep. The club's sponsors also needed to be entertained — the garage proprietor, the local transport operator, one stock firm manager, a banker and two different chemical company reps. The happier they got, the greater the likelihood of them coughing up again next year.

The person with the biggest responsibility as the trial drew to a close was Betty Ross, the secretary. She had to check each of the judge's cards, sort through all the points for the local prizes and put out the final results as quickly as possible — all while everyone else was enjoying themselves at the barbecue and bar. As he pulled up outside the office and switched off, he could hear very convivial laughter from the cookshop. This was a clear sign of the catering committee winding down their operations and dealing with a chateau cardboard or two at the same time. Hearing the rover's distinctive tones, like a tractor with bronchitis, Betty came out and immediately asked James, 'How did you get on?'

'No good,' he replied, 'but at least both dogs got their sheep.' He then paused and gave Betty a quizzical look. 'Why is it that when you have a good run you almost have to force people to ask how it went? When you have a disaster, everyone always wants to know. Now why is that, Betty?'

'I don't know, but,' she smiled, 'if it's any consolation, unless there's a big upset on the zigzag, you and Rag will win both the local and open maidens.'

'I feel better already, not that I get involved so I can win all these big prizes,' he said with tongue firmly in cheek. 'In fact, if I'd got involved to gather the spoils of victory, I'd have got totally disillusioned and left the club years ago.'

THREE SHEEP AND A DOG

There is no James Martin, nor Betty Ross, Colin Black, Mrs Davison, Jack O'Malley nor, for that matter, a Mana Hills Collie Club. But there are hundreds of people just like them right around the country. Many, like James, receive very little, or nothing, in the way of prize money, yet give a tremendous amount of themselves, doing something they obviously enjoy. So, too, do the competitors who visit them.

13

From Top to Bottom

Of all the roles performed by club workers at a dog trial, that of liberator has to be the most important. That statement is based on absolute personal bias and partiality. Apart from winning an open trial or catching up with fellow triallists at the beginning of a new season, putting sheep on the mark for run after run is the next most satisfying part of trialling. I've also found that it's much easier to arrange than an open win! My preference and experience are based amost entirely on heading courses, for reasons that should become apparent. As explained earlier, every heading course has a hook or fenced contrivance of some sort where the sheep stand, waiting for their canine guide to arrive. From the competitor's position, facing the hill, the trio will have been walked out from holding yards, somewhere out on the left. In many cases these will be hidden round the corner of the hill, or just over the top. Where the yard is in sight, it will still be some distance from the hook, and the sheep hidden behind scrim (a long roll of sacking) so the dog isn't tempted to head them instead. Some do, anyway, but only after they've gone too wide round the top of the hill, got lost, then found far more sheep than they ever dreamed of being allowed to work at a trial. The task for the triallist, then, is to get the dog off the multitude and on to the trio.

Liberators do help with dogs which get lost at the back of the hill or involved with the wrong mob. Sometimes it's just a matter of growling at them to go away — 'Grrrr ... they're over there'. At other times they may need their collars felt, and to be dragged towards the right sheep, which is much better than leaving them in the middle of the main mob, with the yard rails about to yield to the pressure. When he was competing north of Gisborne, Bob Bryson saw one of the more unorthodox liberator interventions. 'It was on the long head, and this dog had gone over the back of the hill, out of sight of the man. So the liberators quickly grabbed the dog, put it on the Land Rover and tore down the track and round the bottom of the course. All this time the competitor was whistling and calling the dog, and didn't notice that the young fellas had brought it down and put it in the ring behind him! After a bit more whistling and calling, he gave up and turned to walk out of the ring. There it was, sitting there gazing up at him … he still doesn't know how it got there!'

Between the yard and the hook there will usually be a netting fence on the uphill side to hold the sheep against as they go out. Sometimes it's fenced on either side part of the way and, when it runs out, the liberator and dog take its place. Not all courses use a dog to release sheep, though, as some believe that the first dog a trio meets should be the competitor's. That's all very fine but, when there's trouble, there's nothing like a dog to sort it out. Sheep are also a lot better behaved when they know there's a canine in the vicinity, even if it is a half-broken-in adolescent on the end of a length of twine. When a dog is used, it's important that it doesn't do too much to the sheep, in terms of turning them this way and that, and that the degree of involvement is as consistent as possible from run to run.

The other area where evenness is called for is in the threesomes that are put on the mark. Given that the sheep are supposed to be from the one flock and of the same sex, breed and age, good liberators will still try to match them, according to the variations which exist within any large mob. Whenever possible, they'll put open-faced sheep together or woolly-faced, finer-fleeced, short, stocky ones — whatever. This is because, where the physical characteristics are similar, there is a greater chance of getting a similarity in behaviour and giving the competitor a more even chance. To achieve this and remove any real oddballs or strays, there's often a reject pen at the side of the holding yard where the unmatchables are put. When it gets full, eagle-eyed and evil-minded liberators have been known to wait for the club's president or resident hard case and give him something very special. The best or worst trio I've seen consisted of a very elderly shorn ewe, a woolly wether lamb and a large and extremely arrogant black-faced ram. Not only did this threesome completely break all the rules of same sex and age, it broke the breed conventions too, by being Coopworth, Southdown-Romney cross and South Suffolk, respectively. The other trio of misfits I'll always remember consisted of three very decrepit old creatures I assembled to do someone I'd spotted a real 'favour'. He didn't see it that way but got a re-run, because one of the sheep keeled over and died 50 metres from the ring! He would have got a re-run anway, as did the triallist who was given the ovine all-sorts.

Practical jokes aside, judges and course marshals do have a say in what happens up on the hill, but only if they can be heard. Just as heading dogs can miss hearing vital instructions at the top of a course,

liberators, too, can have bouts of deafness. This can be very frustrating for those down below, trying to attract their attention. The problem is, though, that because the bloke up top doesn't hear, he'll never know that he should be looking downhill for a signal he doesn't want to bloody see! I suppose it would be easier for some club administrators if their liberators were like Mohaka's Jack Midgely, who always did the releasing on the first morning of every trial and almost anonymously, according to former president, Bill Percy. 'He'd arrive from Waiotea Station, do his shift, then go home. I never laid eyes on the man, and don't know what he looks like to this day.'

None of this is to suggest that liberators are a bunch of loners and a breed apart; they're not, well not entirely. In fact, not all of them are liberators; in the South Island, liberating is called 'slipping', which means they slip sheep on to the mark, using slippers. On the occasionally wet and sticky slopes of the North Island, trial workers can also do a bit of slipping, but this only creates more laundry, not trios for trialling. Among the more unusual set-ups on the Mainland is the long head at Takaka, where the yard for the sheep is a cave, but they're not too primitive in nature by the time the slippers have got them into the hook. At Macraes in Otago the sheep are delivered by a couple of shepherds mounted on a tractor. This has a rear-mounted cage, with the trio neatly packed inside. After swooping into the wide hook, the tractor's backed up to the netting, the bloke on the back opens the cage door, out pops the sheep and the tractor departs. The non-driving liberator stays there to keep everyone in their place, until the sheep's official escort arrives. There are as many variations in slipping or releasing set-ups as with everything else about trialling. The main thing is that there are people prepared to do the job, and some who actually enjoy it.

For me, liberating on a heading course is a welcome opportunity to work stock, remind dogs of their manners or teach them new ones and best of all, be out of harm's way on top of a hill. Up there you see everything and, on the courses where I work, have to talk to no one. And when you do have to communicate with the authorities down below, it's either by rather suspect sign language, which they can pretend not to see, or uttered insults, which distance and nor'-westers prevent them from hearing — except on one unfortunate occasion! The urban parallel in this case would be saying something very personal about someone in a crowded restaurant and, just as it's spoken in a good strong voice, the whole place falls completely silent. In this case the covering noise was a howling nor'-wester and just as I vented my spleen at the bloody sheep, a crook hook and a pedantic judge — who was in the right — the wind stopped in mid-gust. As a result, my message to the world in general, and one or two citizens in particular, carried beautifully across the flat. It did not help that the judge's clerk was a lady, and a right and proper one as it turned out. One of the disadvantages of having been trained in voice projection for a microphone is that there are times when you don't need any need electronic assistance.

On many courses, solitude is not possible as either the hill or the hooks into which the sheep are put require two or more to walk them out, then hold them. Liberating in a group can be fun and it certainly was at Martinborough when I was one of several involved in the job. I'm still involved too, though on my own, as the others have passed on to other courses, including the big one in the sky. Martinborough's approach was to have both a team of people, and closed membership, especially up to the 1950s, when the most important liberator was a horse, who pulled the sledge that carried each threesome to the hook. As members of that original group retired to the foot of the hill, they spent their days commenting on the standard of work of their replacements. Just as important was that each year's hook be a precise replica of those of the past. One year, the old timers were adamant that it wasn't right, saying that the netting at the end of the hook didn't reach far enough out towards the other shoulder of the saddle. It should, they said, go within a yard of a certain Scotch thistle that was growing up there that year. This was said on day one, which at Martinborough is local maiden day (locals with maiden dogs), so there was time to rectify the problem before the open trial began on the morrow. When the veterans scrutinised the hill next morning they saw that the hook reached almost to the thistle, so all was well. As a result, the liberation worked much better for the rest of the trial. The only noticeable change up there was, in fact, the thistle itself, which began to wilt. This wasn't surprising as the lads had decided that the best way to get the old boys off their back was to whip the thistle off at ground level and take it to the netting.

Gaining selection in that team was not easy, especially as the only vacancies were those created by the Grim Reaper or rheumatoid arthritis, neither of which you'd wish on anyone. The second year I belonged to the club I was asked to help out on the long head, because a gap had finally appeared. I came down late in the afternoon to run and walked past Masterton stalwart, Jim Hay, who issued a typical challenge. 'Where have you been all day — I thought this was your club?'

'It is,' I replied, 'I've been up there on the long head, liberating.'

'Liberating, here, at Martinborough? No! You've got to belong to the club for 40 years before you're allowed to do that!'

'They must be desperate, Jim,' was the only answer I could come up with. And he walked away, shaking his head in mock disbelief.

The team at that time, the early 1980s, was Mike Langtry, who sorted out the trios in the yards and Simon Beveridge, with whom I alternated in putting the sheep on the mark. Then there was Colin McLeod, who watched over us all. By then he was in his late seventies and had competed and liberated on that hill since the early 1920s. Colin had another claim to it, too — he and his brother Ivan owned it. Their father, Murdoch, had competed at Martinborough's inaugural trial in 1896 and the club moved to the McLeod property, Hillside, around 1913. By the time I made it into the team Colin had a watching brief and usually sat on the bench in front of our canvas and plywood shelter. Every now and then he'd spice the gaps between our chores with stories of runs that had come to a spectacular end, and the men and dogs who created those distant disasters. He and his heading dog, Roy, were responsible for bringing in fresh mobs two or three times a day. We called Roy 'the manager', since whenever the pair left to fetch a new consignment, the deck of the Land Rover was not for him — he sat beside the boss on the passenger's seat. Since those days, the rural community has suffered quite a loss in population, particularly in farm staff, which has had a direct effect on the number of workers at dog trials. As a result, liberators are now seen on that hill one at a time.

My other regular liberating duty has been with the Kapiti-West Coast Club which, when I first helped out, was known as Aokautere-Linton and based at Shannon, south of Palmerston North. It then became dog trialling's most travelled club of recent times because, no sooner did they establish themselves on a new property, than it would be sold. After setting up excellent new courses on grounds near Waikanae, then Paraparaumu, they're now based near Levin and a credit to the determination of a group of volunteers led by Alf Boynton and John Carrad. The first course of theirs I worked on was a huge long head, so big that dogs who attempted it needed to carry a packed lunch for sustenance. The liberator, who walked up the back of the 'mountain', through the straight hunt, needed long-range patrol rations and a tent. What a hill, and what a relief to be given an excellent short head on which to liberate at their next grounds. Two years later, when lifestyle subdivision forced them on again, they moved to Levin, where I'm still the short head liberator, though I was given a year off to judge that event. Being down below, I managed to remember the importance of good liberator-judge relationships. I certainly didn't want a repeat of a confrontation that once happened between an extremely finicky long head judge and an irate liberator. At the top of his voice, the judge had been niggling at the worker for some time, and he, understandably, had got 'very bloody sick of trying to place sheep on the head of a —ing pin!' So he left his sheep, which were nearly in position and stormed all the way down the hill to speak his mind. 'If you want the sheep on that certain point, you can bloody well do it yourself!' With that he marched straight back up the hill, which was a big one too, and, without any further criticism, put the trio in a sensible place.

One of the perks of liberating is what you can see from the hill — the car park, the crowd, the competitor … but not everything. Because of the shape of many courses, after watching the run out and a bit of the lift, that's all you might see for a few minutes, unless you go poking your head over the ridge and run the risk of either altering the action, or becoming directly involved in it. Instead, you watch the triallist work the dog and it's not long before you realise there are as many variations in competitors' behaviour as there are with sheep and dogs. One of the more predictable patterns is in the run out, where there's a direct relationship between a lack of dog speed and effort and the volume of human noise; the less a dog uses its lungs, the more the owner uses his or hers. Another constant sign is that the further a competitor leans to one particular side, the greater the need for the dog to swing out that way. Moreover, the more pronounced the lean, the less likely it'll be that the dog will go that way. A few years ago, there was a chap who competed with a dog who consistently ran as narrow as an arrow. The more the dog leaned into the sheep (the left), the more the triallist leaned out to the right. During extremely narrow run outs, he would tilt so far to the right that everyone thought he'd topple over. I dare say that was true, though I never saw any of this; it was me, working Peg.

As a dog finishes heading it will be either praised, ignored or warned about what fate will befall it if it ever meets up with the boss. Outward displays of dismay are soon over, though; in trialling, what's done is done, and you get on with what's next. Meanwhile the dog fills its lungs with air, and the sheep adjust to the close proximity of a heavy breather with a toothy grin and a loose, liquid tongue falling out of its face. Down below the lull allows for a few quick human breaths, a throat clear or two and time to consider tactics for the lift and pull. For an experienced competitor, with a calm approach and, therefore, dogs of similar bent, this can even mean hunkering down into a stockman's squat. From this super-relaxed position the triallist then makes intermittent, laconic suggestions to the dog as it shepherds its charges straight down the hill. The best exponent at this I've seen was Wanganui's Brian Burke who, when he was working his 1984 New Zealand winner, Lady, would squat on his heels during the greater part of the pull. Other low-key operators will lean forward on-to the top of their crook, which can't be longer than a metre, with one hand over the other. Some will share their weight between one leg and the stick and lean to one side. Then there are those who don't use their crook for support, but as either a baton to conduct proceedings or as something to absorb their tension. My personal favourite is to lay the crook along my shoulders and behind my neck, with my wrists dangling over the shaft. I find this relaxing, though I never seem to be able to maintain the pose for long and, in the sudden switch to emergency mode, my left ear gets a nasty flick as the stick whips by. Some experienced competitors will wander over to one side of the quad and lean on the front marker, if it's strong enough. Many, though, stand centre front of the 20-metre-wide quad and, in imitation of a boxer, lean toward their opposition — sheep, hill and, maybe, dog — keeping their mental guard up, and staying on their toes.

Once the next phase, the pull, gets under way, some quite unusual mannerisms can be displayed. There's the man who, whenever he gives a command, cups a hand behind his left ear, as if he's expecting the dog to give him instructions. Others lean right forward and cup a hand around their mouth as a megaphone, for whistled or spoken commands that are often so low they can barely be heard. Heard by the liberator, that is; dogs can have fantastic hearing, umpteen times better than any human. One of the more unusual stances I've seen was a chap who stood at attention but with one arm out at right angles, as if he were on a bicycle and always about to turn a corner. He would stay like that for half a minute or so at a time and, though it may have been a visual command for a side, it was only with the left arm, not the right. I've seen several who'll work the dog throughout the pull with one hand clamped firmly on top of their head, and some will have both hands clapsed there. Many of us have the habit of shading our eyes with one hand or both, even when the sun's at our back or it's raining! Then there was the chap with a constant choreographic routine of three small steps forward as he uttered a command, then two larger ones back, in the short silence that followed. At the same time, he would swap his crook from armpit to armpit, in the manner of an indecisive sergeant-major.

The crook or, as we usually call it, dog trial stick, is very much the focus of unwitting attention and nervous release. Watching and interpreting what's being done with this, is like seeing a CT scan of a sheep dog triallist's inner frustrations. When a crook is clutched in a

two-handed grip, with a wringing motion just below the handle, the competitor has just wrung the dog's neck. If the stick's held in reverse and pointed at the hill at a 45° angle, this is the schoolteacher syndrome and sooner or later you'll hear the class of one get a verbal warning. Seeing a fist clenched round the shaft of a crook, which is suddenly moved in a quick jarring motion, is visual confirmation of the loud stop command you'll hear at the same time. A series of those jabbing exclamation marks means that the stop is not working, even though the air is full of its repetition. Shortly after that, if the stick's jammed into the ground, or its base drop-kicked, the calamity the command was designed to prevent has just happened! Finally, whenever you see someone firmly holding a stick off the ground, and all of a sudden just let it run through their hands, they've also just let go of the run. It's all over, especially the shouting.

The spoken commands, best described as warnings, which waft towards the top of the hill also give a very good indication of a triallist's mood, especially when the dog needs to be reminded who's in charge. The manner of their delivery is as important as the words themselves. Denny McAloon's 'You'll listen to me, my boy' is said with a wavering, cautionary air. Charlie Anderton's 'Yooo do, Jann … you dooo!' stretches the words for greater emphasis, and Bob Bryson has been known to use an imitation growl, 'Aaaah Bruce!' This worked well if Bruce was getting a bit prick-eared and tip-toed when working round the yard. My favourite warning is the one J.B. Smith used on his good old heading bitch of the 1980s. This he'd utter while shaking his head: 'My wordd, Daisy! … my wooorrdd!' Less pressured is the simple reminder to stay calm, the steady, which is precisely what most say: 'Steady … steadeee!' There are two variations that I particularly like and both come from Taranaki. Lou McCracken, as well as running the aforementioned Hardgraves, had a good bitch called Gipsy. Her steady amounted to the best rhetorical question in dog trialling: 'What are you doing? Gypsy! What are you doing?' Tututawa's Bob Thomson has a dog called Fred, with whom he gets on pretty well and, thanks to the placid nature of both man and dog, the command side of things is rather conversational. The pick of Bob's phrases has to be his steady: 'Just quietly, Fred, just quietly'. One of Fred's side commands, I'm pretty sure it's his left, is 'this side'. One run of theirs I remember well. Bob planned a right turn for the sheep into the first drive, and he and Fred executed it nicely, too, in their understated way: 'This side, Fred, this si… just quietly, Fred … just quietly … thank you.'

We lean forward, stretch unnecessarily onto our toes, give little jumps with each sharp command, twitch, shudder … goodness knows what, and we couldn't give a damn. It's all part of trying to influence events elsewhere and, mentally transporting ourselves and our wishes, no, demands, to that place. This, as with leaning, can lead to doing replicas of some vital commands, without realising it, until it's too late. You give the dog a little left, it takes a couple of paces to that side, and so do you … which is fine if you're not standing on the bridge at Pio Pio! If you are, may the ghost of Ned Hayes tell you about the re-run you won't be having.

Some of what a liberator sees can create frustrations, in the same way as a know-all sports spectator on the terrace gets annoyed when his team ignores bellowed advice. After all, up there on the hill, we know exactly what the competitor should be doing, and say so in low tones, yet the advice is ignored. You just can't help some people — others you mightn't want to assist at all. Personal relationships could form part of that attitude, though the main reason for wondering if a run could have a slight mishap, would be when you've had yours and it was a good one. There's nothing worse than going up the hill on the last morning, fairly sure that you're in front, and staying there till dusk, having watched your position steadily slide to a non-paying eighth. The year our Wairarapa Southern Hawke's Bay Centre held their championships at Kapiti, Clip and I had a very useful run at the end of day one. It was obvious we were well in front, so the last day was pure hell, especially as all the guns turned up. Clip and I liberated every trio that day, and were scrupulously fair with our sheep handling and placement. The only bias was personal and expressed in private, when someone was putting a good run together. One in particular had 'Gordon, you're history' written all over it, but in the last minute a dear little lamb slipped down the side and they didn't yard. Legend has it that my sigh of relief was heard over at the zigzag, during a run! Not long after came a run similar to mine which, I decided, was probably a shade better. The day was much easier from then on, though I did hope I was wrong — and I was.

On a long head course, liberators often see incidents which, had the judge seen them, would have been penalised. Often the judiciary can't see everything and, with flat ground just behind the hook, this is certainly the case at Martinborough, especially as the judge is about 700 metres away. I know of several dogs who wouldn't have withstood closer scrutiny, but that's the way it is for everyone. The best example was a dog who ran out well and arrived behind the sheep in a very relaxed manner. He paid little attention to the sheep, looked around, yawned and wandered over to an interesting piece of ground, which he gave a great big sniff. He then sauntered across to a thistle, and lifted his leg. After irrigating two more thistles, with a beaut sniff between each of them, he returned to the sheep. They'd watched every move, obviously fascinated by this cool and casual canine's routine. He made a couple of 'let's go for a walk' moves, they simply turned round and started walking straight down the hill and the dog just ducked under the wire and followed them. I remember thinking at the time, somewhat indignantly, 'The slack beggar's going to win this!' He didn't, he came third.

There are two other blind spots on that course, as the wide flat between hill and ring is bisected by two gullies. Neither of these is very big, but deep enough for both dog and sheep to be unseen by both judge and competitor. The liberators, though, have an excellent view, especially the year one dog had such a calm, walking pull that he must have been on first-name terms with each of the trio. It was all so cosy that, when they got into the first depression, the dog trotted right up beside the sheep, walked right out in front and continued on round to return to the rear. This is known as 'ringing the sheep' and, out in the open, would cost several points. In the privacy of the gully it wasn't noticed nor, because the sheep were not disturbed in any way, could anyone have suspected a severe misdeed. Anyway, it was a very good pull and at the end of it the sheep stood perfectly for a full-point hold. Rightfully, it was the winning run.

Martinborough's second gully is right in front of the ring, with the nearest side being rather steep. This is blind too, but now that there's a proper judge's box on stilts, there's a better view. Before this was erected, a dog was having an excellent pull, and reached the gully in perfect form, but only two of the trio came out the other side. They walked quietly into the ring, ready for the hold, but sheep number three and the dog weren't to be seen, except from the rear, up in liberators'-ville. As they were climbing out of the gully, the back sheep decided that it was a bit to steep for her, stopped, turned and gave the dog a rather aggressive look. The latter took exception to this and dived at the ewe, to show who was boss. This meant that they both lost their footing, went into orbit and finished up in the ditch at the bottom of the gully, with the ewe on top of the bitch! Not knowing any of this, the competitor was getting quite agitated and issued several 'walk-up, walk-up' commands in a very insistent manner. Eventually the ewe rolled off the dog, and they both got up and made their way into the ring, in the right order. The competitor got a good hold too but, even though the judge didn't know what had happened, the prolonged absence of both the dog and a third of the mob kept them out of the results.

Some of the doings that liberators and slippers have got up to over the years have become legend. At local maiden trials or shepherds' events where there isn't too much at stake, it hasn't been uncommon for one of a trio to have an empty beer bottle tied round its neck. The first time I saw this happen, the judge decided it was unfair, as only one sheep was wearing a bottle. He ordered a re-run and said that each sheep should have a bottle of its own. This called the bluff of the boys up the hill as it was early in the day and they hadn't produced enough empties. At other times innocent sheep have carried the contents, not the bottle. The most celebrated of these incidents occurred at least 80 years ago and concerned W.V. McIntyre, who was competing on East Coast's grounds at Porangahau. The story was originally told by another trialling stalwart, Ronny McDonald who, years later, passed it on to Doug Cochrane, who passed it … 'The young fellas were liberating this day and they were waiting for W.V. Everyone took a bottle of whisky up there in those days, and they filled this poor bloody sheep up with whisky till it was coming out its ears. Old Mac comes out on the mark, away he goes. Ronny tells the story: "When the dog got up there it must have looked as big as a bloody elephant — to that sheep that was full of the stuff — and it just took off! Straight down the course, straight as a bloody die, right through the ring, hopped through the fence, over the road, then into the school paddock and dropped dead." Then he said, "You know we told McIntyre years afterwards, and he still couldn't see the joke!" '

In the early 1970s, after competing at the Expo International trial at Rotorua, a Welsh triallist went with other overseas competitors to the Gisborne Charity Trial. This is an excellent yarding event, held every January, to raise money for local causes. The Welshman offered to give a demonstration of shedding sheep, using a dog to cut, then hold, two or three sheep off a mob. 'Unfortunately,' recalls Bob Bryson, 'he rubbed us liberators up the wrong way, so we tied the sheep together. The string broke after a while, but it made things pretty difficult for him for quite a time!' A more regular trialling practical joke is taking someone's favourite hat. Out at Akitio, on the Southern Hawke's Bay coast, one year, someone flogged a young club member's hat. 'He got really annoyed about it too — "Where's my hat!" Next morning he had first run on the short head and yard and had to go out and run without it. He cast the dog, pulled them down to the quad, and there he saw his hat, strapped to the back of one of the sheep! He had to yard them to get it back. He did too, and said how well the liberators had tied it on … didn't worry the sheep at all.' At other times sheep have carried notes down hill, and not the kind a grateful competitor could cash in at the bar. In the days before radio telephones and cell-phones, these messages, tied to a lock of wool in the middle of a sheep's back, wanted important issues resolved, such as 'Where the hell are our replacements?' A regular on hot days was: 'Please send half a dozen bottles of beer with the lunch', and, if it was after 1 p.m., 'Where's our bloody lunch?'

Another area of concern for liberators, especially as the trial draws to a close, is wondering if they're going to get a run themselves. Missing out has happened to me, and one year it nearly did to Mick Takarangi on Taupo's long head, but he resolved the issue himself. Apart from him, the last competitor had run and with no one on their way up to liberate for his run, he did it himself. Mick then got the rest of his dog team and went straight down the hill. At the bottom he tied his hunt-aways up, ran to the ring, 'time' called the judge, and away the dog went to fetch the trio it had put in place minutes before. To make the point that there's no advantage to be gained from putting your own sheep on the mark, Mick was unplaced. I tried doing something similar at Martinborough one year, but left the club secretary up there to keep the sheep in place. Unfortunately he didn't have a dog; the trio took advantage of this and simply walked out of the hook and round the side of the hill. This proves another point: in most cases liberators and slippers wouldn't be any use at all if they didn't have a capable canine with them. Some dogs really love the job, and quickly fall into a set routine. They move away as soon as the competitor's dog arrives, and go straight to the mouth of the release set-up, waiting for the next three to be let out, and all for the joy of working sheep and the chance of half a mutton and pickle sandwich at smoko.

Some liberators' dogs are so enthusiastic that they can become a problem, as was the case at Martinborough when the time came for a keen young dog to have his run. A little fellow, he headed the hill well and, in due course, lifted the sheep quietly enough to start the pull. Tucked nicely behind them, he had steered the procession little more than 10 metres before he was hit by a major memory flash and thought, 'Oh no, this isn't what you do!' Quicker than a terrier on a rabbit, he was round the front, stopped and turned the trio, and had them back in the hook before his totally unprepared boss could stop him. No matter what was said after that, and there was plenty, he stayed there minding his charges for the next dog — not comprehending that it was himself who was next … now! After a while the liberator, who'd replaced the dog's owner, went out and, in concert with assorted 'wayleggos' and call off whistles, physically encouraged the dutiful dog to leave.

Though slippers and liberators can be a law unto themselves, they do try to do their best by the competitors and take a pride in giving everyone a fair chance. Despite that, when you've finally wrangled a troublesome trio into the hook, you know that the best dog in the world wouldn't have a hope in hell with them. Conversely, there are those who walk to the hook like lambs and you think, 'They've got 98–99 written all over them.' But up comes a brash bully of a dog, who dives in and starts harassing them and, naturally, their attitude changes in seconds. Then you think, 'What a waste of good sheep!' Then you remember when your dog did much the same thing. That day, though, the liberator came down for lunch and in the middle of a crowded bar, which immediately fell silent, walked straight up and eyeballed me with: 'You got the best bloody sheep I put out all morning, and you stuffed them up!'

14

ONE TRIAL AFTER ANOTHER

Each autumn, February to May, the keenest triallists become nomads and think nothing of visiting as many trials in out of the way places as circumstances will allow. This means a lot of early mornings, long drives, late nights, and criticism from those with whom you occasionally live. It's a way of life that often puzzles the uninitiated — 'Why drive around at all hours to chase someone else's sheep? You've got plenty at home!' An alternative view is found in an old fisherman's quotation which, with a minor change, fits sheep dog trialling.

Behold the dog triallist.
He ariseth early in the morning, and disturbeth the whole household.
Mighty are his preparations.
He goeth forth full of hope, and when the day is spent, he returneth smelling of strong drink.
And the truth is not in him.

My mother summed up the early morning aspect well when I stayed with her on the way to a trial. I was having a solitary 4.30 a.m. cup of coffee when, from the dim recesses of the morning, came the observation: 'This does seem a strange time to start a day of pleasure.' At such an hour that's a piece of common sense you can't really argue with. Soon you gather yourself and most of your belongings and, still drowsy, get in behind the wheel and begin another day of hope. How much easier and more pleasant it is when you don't have to drive; you're already there, over-nighting on a trip of several trials.

The ringing echo of an insomniac tui peels out from the nearby bush, and the black mid-February morning is penetrated by a gentle tap on the door. Creaking a little, the door finishes its opening arc and a discreet rattle of crockery on the bedside table announces the first of Bernard Murphy's daily dog trial rituals, all designed to make visitors welcome. This is just a tiny part of what makes such a success of one of the country's more isolated trials, Whangamomona, which has always been associated with the Murphy family. With a trial ground hidden in a basin nearly halfway between Stratford and Taumarunui, competitors from outside Taranaki stay at least one night in the district. It's an area that's best described as an endless series of quite closely packed gullies which, from a high ridge, look rather like a cliff-top view of a rough, green sea, except that it doesn't move. His first sight of it extracted an immediate 'Hell, look at that!' from Central Otago's Eric Stringer, who's used to one thing or another — steep mountains and upland plains — not a world resembling an upturned saw. Earlier the same day we had passed a road sign bearing the warning, 'Winding road next 15 kilometres'. Noticing this, Eric turned and said quite indignantly, 'What do they mean? The road's already been winding for the last 15 kilometres!' To the locals, the real twists and turns were just beginning. Whangamomona's first trial was held in 1925 and, with the tortuous roads and stretches of gravel that still exist thereabouts, it's obvious that it's never been easy to get to. Until the mid-1950s, they held a three-day trial, with all the events being run, in turn, on the same hill. Now all four run concurrently — two of them on Murphy land — with well-built, good-mannered Murphy sheep on each of them. So the three- to six-hour drive many competitors make to get there is well worthwhile.

Plenty of effort has also been made by those who run the trial. February days in this valley are incredibly hot, so trees have been strate-gically planted to provide shade for dogs, triallists and their woolly competition. Down on the flat, specimen trees act as sun umbrellas for

competitors. As these have grown, the wooden fences that once pro-
tected them from stock have been turned into circular seats. By edging your way around one, you can see most of three courses and the
top of the straight hunt. At the foot of the zigzag, the holding pen
looks like a copse of willows and little else, until you realise that a fair-
sized mob of sheep is contained within. When these yards were erected,
Bernard used poles of twisted willow as posts, knowing that it wouldn't
be too many years before they were shading sheep before their runs,
and liberators in between them. Standing like an upland oasis on a high
ridge, the holding yard to the left of the long head is also alive. In a
rugged environment of dry summers and winter storms, Bernard's
choice for this pen's posts was paulownia poles; they, too, have grown
arms and leaves to put sheep in the shade. The hot and humid climate
of the hinterland also means early morning mists that completely
choke the valleys, and they can stay clagged up till 9 o'clock or later.
My first morning at Whanga' was no exception and, as the sun vapor-
ised the fog, it revealed one of the bigger long head courses in the
country, made even tougher by the heat that had just cleared it. I
described the subsequent action in an earlier chapter, and judged the
course thirteen years later. That was an interesting experience, which
required great care with competitors' initials, especially when compil-
ing the results. Four of the five had the same surname — Murphy.
Bernard was fifth, Steve, a son, second and Bernard's two brothers, Des
and Gary, were first and third respectively. They kindly left a small gap
so that I could put Ian Jeffery from Hawke's Bay into fourth place.

Until very recently, both Whangamomona's heading courses had
unusual but practical judges' shelters. For 362 days of the year they
looked distinctly Druid-like — four poles, set in a square, with beams
joined around the top, and nothing else. Come trial time, a tarpaulin
was simply thrown over this arrangement and table and chairs installed.
They still do this for the short head and, with no windows to steam
up, there's an uncluttered view from the hub of a course that almost
completely encircles the shelter. Tarpaulins are a regular addition to trialling structures. Apart from their importance as shelter and shade
providers, during rain they can also catch a lot of water, and become

aerial ponds. The next important point to understand is where to stand in relation to the prevailing wind, when you want to get rid of that water by pushing the pond up with your dog trial stick!

Like many grounds, Whangamomona is not connected to the national grid, but they do have plenty of wood for their copper and an ancient water boiling contraption that stands near the cookshop. There's another copper standing near the bar, which is not used to brew tea. It's a very elderly Methven, complete with curved, cast iron legs and clawed feet, and its role in life is drinker hygiene. After use and a rinse, or whatever, the glassware's put in a tray made of chook netting and left immersed to simmer for the required time; the Health Department would be proud of them. Their bar is a hut that opens up at the front for serving, with a tin verandah stretched round it, and a 4 x 2 rail at elbow height for the correct laconic lean, while telling lies. Conversely, you can face out and rest on both forearms, while watching a run. Their weatherboarded cookshop has the best view, though, as the wall facing three of the courses is a series of shutters that are lifted to become a verandah with glassless windows beneath. On the last night, the cookhouse is retired and all the cooking and consuming's done in the paddock, at their excellent barbecue. Before it was introduced, Fay, Bernard's wife, would have 25 or more sit down to tea at her table. This after she had fed at least eight house guests a 5.30 a.m. breakfast, followed by a full day's work in the cookhouse.

Whangamomona's programme sums up the means by which we're fed at all trials: 'Catering by courtesy of local ladies.' Every club in the country is supported by a group of women who serve lunch each day, plus morning and afternoon smokos for competitors, and prepare baskets of same for the judges and workers on all courses. Some catering committees go to almost too much trouble, for the size of our waists anyway. For all that, I've never heard anyone do anything other than praise and encourage them. At Waiau in North Canterbury, the meal could only be described as a hotel smorgasbord, with one table laden with cold meats and salads and another with an amazing array of puddings. My favourite dessert at a trial is apple or apricot slice and the flavour of those of the pip fruit variety I had at the Malvern trial over a dozen years ago is still fresh in my taste buds' memory bank. Not that I would ever complain about the wonderful steam puddings, complete with custard, fruit and cream, I've had at the Wairau Valley and Marlborough clubs. Marlborough's grounds are just out of Blenhiem, and they also have flowers on the table and proper tablecloths — very flash. As the season gets cooler, dishes such as curried sausages, farmhouse mince, shepherd's pie and Irish stew can appear, all accompanied by mashed spud and green peas. The same weather also sees the appearance of a variety of home-made soups, all guaranteed to stick to your ribs. If there is one traditional dog trial staple, it would have to be cold mutton: hindquarter on the bone, stuffed and rolled forequarter and mutton ham — as in Cumberland ham. Accompanying these will be salads, spuds, peas and someone's special relish or chutney. The usual price for lunch these days would be $5 to $6; I don't think I've ever paid more. As Alf Boynton says, 'You'll never eat or drink cheaper than at a dog trial.' The main reason is that most of the food, particularly the meat, is donated.

Morning and afternoon teas usually cost $2 and, in the far South, the morning fare can include hot cheese rolls. Down there, and everywhere else, scones are a regular item — with or without jam and cream — and sandwiches, two or three of which will quickly fill the gap left by a missed meal. There's always an assortment of home-made cakes, and fruit and date rolls that can't be ignored, especially when the latter are spread thickly with butter. At the beginning of the day most clubs have an early morning cuppa and snack but only one that I know of puts on a full cooked breakfast. This, prepared on a gas-fired barbecue trailer, is a Kapiti West-Coast speciality and, what's more, it's free! Other club traditions I've encountered include Kyeburn providing saveloys in the bar at night and Lumsden putting on free oysters, though I imagine that economics and availability have ended that tradition. With the awareness of drink driving that now exists, all clubs have food in the bar, a barbecue, or both. The alternative is a hangi, which is often put on as a fundraiser by a local organisation, such as a school committee or playcentre. To Southern Hawke's Bay's Wainui club, the term barbecue doesn't just mean chops, sausages and steaks;

they also grill paua patties. That's not all — their speciality is deep-fried cod and snapper, encased in batter, and cooked on a portable device operated by a couple from the nearby village of Herbertville. In Northland the barbecues some clubs put on have all but attained the status of an art form. Not only do they have baked-in-foil potatoes and a full range of marinated meats, they even do Mediterranean-style shish kebabs. As with all the after-trial barbecues I've been to, there's no charge.

Club by club, specialities extend to other elements of trialling. One of the more uplifting of these is well suited to the early hours of April mornings in the Hunterville hinterland. Otairi-Pukeroa have always shouted a heart starter of whisky or gin to each competitor when they've entered at the secretary's office. David Duncan, who plays mine host at early hour, doesn't make this a compulsory drink, but very few refuse. Otairi was Alf Boynton's trial before he went to Kapiti, and the tradition of the sunrise snifter came with him, making this a trial where you can have a bracer and breakfast without having to trouble your wallet. In other places you may get a sample pack of dog biscuits or nuts, a dog roll, notebook, pen or key ring, all depending on the trial's main sponsor. They're good gestures, too, but they lack the edge of David Duncan's 'You'll have one?' while he's pouring your tot. Many clubs give their president or a designated 'hospitality steward' an allowance to shout for visitors in the bar, albeit a bit later in the day. The bar itself is usually run by a non-triallist, who's prepared to help out at a district function, and the licence is often taken out in his name too. The best title I've come across for a barman in a club's list of officials is 'entertainment steward'. Clubs with real class, though, don't call their watering hole a bar, nor the person responsible a barman. It's a 'refreshment booth', presided over by a 'steward'.

There are some clubs in the South that have never had a booth or bar and, if they do now, it may only have begun serving in the last decade or so. I competed at the Gore club's trial, in 1987, the first year they had licensed, indoor drinking, as opposed to impromptu gatherings around various vehicles. They celebrated their new-found, official, wetness in some style, to make up for the preceding decades of drought. The visitors, of whom I was one, were a bit more restrained, but even so it became an evening I will never forget. After what I considered sufficient imbibement and well fed with with pork sausage blotting paper from the barbecue, I prepared to head back up the road to my temporary base at Balclutha. The night was as black as the inside of an Angus cow and as I stood in the car park adjusting to the dark, before I tried to pick my vehicle, I remembered the technique W.V. Kerr used in similar circumstances.

W.V., or Bill, is one of trialling's long-term characters and, on at least one occasion, I found myself walking out of the Omarama pub at the same time as he did. We took a right turn on to the edge of the main road and walked a few paces alongside various utilities, Land-Cruisers and Land Rovers when suddenly Bill stopped, looked up and down the road and said, 'Where's my truck?' He followed this with his bark-up whistle, the one he'd use on the hill to get his whole team to sing and either start lifting the sheep on a distant face or signal to fellow musterers that he was ready to start his beat. In this case it was to trigger a canine location beacon in the dark of a High Country evening. It worked too. No sooner did his two-bar call begin to fade than an enthusiastic chorus of loud, though, muffled barking began, some distance away in the other direction. 'Ah-ha,' said W.V., 'there it is', and immediately turned to the left and disappeared into the night. His team were obviously delighted at being given the opportunity to bark legally in the truck, and kept their loud and happy chorus going until a sharp and shrill whistle pierced the night, followed by a spoken comment or two, and they fell silent. It's not easy being a sheep dog. One minute you're told to do something and, next thing, you get insulted for doing it — you can't win!

I didn't use W.V.'s technique at Gore since I knew roughly where the car was and, as my eyes adjusted to the moonless night, its white shape became apparent. In those days I had a lightweight aluminium dog box mounted on the back of the car so I went over to open the door at the side to let Peg and Shorty out for a pit stop before we hit the road — touring with dogs can be likened to travelling with small children, except that dogs don't cry when they're tired! Dogs are also creatures of habit and my duo were no exception. Peg was always last in and first out and Shorty vice versa, so when a brown shape (Shorty) shot out of the box, I closed the door to wait the mandatory few minutes for them to sniffle and snuffle about until they found the best place to water the local pasture. In due course I went and opened the door and, without looking, waited for the two bounces that always signified their arrival, closed their door, climbed into my compartment and drove off. Arriving at Balclutha, I let them out to be tied up and fed. Out popped Shorty — alone! I had been trialling several years by then so I was used to a sinking feeling in my stomach, though, I doubt that it sank as low or as quickly than it did when I realised I had lost Peg. Hell's bells! I'd heard of people forgetting to take their dogs to a trial and others who'd sold them on the spot, but leaving them behind? No! Without a phone on the ground that I knew of, I rang Gore's president, Les Roughan, at his home. He was, of course, still presiding over the end of prohibition celebrations at the clubrooms. Understandably, it was quite some time before I got an answer and when I identified myself, Les didn't wait for my stumbling, worried preamble, but immediately said, 'I've got your dog, John.'

We arranged for Peg's return at a trial two days away and I began to relax. Thinking back, I realised there must have been a change of position in the dog box, which meant that Shorty came out first. Seeing her exit, I closed the door. Therefore, when I opened it for them to get back in, the first of the two bounces I felt was obviously Peg leaving, and the second was Shorty arriving. Left behind, Peg went out on to the road and started the 75-kilometre journey to Balclutha on foot. Fortunately it wasn't long before another departing competitor spotted her and took her back to the grounds, where she was recognised. I also recalled that, earlier in the day, when Peg crashed the top, and a fair portion of the side, of Gore's very big long pull hill, I told her of a couple of places she could go … hell and buggery. When she was missing, I wanted her back, immediately! Fickle fellows, dog men.

Among the dog trial bars in which I've slaked my thirst, one of the most characterful would be Ohingaiti's old, verandah-fronted cottage, with an ancient stove burning away in the corner of the one room within. Whenever I was there, it provided little heat, but filled the room with enough smoke to make you think that you should be warm. In the heart of the Maniototo, Kyeburn's establishment has always had a very good last night, whenever I've been there. This club has a couple of great characters. There's John Steele, their straight hunt marshal, who has also performed that role at six island and national championships — and always with a quick quip for each competitor to relax them on their way to the mark. The other notable is the High Country poet, Blue Jeans — Ross McMillan. He's been a Maniototo musterer for many years, a regular liberator on the short head and has had at least two collections of his poetry published. He has been known to recite a few in Kyeburn's bar, just as John Steele often delivers some very funny stories in his typically bluff, and 'brrroad' way. Alas, I'm unable to repeat any of them, unlike an excerpt from one of Ross's pieces on dog trialling.

> I've put sheep in the cookhouse and in the booth, too,
> It's hard to believe what my old dog can do.
> He hunted sheep once in the ladies' outhouse,
> And a sheila shot out like she sat on a mouse,
> With her pants round her ankles (I couldn't help grin)
> But the way that she swore at me — sure t'was a sin.

Methven's low-roofed, barn-red establishment perched on the lip of one of the shelves that step up from the Rakaia Gorge bridge, is another which has a very special flavour; especially when there's a nor'-wester blowing (always) and constantly stirring the sawdust carpet. Sections of the roof are carried by manuka props that can be kicked out by ungainly drinkers as the proceedings wear on. When 'Big Jim' Morris owned Manuka Point Station up at the head of the gorge, this wasn't a problem. When an upright was taken out, Jim would fill in till the prop went back or, in the case of a breakage, a replacement found and cut to length. Unfortunately, according to the locals, it was Jim and his legendary hobnail boots, sized somewhere in the mid teens, who usually took the props out in the first place!

Another favourite of mine which, like Ohingaiti's old hut, has now gone, was the Waihemo bar at Dunback, in North Otago. It was part of an elderly cookshop and bar complex that was accidentally burnt down. Open fronted, it looked out on to a big, well-tussocked long pull course. During the pre-lunch cocktail hour(s) the sun streamed in, its harsh glare removed by the dusty screen that rose from the sawdust floor, making it all very cosy, thank you. In the case of the evening gatherings, the cosiness would be replaced with a more raucous atmosphere. After the fire a flash new dining and drinking establishment was erected, with all the outward charm and atmosphere you'd expect from a modern building. Inside, the hospitality was as genuine as ever but it wasn't the same, especially for some local identities. A major problem was the well-finished, polyurethane-coated particle board floor. For trialling's traditionalists, and especially local workers, the standard footwear is hobnail boots. Alas, a happy wearer of hobnails, plus five beers, plus a shiny new floor, equals beer number six being wasted, as its owner finally loses his balance and goes to ground. I attended the last night revelry in the first year of the new building's life and, warm and comfy that we were, it all got too much for local stalwart, Russell Heckler. Sick of the floor and the sterility of the new surroundings, he disappeared to return with some sawdust, which he immediately sprinkled underfoot. It barely covered where he was standing, but it was the symbolism of the act that counted, and the evening rollicked on, echoing out among the lower peaks of the Kakanui Mountains.

There are two official means of informing triallists when a club's annual event will be held: a nationally published, annual trial dates and judges list, and each club's own programme, which is posted to the regulars. Reading a few of these gives an insight into trialling and underlines some of its unique qualities. Most programmes are printed on coloured light cardboard and folded, concertina-like. There are some immense variations, ranging from computer-generated letters to Whanga-momona's tiny and tidy 10- x 13.5-centimetre eight-page booklet. Invariably the front page announces the date, time and location of the event and continues with a detailed list of office-bearers. This includes the full committee, to which all club members automatically belong, and the various duties each will perform at the trial. Life members are also listed, along with the judges and timekeepers, suppliers of sheep, the property owners and, if there's room, a sponsor's logo. And that's just page one! As the programme's unfolded — one column per fold — the events, prize money and special trophies are all revealed. There'll also be a few advertisements, to cover the cost of the exercise, and some standard information under the heading 'Rules'.

> All persons enter grounds at their own risk.
> All dogs must be tied up when not competing.
> All dogs not competing must be under control.
> All dogs must be kept away from the luncheon pavilion.
> Any dogs interfering with another dog's run will be disqualified.
> Competitors not taking their runs as directed, risk disqualification.
> Owners of dogs on grounds must produce current hydatids certificates.
> Onus on competitor to ensure dogs are entered in correct categories.
> Starting times on all courses, as soon as possible.
> Affiliated with the NZSDT Assn and run under their rules.
> The Committee reserves the right to alter or amend any condition, at their discretion.

As all clubs have prizes for locals, to encourage their support and participation, a regular programme listing is the definition of a local. At Ohingaitai where, within a 30-minute drive, there are another six clubs — Moawhanga, Mataroa, Kawhatau, Ruahine, Poukiore, and Otairi-Pukeroa — membership of any of those is sufficient for local status. For Raetihi, it's just as straightforward: 'Local — Residing within 50 km by road of Raetihi.' Other clubs have an even simpler formula: 'Locals are workers at trials.' In some clubs, where the criterion is a residential address, an accurate definition may require either a map reading badge or local knowledge, which you will have, if you belong there. Understanding Waimarama-Maraetotara's local boundaries could call on both: 'From sea to Atua Road, to Patangata, to Middle Road, to Te Mata, and down the Tuki Tuki River to its mouth at Haumoana.' At

Kaitieke, in the southern King Country, you need to know your local history: 'Local Dog — means a dog owned (Bona fide owner) within the Old Taumarunui County, six weeks prior to the trials.'

It's worth being a local because, in many instances, there are so many prizes it seems impossible to miss out, though I often do! Within each of the standard events there are local classes, which can include an open as well as a local maiden, and maiden man, maiden dog — for which a maiden woman with a maiden dog is also eligible. There are plenty of special classes too, such as local or liberator with the highest-pointed run, and aggregates and team prizes, such as 'highest aggregate points, local musterer with two huntaways and one heading dog'. In Otago, Tuapeka West used to have the 'G and B Store's special for local with highest aggregate, who has not won a prize.' Neighbouring club, Waitahuna, had an award for the local with the lowest points, and another for committee men not running a dog. The latter involved nothing more than a draw out of a hat. In direct contrast to a local prize is Kyeburn's, 'Naseby Royal Hotel Special; $20 for the maiden competitor who has travelled the furthest.' Having a Wellington address, I won that sixteen years ago, by several hundred kilometres, the clearest victory I've ever had in anything.

When I first started trialling, the competitive category that puzzled me most was a thing called a 'bracelet'. This is a very common class with intermediate dogs, 'Intermediate Hunt [or head] Bracelet, $2'. I thought 'Why would a reasonably macho bunch like dog triallists want to compete for some sort of bangle?' What it refers to — and fortunately I managed to solve this myself — is the total gained by a dog over a brace, the two courses for its type (two heads or two hunts). Another programme regular reminds me of a bread advertisement: 'FRESH SHEEP EACH DAY.' That's a guarantee that what was used today won't be used tomorrow. Sometimes they are, though, and if you run tomorrow, you don't really mind. But, if you ran the day before, and got shoved off the prize list by one of tomorrow's men, working the sheep you battled hard to tame, you mind very bloody much! The most eye-catching statement I've read is on the Parapara-Makirikiri programme: 'NO RIFLE SHOOTING ON TRIAL DAYS.' Not only is this a guarantee that your dog won't get killed in action, but it also means that the local rifle club won't be at home on their range, which is adjacent to the long head. Quite a few sheep dogs are gun shy and if their owners thought there was a chance of a loud report or two, they wouldn't bother coming. Others, though, may well try and fit these sound effects into their runs.

There are few competitive sports as rural as sheep dog trialling, which means that, wherever you are, you'll be surrounded by great scenery. In time you take for granted that trialling is a passport to some amazing country, both the courses themselves and the back roads and overland passes you travel over to reach them. Among the most memorable for me is the magnificent drive between the Tokirima and Whangamomona trials on a February evening. This stretch includes the winding, riverside and bush-clad Tangarakau Gorge, the rough-hewn limestone tunnel leading on to the Tahora Saddle and the switchback road, with a view of ridge after ridge disappearing into the sunset. The drive to Tututawa a couple of mornings later has its moments too, especially the first rays of sun on Mount Taranaki, through the mists lingering round the Pohokura and Strathmore saddles. Heading to Kaitieke's trial, west of the Raurimu Spiral, you get a magnificent view of that bush-enveloped valley in the Whanganui River catchment. The drive between a couple of Kaitieke's courses would also have any tourist bus stopping to disgorge its passengers and boost Kodak's profits. To get to the long head, the track follows a clear and busy river and then crosses another as it tumbles and twirls down a limestone chasm to join the other. What makes it even better is that their long head course would be worth crossing a desert for anyway, so travelling by the babble and blather of the creeks, surrounded by bush, birdsong and the moist gleam of a misty morning, is a real bonus. In my own centre, the trip up SH52 from Masterton to Waipukurau is one of the last back country, non-tourist drives in the country. It's a 214-kilometre route that wanders in and out of valley after pleasant valley and, most important, takes you to six different trial grounds.

In the South Island, one of my most memorable journeys was early one autumn morning through North Canterbury to the Waiau club's grounds. It was one of those days when everything seemed as close to perfect as it could get, especially the autumn tonings, the cookshop, the company and the huntaway sheep. The overland drive to Cheviot, ready for that district's trial next morning, was another reminder of how good it is that we don't compete in town. Coming off the Pigroot and down into the Maniototo, with the promise of two or three good trials to come, is always a great feeling, as is approaching Mount Nessing's grounds, near Fairlie. From the turn-off at Albury to their headquarters below the foothills of the Rollesby Range, the road and farm track climb 300 metres just to get to their huts above the Opawa River. As a rule, what follows will be a searing hot March day, typical of inland Canterbury but, towards its end, the air will become cool, clear and relaxing. By early evening you can be sitting by a boulder-strewn stream, watching huntaways shift half-bred two-tooths up a steep face, with nothing more to worry about but your next run. Next day it's the Levels trial, on the other side of the broad valley, and from their hunt courses, which seem to start halfway up the Brothers Range, you look back to yesterday's location. In mid-afternoon sun, the detail on the tussock-clad hills is lost — it's just a warm blur of tan and gold, sheep and dog country, all the way west to the Southern Alps.

Liberators get good views too, and those include a brief stint on top of Kyeburn's very tall and well-tussocked long pull course. At 7 a.m., with the panorama of the entire Maniototo Basin before you, the Rock and Pillar, Hawkdun and Kakanui Ranges at its edge and the craggy peaks of the Remarkables in the distance, you realise that it was well worth the climb. This was my first attempt at slipping sheep into the strings and I have to admit that the trio did slip — right through Peg's and my clutches. I soon learned to look at the sheep first, the scenery second. From the long head at Martinborough, although the heights aren't nearly as lofty, it's still a great view across to the Rimu-taka and Tararua Ranges. The river flats in between the trial grounds and the hills are now best known for fermented grape juice produc-tion. It's a good drop too, though we don't bother with it in our refreshment booth. The reason we're in that locale is because, just a little way down the flat, three gentlemen by the name of Weld, Clifford and Vavasour, in 1844 took up the Wharekaka Run, which was New Zealand's first pastoral lease and heralded the birth of our sheep industry. Wharekaka's Merinos didn't like the then undrained river flats so Weld and co. moved their operation to the more open tussock and range country of the South Island, which can also be seen from the Martinborough long head.

The sights, animal instances and quirks of tradition that contribute so much to the special world of sheep dog trialling wouldn't exist without the most important ingredient of all, the people. Remove any practising triallist from dogs, sheep and hills and, as long as there was someone in the vicinity with the same interest, he or she would be as happy as a pig in mud. Happier still, if a dog or two were sniffing around a group of rural vehicles, with some weatherbeaten faces nearby, squinting into the hills and yarning at the same time. Some of the best memories I have are of the people I've met and what they've given me in the way of companionship, help and support. The first time I gained an open place I was staying with Tony and Puddy Sheild in Marlborough. When the news was phoned through, out came a silver salver, bearing bottled bubbly to celebrate. True triallists get as much pleasure out of their colleagues' successes as they do their own. I'll always regard as a privilege being able to watch runs with Cyril Perry, Les Knight, Charlie Crutchley, Alf Boynton, Ellis Child, Ginger Anderson, the Weir brothers, numerous Murphys, two Bartletts, the same number of Stringers, Brysons, Sheilds and Smiths, and many more. These are the people who have taught me and many others all they know about the game. Not just the finer points of competing, but how to walk away from a disaster and learn from it. Sometimes sheep, dogs, contour and climate all combine to conspire against you and there's no way anything practical can be done — without a knife! Following the example set by your friends, you remind yourself that there will be another trial tomorrow, shrug your shoulders and say, 'That's dog trialling.'

I've also been fortunate to see the top competitor and dog combinations of the last couple of decades in action, all of them providing unforgettable moments. There are other moments, too, that a trial-list never forgets. There's that very personal six- to fourteen-minute moment, which starts when the dog leaves you and, as it unfolds, becomes something that you'd dreamt about, but never really dared to expect. The more it continues, the more you determine not to let it go, becoming increasingly aware that this could be *the* one. More and more you and your other self reach out, across the flat or up the hill, to steady and steer the dog, to maintain what, so far, is the closest you've ever been to perfection. There are a couple of flaky moments as nerves, a dry throat, then a testy ewe, cause heart flutters, but it all holds together, steady and true. You make the last moves and com-mands almost as an automaton, without drawing breath, and the other world to which you seem to have ascended is suddenly broken by the reality of the judge's call, 'Right!' You show no emotion, certainly don't look at the judge, call the dog off, praise it and walk away — all the time becoming increasingly aware that you just might have pulled it off. Still stoic and betraying no emotions, you walk past the judge's hut and say 'thank you', avoiding any eye contact. Behind the box and out of sight, you stop, heave a huge sigh, tilt your head, bend your right forearm, clench your fist and say 'Yeess!' Now *that* really is dog trialling.

Time!

Bibliography

Books

Acland, L.D.G., *A Sheep Station Glossary*. Press, Christchurch, 1933.

Beilby, Walter, *The Dog in Australia*. George Robertson & Company, Sydney, 1897.

Cavanagh, Rod, *Australian Sheep Dogs, Training and Handling*. Rod Cavanagh, Victoria, 1990.

Dalton, Clive, *Farm Dogs — Breeding, Training & Welfare*. NZ Rural Press, Auckland, 1996.

Drabble, Margaret (ed.), *The Oxford Companion to English Literature*. Oxford University Press, Oxford, 1985.

Fyfe, Frank, *Martinborough Collie Club, 1896–1996*. Martinborough Collie Club, Greytown, 1996.

Hartley, C.W.G., *The Shepherd's Dogs*. Whitcoulls Publishers, Christchurch, 1979.

Hore, Arthur, *Tokarahi Dog Trial Club, 1934–1967*. Arthur Hore, Oamaru, 1968.

Kelley, R.B., D.V.Sc, *Sheep Dogs: Their Breeding, Maintenance and Training*. Angus & Robertson, Sydney, 1958.

Knight, L.J., *A Guide to Training Sheep Dogs in New Zealand*. Les Knight, Te Kuiti, 1984.

Lilico, James, *The Breeding and Training of Sheep Dogs*. James Lilico, Invercargill, 1919.
Fifty Years Amongst Sheep Dogs. James Lilico, Invercargill, 1926.
Sheep Dog Memoirs. James Lilico, Invercargill, 1934.

Longton, Tim and Edward Hart. *The Sheep Dog: Its Work and Training*. David & Charles, Newton Abbot, 1984.

McCulloch, J. Herries, *Sheep Dogs and Their Masters*. Moray Press, Edinburgh, 1946.

Macgregor Redwood, Miriam, *A Dog's Life: Working Dogs in New Zealand*. A.H. & A.W. Reed, Wellington, 1980.

McLeod, David, *Kingdom in the Hills*. Whitcombe & Tombs, Christchurch, 1974.

McMillan, Ross (Blue Jeans), *Tales of the High Country*. Central Otago News, Alexandra, 1981.

Mills, A.R., *Huntaway*. A.H. & A.W. Reed, Wellington, 1966.

Mills, A.R., S.F. Herbert and W.V. McIntyre, *A Practical Guide to Handling Dogs and Stock*. A.H. & A.W. Reed, Wellington, 1964.

Minty, J.G. and E.J. Neilson (compilers), *New Zealand Working Sheep Dog Stud Book*, Vol. V. New Zealand Working Sheep Dog Stud Book Association, Christchurch, 1958.

Moore, V. and L. (compilers), *New Zealand Working Sheep Dog Stud Book*, Vol. I. New Zealand Working Sheep Dog Stud Book Association, Christchurch, 1951.

Moorhouse, Sydney, *The British Sheepdog*. H.F. & G. Witherby, London, 1950.

Newton, Peter, *Wayleggo*. A.H. & A.W. Reed, Wellington, 1947.
Ten Thousand Dogs. A.H. & A.W. Reed, Wellington, 1971.
In the Wake of the Axe. A.H. & A.W. Reed, Wellington, 1972.
Sixty Thousand on the Hoof: Big Country South of the Rangitata. A.H. & A.W. Reed, Wellington, 1975.

Orsman, Elizabeth & Harry, *The New Zealand Dictionary*. New House Publishers, Auckland, 1994.

Osborne, Sonny, *Droving Dogs and Sheep*. Sonny Osborne, Feilding, 1987.

Pinney, Robert, *Early South Canterbury Runs*. A.H. & A.W. Reed, Wellington, 1971.
Early Northern Otago Runs. Collins, Auckland, 1981.

Pollard, Jack (ed.), *Wild Dogs Working Dogs Pedigrees and Pets*. Lansdowne Press, Sydney, 1968.

Rennie, Neil, *Working Dogs*. Shortland Publications, Auckland, 1984.

Ries, Rex, *A History of the Northland Sheep Dog Trial Movement*. Northland Sheep Dog Trial Centre, Whangarei, 1996.

Robertson, B.T. *A Century of Waitangi Station*. Waitangi Station, Oamaru, 1982.

Rutherford, Ben, *A View From The Brothers*. A.H. & A.W. Reed, Wellington, 1970.

Saunders, Roy, *Sheepdog Glory*. Andre Deustch, London, 1956.

Sharpe, R.D, *Country Occasions*. A.H. & A.W. Reed, Wellington, 1962.

Sinclair, Ian, *Boot in the Stirrup*. A.H. & A.W. Reed, Wellington, 1973.

Stronach, Bruce, *Musterer on Molesworth*. Whitcombe & Tombs, Christchurch, 1953.

Sutton, Catherine G., *The Observer's Book of Dogs*. Frederick Warne, London, 1978.

Thomson, Bob, *Taranaki Dog Trialling*. Bob Thomson, Stratford, 1993.

Whalan, W.J., *Waitaki Collie Dog Club: 1885–1985*. Waitaki Collie Dog Club, Oamaru, 1985.

Wright, Christine, *Whistles in the Wind*. Methven Collie Club, Methven, 1996.

Whyte, William, *The Sheep-dog: Judging and Conduct of Trials and The Art of Breaking-in*. W. Whyte, Napier, 1927.

Winstanley, Lionel, *Hobnails Hounds & Humour*. Lionel Winstanley, Blenheim, 1994.

Sheep Dog Trial Club Jubilee Programmes and Booklets

Akitio Sheep Dog Trial Club, 75th Jubilee, 1990.

Dannevirke & District Sheep Dog Trial Club, 75th Jubilee, 1982.

East Coast Sheep Dog Trial Club, 90th Jubilee, 1979.

East Coast Sheep Dog Trial Club, Centennial, 1989.

Kawhatau Collie Club, Golden Jubilee, 1984.

Kumeroa Sheep Dog Trial Club, 75th Jubilee, 1989.

Mangamahu Sheep Dog Trial Club, 50th Jubilee, 1976.

Maungakaramea Sheep Dog Trial Club, 75th Jubilee, 1988.

Moawhanga Collie Club, 75th Jubilee, 1974.

Mohaka Dog Trial Club, Centennial, 1996.

Omarama Collie Dog Club, 75th Jubilee, 1990.

Otairi-Pukeroa Collie Club, 50th Jubilee, 1990.

Pio Pio Collie Club, 75th Jubilee, 1992.

Poukiore Collie Club, 50th Jubilee, 1994.

Taupo Dog Trial Club, 25th Jubilee, 1992.

Tikokino Sheep Dog Trial Club, 75th Jubilee, 1986.

Waitaki Collie Dog Club, Diamond Jubilee, 1945.

Periodicals

New Zealand Listener
New Zealand Farmer
New Zealand Journal of Agriculture
The Field
Oamaru Times
Pastoral Review
Press (Christchurch)
Southland Times
Straight Furrow
Timaru Herald
Trial Dates and Official Judges List, New Zealand Sheep Dog Trial
  Association.
Various club and championship programmes, 1922–1997.